J.K. Lasser's
Business Forms
for Managing
the Smaller Business

ARNOLD GOLDSTEIN, EDITORIAL CONSULTANT

J.K. LASSER INSTITUTE
New York   London   Toronto   Sydney   Tokyo   Singapore

J.K. LASSER INSTITUTE

Simon & Schuster, Inc.
15 Columbus Circle
New York, NY 10023

DISTRIBUTED BY PRENTICE HALL TRADE SALES

Manufactured in the United States of America

1 2 3 4 5 6 7 8 9 10

This book is sold with the understanding that neither the author nor the publisher is engaged in rendering legal advice. If legal advice is required, the services of an attorney should be sought. Publisher and author cannot in any way guarantee that the forms in this book are being used for the purposes intended and, therefore, assume no responsibility for their proper and correct use.

ISBN 0-13-508276-5

Library of Congress Cataloging-in-Publication Data

J.K. Lasser's business forms for managing the smaller business /
  Arnold Goldstein, editorial consultant.
     p.   cm.
  Compiled from J.K. Lasser's executive's personal organizer forms
and J.K. Lasser's operations forms for smaller businesses.
  ISBN 0-13-508276-5 : $34.95
    1. Business—Forms.   2. Small business—Forms.   3. Time
management—Forms.   I. Goldstein, Arnold S.   II. J.K. Lasser
Institute.   III. J.K. Lasser's executive's personal organizer forms.
IV. J.K. Lasser's operations forms for smaller businesses.
V. Title: Business forms for managing the smaller business.
HF5371.J18   1990
651'29—dc20
                                              90-30246
                                                   CIP

LIST OF FORMS

Section 2   General Planners   B 109

Section 3   Projects   B 127

Section 4   Executive and Administrative   B 149

Section 5   Accounting and Finance   B 201

Section 6   Purchasing and Shipping   B 241

Section 7   Sales and Marketing   B 297

Section 8   Personnel   B 329

Section 9   Graphs and Charts   B 391

Section 10 Maps   B 443

ABOUT THIS BOOK

Even the smallest business needs hundreds of different forms to run smoothly. The forms in this book are specifically designed to help you increase efficiency, improve productivity, and organize yourself for peak managerial performance. You'll find forms for just about every need and function—forms for setting goals, defining projects, organizing important records, documenting business transactions, hiring or firing employees, and much more. With *J.K. Lasser's Business Forms for Managing the Smaller Business*, you can set up a personalized planning system that will help you take control of the one commodity you can't afford to waste—your time.

Now with this complete business and executive form-file, you'll have the most extensive compilation of time management forms available. With over 450 pages of forms for every business need, you'll have a complete and valuable collection of ready-to-use forms to help you run a more efficient and profitable business.

Convenient: No more searching for those hard-to-find or only rarely used forms. This book puts virtually every type of form at your fingertips.

Economical: No more expensive form suppliers, printers, or designers who can charge up to $100 to prepare routine forms found in this book. *J.K. Lasser's Business Forms for Managing the Smaller Business* is the low-priced alternative, with each master form available for pennies.

Efficient: No more tying up valuable storage space and money with unused quantities of seldom-used forms. Whether you need one copy or dozens of copies, you can print precisely the quantity of forms needed.

Effective: No more doing without important forms or patching together makeshift forms. Now J.K. Lasser offers these professionally designed forms to help every size and type of organization get much more done in less time.

* Over 200 business forms to improve every phase of operations—personnel, sales,

credit and collection, bookkeeping, inventory and purchasing, expense control, routine office procedure . . . and much more.

* Over 200 of the most effective time management forms created exclusively for this book by a leading systems analyst. From day organizers to project planners, these time savers belong on the desk of every manager who wants to increase efficiency and improve productivity.

* The bookkeeping department will welcome the more than 40 data sheets and columnar forms proven ideal for the collection, analysis, and review of operating data. Whether it be daily or annual summaries, these multi-purpose forms quickly put the numbers into focus.

* And with the business and executive form-file there is an instant source of charts, graphs, and tables. These popular graphics give every presentation the perfect professional touch.

* To plan and review activities geographically, this book also includes world and state maps. These master maps encompass the key areas of interest to most organizations.

Browse through this book and discover for yourself the many useful forms you can put to work today.

HOW TO USE THIS BOOK

The form-file has been thoughtfully designed for convenient, professional use.

* Durable, heavy stock paper allows long use: clear, crisp copies; and easy perforation. Perforation is fast: just fold along the perforated line to insure a clean tear, then pull gently starting at the top. Store the original after use, so it can be located easily for reuse when needed. Wide margins allow forms to be hole-punched for binder storage.

* Every form can be quickly and easily modified or customized to specific needs. Use the forms ''as is'' or as a reference for designing your own forms, easily created by desktop publisher or typesetter.

* Appropriate forms can be personalized with your company name, address, logo, etc. simply by typeset, rubber stamp, or overlay on your business card.

* Just as these forms can be customized and personalized to match your particular needs, your plain paper copier can be loaded with a variety of paper stocks to give you added flexibility. This will enable you to copy your forms on colored paper, letterhead, or special paper stock.

Now you are all set—simply push the copier button to enjoy the easiest and most economical way to produce the forms your company needs.

THE FORM YOU NEED
IS EASY TO FIND

The forms in this book are both grouped by section and cross-indexed alphabetically. It's easy to find just the form you need:

Section 1 - Administrative & Planning

Section 2 - General Planners

Section 3 - Projects

Section 4 - Executive & Administrative

Section 5 - Accounting & Finance

Section 6 - Purchasing & Shipping

Section 7 - Sales & Marketing

Section 8 - Personnel

Section 9 - Graphs & Charts

Section 10 - Maps

There may be several formats for the more popular forms, so check and compare the various forms to find the one most appropriate for your purposes. Once you have selected the forms you will be using, set them up in a file or notebook at your desk and see how productive they will be in making time work for you.

Administrative
and
Planning

APPOINTMENTS

	APPOINTMENT	MEMORANDUM
7:00		
7:15		
7:30		
7:45		
8:00		
8:15		
8:30		
8:45		
9:00		
9:15		
9:30		
9:45		
10:00		
10:15		
10:30		
10:45		
11:00		
11:15		
11:30		
11:45		
12:00		
12:15		
12:30		
12:45		
1:00		
1:15		
1:30		
1:45		
2:00		
2:15		
2:30		
2:45		
3:00		
3:15		
3:30		
3:45		
4:00		
4:15		
4:30		
4:45		
5:00		
5:15		
5:30		
5:45		
6:00		
6:15		
6:30		
6:45		

DAILY PLANNER

DATE _____

FROM YESTERDAY	✔

TODAY'S APPOINTMENTS	✔

PHONE CALLS	✔	REMINDERS	✔

DAILY DIARY

DATE _____

TIME	

PROFESSIONAL CHARGE SHEET

HOUR	DIARY	TIME	
		HRS.	MIN.

DAILY NOTES

FOR TOMORROW

DATE _____

PRIORITY		✔

MEETING NOTICE AND AGENDA

Name of group _____   Date _____

Title of meeting _____   Starting time _____

Called by _____   Place _____

Purpose of meeting _____

Background materials _____

Please bring _____

Desired outcomes _____

Manager/Chairperson _____   Recorder _____

Group members _____

Order of agenda items	Time allocated
1.	
2.	
3.	
4.	
5.	

MEETING AGENDA

Location: _____ Date

Time: _____

Participants: _____

_____

_____

_____

_____

_____

Topics:	Outcome:
_____	_____
_____	_____
_____	_____
_____	_____
_____	_____
_____	_____
_____	_____
_____	_____
_____	_____
_____	_____
_____	_____
_____	_____
_____	_____
_____	_____
_____	_____
_____	_____
_____	_____
_____	_____
_____	_____
_____	_____
_____	_____
_____	_____
_____	_____
_____	_____
_____	_____
_____	_____
_____	_____
_____	_____
_____	_____
_____	_____
_____	_____
_____	_____
_____	_____
_____	_____

MEETING PLAN

Function: _____   Location: _____

Date: _____   Attending: _____

8:00 - 8:30	_____
8:30 - 9:00	_____
9:00 - 9:30	_____
9:30 - 10:00	_____
10:00 - 10:30	_____
10:30 - 11:00	_____
11:00 - 11:30	_____
11:30 - 12:00	_____
12:00 - 12:30	_____
12:30 - 1:00	_____
1:00 - 1:30	_____
1:30 - 2:00	_____
2:00 - 2:30	_____
2:30 - 3:00	_____
3:00 - 3:30	_____
3:30 - 4:00	_____
4:00 - 4:30	_____
4:30 - 5:00	_____
5:00 - 5:30	_____
5:30 - 6:00	_____
6:00 - 6:30	_____
6:30 - 7:00	_____
7:00 - 7:30	_____
7:30 - 8:00	_____
8:00 - 8:30	_____
8:30 - 9:00	_____

MEETING PLANNER

_____ Meeting   Date _____   Time _____

ISSUES/TOPICS	PRIORITY A/B/C	RESULTS EXPECTED	PROBLEMS/ DECISIONS/ PLANS	INFO OR PRE-WORK REQUIRED	WHO SHOULD BE INVOLVED	TIME

Follow-Up (After the meeting)

ISSUES/TOPICS	(WHO) RESPONSIBILITY	RESULT	DUE DATE

DAILY GOALS

DATE _____

GOALS FOR THE DAY

	PRIORITY	GOAL	✔
1			
2			
3			
4			
5			
6			
7			
8			
9			
10			

	GOAL #	TASK	PRIORITY	TARGET DATE	✔
1					
2					
3					
4					
5					
6					
7					
8					
9					
10					
11					
12					
13					
14					
15					
16					
17					
18					
19					
20					
21					
22					
23					
24					

DAILY PRIORITY PLANNER

DATE_____

HIGH PRIORITY	COMPLETED ✔	FOLLOW-UP
1.		
2.		
3.		
4.		
5.		
6.		
7.		
8.		
9.		
10.		

LOW PRIORITY	COMPLETED ✔	FOLLOW-UP
1.		
2.		
3.		
4.		
5.		
6.		
7.		
8.		
9.		
10.		

TODAY'S ACTIVITIES

TODAY'S DATE _____

NOTES

	EXPENSES	AMT.
1.		
2.		
3.		
4.		
5.		
6.		
7.		
8.		
9.		
10.		
11.		
12.		
13.		
14.		
15.		
16.		
17.		
18.		
19.		
20.		

DAILY PLANNER AND APPOINTMENTS

DATE _____

FROM YESTERDAY	✔	TIME SCHEDULE
		6:00
		6:30
		7:00
		7:30
		8:00
TODAY'S PRIORITIES	✔	8:30
		9:00

		✔	TIME
D O			9:30
			10:00
			10:30
			11:00
			11:30
P H O N E			12:00
			12:30
			1:00
			1:30
			2:00
W R I T E			2:30
			3:00
			3:30
			4:00
			4:30

FOLLOW-UP	✔	TIME
		5:00
		5:30
		6:00
		6:30
		7:00
		7:30

FOR TOMORROW	NOTES

THINGS TO DO TODAY

DATE_____

SEE	✔

PHONE	✔

WRITE	✔

DAILY PLANNER AND APPOINTMENTS

DATE _____

FROM YESTERDAY	✔	TIME SCHEDULE
		6:00
		6:30
		7:00
		7:30
		8:00

TODAY'S PRIORITIES	✔	
		8:30
		9:00

D O			9:30
			10:00
			10:30
			11:00
			11:30
P H O N E			12:00
			12:30
			1:00
			1:30
			2:00
W R I T E			2:30
			3:00
			3:30
			4:00
			4:30

FOLLOW-UP	✔	
		5:00
		5:30
		6:00
		6:30
		7:00
		7:30

FOR TOMORROW	NOTES

URGENT ACTIVITIES

DATE _____

TIME NEEDED	ACTIVITY	✔

TIME ANALYSIS

DATE _____

	SCHEDULED		ACTUAL		ACTIVITY	✓
	TOTAL TIME	% OF TIME	TOTAL TIME	% OF TIME		

DAILY TIME SHEET

NAME		DEPARTMENT		LOCATION

DATE	EMPLOYEE NUMBER	SOCIAL SECURITY NUMBER	PAYROLL CLASSIFICATION	FILE NUMBER

TIME RECORD FOR:
☐ SHIFT ☐ JOB ☐ CONTRACT ☐ _____ EXPLANATION _____

	CLIENT	PROFESSIONAL SERVICE	SCHEDULED APPOINTMENT	TIME STARTED	TIME STOPPED	TOTAL TIME	NEXT APPOINTMENT DAY/TIME
1							
2							
3							
4							
5							
6							
7							
8							
9							
10							
11							
12							
13							
14							
15							
16							
17							
18							
19							
20							

REVIEW OF SERVICES RENDERED

☐ _____ # APPOINTMENTS _____ TIME _____

☐ _____ # APPOINTMENTS _____ TIME _____

☐ _____ # APPOINTMENTS _____ TIME _____

☐ _____ # APPOINTMENTS _____ TIME _____

☐ _____ # APPOINTMENTS _____ TIME _____

EMPLOYEE SIGNATURE   DATE

SUPERVISOR SIGNATURE   DATE

PAYROLL SIGNATURE   DATE

DAILY TRACKING

COMMITTEE/GROUP

Name of Committee: _____ Date _____

Functions: _____
_____

Specific Objectives: _____
_____

Chairman: _____
_____

Participants: _____

Title	Name	Address	Phone

COMMITTEE REPORT

Accomplished: Date

_____

Planned Activities:

_____

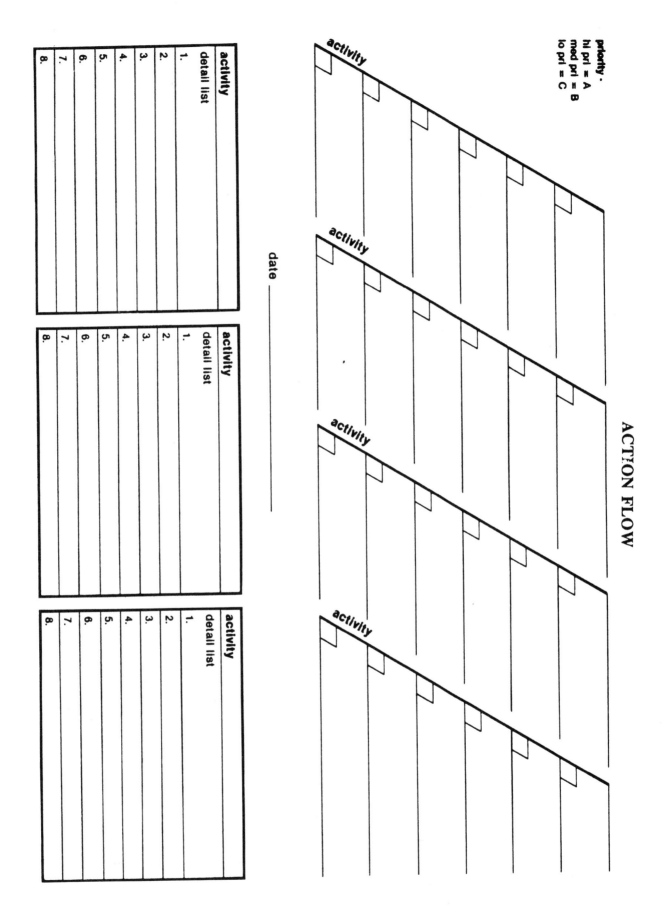

ACTION FLOW

priority :
hi pri = A
med pri = B
lo pri = C

activity

activity

activity

activity

date _____

activity	
detail list	
1.	
2.	
3.	
4.	
5.	
6.	
7.	
8.	

activity	
detail list	
1.	
2.	
3.	
4.	
5.	
6.	
7.	
8.	

activity	
detail list	
1.	
2.	
3.	
4.	
5.	
6.	
7.	
8.	

HOURS WORKED

NUMBER _____ NAME _____

19__	1	2	3	4	5	6	7	8	9	10	11	12	13	14	15	16	17	18	19	20	21	22	23	24	25	26	27	28	29	30	31	LATE HRS	LATE MIN	SICK	DAYS ABSENT EXC	DAYS ABSENT INEXC
JAN.																																				
FEB.																																				
MARCH																																				
APRIL																																				
MAY																																				
JUNE																																				
JULY																																				
AUG.																																				
SEPT.																																				
OCT.																																				
NOV.																																				
DEC.																																				

TOTAL

19__	1	2	3	4	5	6	7	8	9	10	11	12	13	14	15	16	17	18	19	20	21	22	23	24	25	26	27	28	29	30	31
JAN.																															
FEB.																															
MARCH																															
APRIL																															
MAY																															
JUNE																															
JULY																															
AUG.																															
SEPT.																															
OCT.																															
NOV.																															
DEC.																															

TOTAL

CODE:
I – INEXCUSED ABSENCE
E – EXCUSED ABSENCE
V – VACATION
S – SICK
L – LATE (SHOW NO. OF MINUTES LATE)
J – JURY DUTY

NOTES:

PERSONAL ATTENDANCE

WEEK OF_____

	HOURS						
	SUN	MON	TUE	WED	THU	FRI	SAT

OVERTIME SUMMARY

Day	Began Work	End Work	Over Time	Comments

Date

DAILY TIME AND EXPENSE LOG   DATE _____

SERVICES RENDERED	TIME	
	HRS.	MIN.

EXPENSE	AMOUNT	REASON FOR EXPENSE
Travel		
Breakfast		
Lunch		
Dinner		
Lodging		
Tips		
Auto		
Tolls/Parking		
Telephone		
Entertainment		
TOTAL		

FOR TODAY

DAY _____

Appointments and Telephone Calls:	
_____	_____
_____	_____
_____	_____

Done

1. _____ ☐

2. _____ ☐

3. _____ ☐

4. _____ ☐

5. _____ ☐

6. _____ ☐

7. _____ ☐

8. _____ ☐

9. _____ ☐

10. _____ ☐

11. _____ ☐

12. _____ ☐

13. _____ ☐

14. _____ ☐

15. _____ ☐

DAILY TIME AND EXPENSE LOG

DATE _____

SERVICES RENDERED	TIME	
	HRS.	MIN.

EXPENSE	AMOUNT	REASON FOR EXPENSE
Travel		
Breakfast		
Lunch		
Dinner		
Lodging		
Tips		
Auto		
Tolls/Parking		
Telephone		
Entertainment		
TOTAL		

PROFESSIONAL CHARGE SHEET

HOUR	DIARY	TIME	
		HRS.	MIN.

PROFESSIONAL TIME RECORD

	PERSON	CHARGES		PAID		BALANCE	
7:00							
7:15							
7:30							
7:45							
8:00							
8:15							
8:30							
8:45							
9:00							
9:15							
9:30							
9:45							
10:00							
10:15							
10:30							
10:45							
11:00							
11:15							
11:30							
11:45							
12:00							
12:15							
12:30							
12:45							
1:00							
1:15							
1:30							
1:45							
2:00							
2:15							
2:30							
2:45							
3:00							
3:15							
3:30							
3:45							
4:00							
4:15							
4:30							
4:45							
5:00							
5:15							
5:30							
5:45							
6:00							
6:15							
6:30							
6:45							

30 MINUTE TIME LOG

7:00	
7:30	
8:00	
8:30	
9:00	
9:30	
10:00	
10:30	
11:00	
11:30	
12:00	
12:30	
1:00	
1:30	
2:00	
2:30	
3:00	
3:30	
4:00	
4:30	
5:00	
5:30	

CHECK DAY PLANNED							TIME NEEDED		FOLLOW-UP	✔
S	M	T	W	T	F	S				

THIS WEEK'S DEADLINES   WEEK OF _____

WEEKLY ORGANIZER

DATE _____

GOALS FOR WEEK				FROM LAST WEEK
GOAL	✔	GOAL	✔	

MONDAY

D O

P H O N E

W R I T E

TUESDAY

D O

P H O N E

W R I T E

WEDNESDAY

D O

P H O N E

W R I T E

THURSDAY

D O

P H O N E

W R I T E

FRIDAY

D O

P H O N E

W R I T E

SATURDAY/SUNDAY

D O

P H O N E

W R I T E

WEEKLY GOALS

WEEK OF _____

	PRIORITY	GOAL	✔
1			
2			
3			
4			
5			
6			
7			
8			
9			
10			

	GOAL #	TASK	PRIORITY	TARGET DATE	✔
1					
2					
3					
4					
5					
6					
7					
8					
9					
10					
11					
12					
13					
14					
15					
16					
17					
18					
19					
20					
21					
22					
23					
24					

WEEKLY PROJECTS

WEEK OF _____

CHECK DAY PLANNED								DATE NEEDED	FOLLOW-UP NEEDED	FOLLOW-UP DATE	✔
S	M	T	W	T	F	S					

THIS WEEK'S PLANS

MONDAY   Date: _____   ✔   ✔

1. _____ ☐   7. _____ ☐
2. _____ ☐   8. _____ ☐
3. _____ ☐   9. _____ ☐
4. _____ ☐   10. _____ ☐
5. _____ ☐   11. _____ ☐
6. _____ ☐   12. _____ ☐

TUESDAY   Date: _____   ✔   ✔

1. _____ ☐   7. _____ ☐
2. _____ ☐   8. _____ ☐
3. _____ ☐   9. _____ ☐
4. _____ ☐   10. _____ ☐
5. _____ ☐   11. _____ ☐
6. _____ ☐   12. _____ ☐

WEDNESDAY   Date: _____   ✔   ✔

1. _____ ☐   7. _____ ☐
2. _____ ☐   8. _____ ☐
3. _____ ☐   9. _____ ☐
4. _____ ☐   10. _____ ☐
5. _____ ☐   11. _____ ☐
6. _____ ☐   12. _____ ☐

THURSDAY   Date: _____   ✔   ✔

1. _____ ☐   7. _____ ☐
2. _____ ☐   8. _____ ☐
3. _____ ☐   9. _____ ☐
4. _____ ☐   10. _____ ☐
5. _____ ☐   11. _____ ☐
6. _____ ☐   12. _____ ☐

FRIDAY   Date: _____   ✔   ✔

1. _____ ☐   7. _____ ☐
2. _____ ☐   8. _____ ☐
3. _____ ☐   9. _____ ☐
4. _____ ☐   10. _____ ☐
5. _____ ☐   11. _____ ☐
6. _____ ☐   12. _____ ☐

WEEKLY WORKSHEET

		MONDAY	TUESDAY	WEDNESDAY	THURSDAY	FRIDAY

APPOINTMENTS THIS WEEK

	MONDAY	TUESDAY	WEDNESDAY	THURSDAY	FRIDAY	
8:00						8:00
8:30						8:30
9:00						9:00
9:30						9:30
10:00						10:00
10:30						10:30
11:00						11:00
11:30						11:30
12:00						12:00
12:30						12:30
1:00						1:00
1:30						1:30
2:00						2:00
2:30						2:30
3:00						3:00
3:30						3:30
4:00						4:00
4:30						4:30
5:00						5:00
5:30						5:30

WEEKLY PLANNER

MONDAY	TUESDAY	WEDNESDAY	THURSDAY	FRIDAY

WEEKLY WORKSHEET

MON				
TUE				
WED				
THU				
FRI				

	MONDAY	TUESDAY	WEDNESDAY	THURSDAY	FRIDAY

WEEKLY WORKSHEET

WEEK-TO-WEEK ACTIVITIES DATE _____

PRIORITY KEY:
1 - URGENT   2 - IMPORTANT   3 - LOW PRIORITY   4 - VERY LOW PRIORITY   5 - CAN WAIT

FROM LAST WEEK

PRIORITY		✔	PRIORITY		✔

FOR THIS WEEK

PRIORITY		✔	PRIORITY		✔

FOR NEXT WEEK

PRIORITY		✔	PRIORITY		✔

52 WEEK RECORD

1							1
2							2
3							3
4							4
5							5
6							6
7							7
8							8
9							9
10							10
11							11
12							12
13							13
14							14
15							15
16							16
17							17
18							18
19							19
20							20
21							21
22							22
23							23
24							24
25							25
26							26
27							27
28							28
29							29
30							30
31							31
32							32
33							33
34							34
35							35
36							36
37							37
38							38
39							39
40							40
41							41
42							42
43							43
44							44
45							45
46							46
47							47
48							48
49							49
50							50
51							51
52							52

TWO WEEK WORKSHEET

		MONDAY	TUESDAY	WEDNESDAY	THURSDAY	FRIDAY		MONDAY	TUESDAY	WEDNESDAY	THURSDAY	FRIDAY

14 DAY PLANNER

	SUNDAY	
	MONDAY	
	TUESDAY	
	WEDNESDAY	
	THURSDAY	
	FRIDAY	
	SATURDAY	

	SUNDAY	
	MONDAY	
	TUESDAY	
	WEDNESDAY	
	THURSDAY	
	FRIDAY	
	SATURDAY	

TWO WEEK PLANNER

SUNDAY	MONDAY	TUESDAY	WEDNESDAY	THURSDAY	FRIDAY	SATURDAY

SUNDAY	MONDAY	TUESDAY	WEDNESDAY	THURSDAY	FRIDAY	SATURDAY

TWO WEEK PLANNER

	MONDAY	TUESDAY	WEDNESDAY	THURSDAY	FRIDAY

MONDAY	TUESDAY	WEDNESDAY	THURSDAY	FRIDAY

B 50

TWO WEEK TRACKING

1										
2										
3										
4										
5										
6										
7										
8										
9										
10										
11										
12										
13										
14										

TWO WEEK TRACKING

1		
2		
3		
4		
5		
6		
7		
8		
9		
10		
11		
12		
13		
14		

□ 1990 □ JANUARY
□ 1991 □ FEBRUARY
□ 1992 □ MARCH
□ 1993 □ APRIL
□ 1994 □ MAY
□ 1995 □ JUNE
□ 1996 □ JULY
□ 1997 □ AUGUST
□ 1998 □ SEPTEMBER
□ 1999 □ OCTOBER
□ 2000 □ NOVEMBER
□ 2001 □ DECEMBER

DETERMINE WHICH DAY THIS, THE PREVIOUS AND THE FOLLOWING MONTH BEGAN ON AND LABEL MONTHS BELOW.

M   T
T   F
S   S

PRIORITY
ITEMS FOR
THIS
WEEK

MONDAY   DATE
TUESDAY   DATE
WEDNESDAY   DATE
THURSDAY   DATE
FRIDAY   DATE
SATURDAY   DATE
SUNDAY   DATE

A HUNDRED YEAR CALENDAR

How to use the 100-year calendar: First find the proper year in question. It is listed in the table on the facing page. The months of the year are identified by reference numbers 1-7. Select the desired month and refer to the corresponding tables shown on this page.

1

S	M	T	W	T	F	S
1	2	3	4	5	6	7
8	9	10	11	12	13	14
15	16	17	18	19	20	21
22	23	24	25	26	27	28
29	30	31				

2

S	M	T	W	T	F	S
	1	2	3	4	5	6
7	8	9	10	11	12	13
14	15	16	17	18	19	20
21	22	23	24	25	26	27
28	29	30	31			

3

S	M	T	W	T	F	S
		1	2	3	4	5
6	7	8	9	10	11	12
13	14	15	16	17	18	19
20	21	22	23	24	25	26
27	28	29	30	31		

4

S	M	T	W	T	F	S
			1	2	3	4
5	6	7	8	9	10	11
12	13	14	15	16	17	18
19	20	21	22	23	24	25
26	27	28	29	30	31	

5

S	M	T	W	T	F	S
				1	2	3
4	5	6	7	8	9	10
11	12	13	14	15	16	17
18	19	20	21	22	23	24
25	26	27	28	29	30	31

6

S	M	T	W	T	F	S
					1	2
3	4	5	6	7	8	9
10	11	12	13	14	15	16
17	18	19	20	21	22	23
24	25	26	27	28	29	30
31						

7

S	M	T	W	T	F	S
						1
2	3	4	5	6	7	8
9	10	11	12	13	14	15
16	17	18	19	20	21	22
23	24	25	26	27	28	29
30	31					

Year Reference Table

Year	JAN	FEB	MAR	APR	MAY	JUNE	JULY	AUG	SEPT	OCT	NOV	DEC
1900	2	5	5	1	3	6	1	4	7	2	5	7
1901	3	6	6	2	4	7	2	5	1	3	6	1
1902	4	7	7	3	5	1	3	6	2	4	7	2
1903	5	1	1	4	6	2	4	7	3	5	1	3
1904	6	2	3	6	1	4	6	2	5	7	3	5
1905	1	4	4	7	2	5	7	3	6	1	4	6
1906	2	5	5	1	3	6	1	4	7	2	5	7
1907	3	6	6	2	4	7	2	5	1	3	6	1
1908	4	7	1	4	6	2	4	7	3	5	1	3
1909	6	2	2	5	7	3	5	1	4	6	2	4
1910	7	3	3	6	1	4	6	2	5	7	3	5
1911	1	4	4	7	2	5	7	3	6	1	4	6
1912	2	5	6	2	4	7	2	5	1	3	6	1
1913	4	7	7	3	5	1	3	6	2	4	7	2
1914	5	1	1	4	6	2	4	7	3	5	1	3
1915	6	2	2	5	7	3	5	1	4	6	2	4
1916	7	3	4	7	2	5	7	3	6	1	4	6
1917	2	5	5	1	3	6	1	4	7	2	5	7
1918	3	6	6	2	4	7	2	5	1	3	6	1
1919	4	7	7	3	5	1	3	6	2	4	7	2
1920	5	1	2	5	7	3	5	1	4	6	2	4
1921	7	3	3	6	1	4	6	2	5	7	3	5
1922	1	4	4	7	2	5	7	3	6	1	4	6
1923	2	5	5	1	3	6	1	4	7	2	5	7
1924	3	6	7	3	5	1	3	6	2	4	7	2
1925	5	1	1	4	6	2	4	7	3	5	1	3
1926	6	2	2	5	7	3	5	1	4	6	2	4
1927	7	3	3	6	1	4	6	2	5	7	3	5
1928	1	4	5	1	3	6	1	4	7	2	5	7
1929	3	6	6	2	4	7	2	5	1	3	6	1
1930	4	7	7	3	5	1	3	6	2	4	7	2
1931	5	1	1	4	6	2	4	7	3	5	1	3
1932	6	2	3	6	1	4	6	2	5	7	3	5
1933	1	4	4	7	2	5	7	3	6	1	4	6
1934	2	5	5	1	3	6	1	4	7	2	5	7
1935	3	6	6	2	4	7	2	5	1	3	6	1
1936	4	7	1	4	6	2	4	7	3	5	1	3
1937	6	2	2	5	7	3	5	1	4	6	2	4
1938	7	3	3	6	1	4	6	2	5	7	3	5
1939	1	4	4	7	2	5	7	3	6	1	4	6
1940	2	5	6	2	4	7	2	5	1	3	6	1
1941	4	7	7	3	5	1	3	6	2	4	7	2
1942	5	1	1	4	6	2	4	7	3	5	1	3
1943	6	2	2	5	7	3	5	1	4	6	2	4
1944	7	3	4	7	2	5	7	3	6	1	4	6
1945	3	6	6	2	4	7	2	5	1	3	6	1
1946	4	7	7	3	5	1	3	6	2	4	7	2
1947	5	1	1	4	6	2	4	7	3	5	1	3
1948	6	2	3	6	1	4	6	2	5	7	3	5
1949	1	4	4	7	2	5	7	3	6	1	4	6
1950	2	5	5	1	3	6	1	4	7	2	5	7
1951	3	6	6	2	4	7	2	5	1	3	6	1
1952	4	7	1	4	6	2	4	7	3	5	1	3
1953	6	2	2	5	7	3	5	1	4	6	2	4
1954	7	3	3	6	1	4	6	2	5	7	3	5
1955	1	4	4	7	2	5	7	3	6	1	4	6
1956	2	5	6	2	4	7	2	5	1	3	6	1
1957	4	7	7	3	5	1	3	6	2	4	7	2
1958	5	1	1	4	6	2	4	7	3	5	1	3
1959	6	2	2	5	7	3	5	1	4	6	2	4
1960	7	3	4	7	2	5	7	3	6	1	4	6
1961	1	4	4	7	2	5	7	3	6	1	4	6
1962	2	5	5	1	3	6	1	4	7	2	5	7
1963	3	6	6	2	4	7	2	5	1	3	6	1
1964	4	7	1	4	6	2	4	7	3	5	1	3
1965	6	2	2	5	7	3	5	1	4	6	2	4
1966	7	3	3	6	1	4	6	2	5	7	3	5
1967	1	4	4	7	2	5	7	3	6	1	4	6
1968	2	5	6	2	4	7	2	5	1	3	6	1
1969	4	7	7	3	5	1	3	6	2	4	7	2
1970	5	1	1	4	6	2	4	7	3	5	1	3
1971	6	2	2	5	7	3	5	1	4	6	2	4
1972	7	3	4	7	2	5	7	3	6	1	4	6
1973	2	5	5	1	3	6	1	4	7	2	5	7
1974	3	6	6	2	4	7	2	5	1	3	6	1
1975	4	7	7	3	5	1	3	6	2	4	7	2
1976	5	1	2	5	7	3	5	1	4	6	2	4
1977	7	3	3	6	1	4	6	2	5	7	3	5
1978	1	4	4	7	2	5	7	3	6	1	4	6
1979	2	5	5	1	3	6	1	4	7	2	5	7
1980	3	6	7	3	5	1	3	6	2	4	7	2
1981	5	1	1	4	6	2	4	7	3	5	1	3
1982	6	2	2	5	7	3	5	1	4	6	2	4
1983	7	3	3	6	1	4	6	2	5	7	3	5
1984	1	4	5	1	3	6	1	4	7	2	5	7
1985	3	6	6	2	4	7	2	5	1	3	6	1
1986	4	7	7	3	5	1	3	6	2	4	7	2
1987	5	1	1	4	6	2	4	7	3	5	1	3
1988	6	2	3	6	1	4	6	2	5	7	3	5
1989	1	4	4	7	2	5	7	3	6	1	4	6
1990	2	5	5	1	3	6	1	4	7	2	5	7
1991	3	6	6	2	4	7	2	5	1	3	6	1
1992	4	7	1	4	6	2	4	7	3	5	1	3
1993	6	2	2	5	7	3	5	1	4	6	2	4
1994	7	3	3	6	1	4	6	2	5	7	3	5
1995	1	4	4	7	2	5	7	3	6	1	4	6
1996	2	5	6	2	4	7	2	5	1	3	6	1
1997	4	7	7	3	5	1	3	6	2	4	7	2
1998	5	1	1	4	6	2	4	7	3	5	1	3
1999	6	2	2	5	7	3	5	1	4	6	2	4
2000	7	3	4	7	2	5	7	3	6	1	4	6

THIS MONTH'S DEADLINES

MONTH _____

DATE NEEDED	TIME NEEDED		FOLLOW-UP	✔

MONTHLY CHECKLIST

MONTH OF

	1	2	3	4	5	6	7	8	9	10	11	12	13	14	15	16	17	18	19	20	21	22	23	24	25	26	27	28	29	30	31

ONE MONTH RECAP

1																		
2																		
3																		
4																		
5																		
6																		
7																		
8																		
9																		
10																		
11																		
12																		
13																		
14																		
15																		
16																		
17																		
18																		
19																		
20																		
21																		
22																		
23																		
24																		
25																		
26																		
27																		
28																		
29																		
30																		
31																		

ONE MONTH RECAP

1					
2					
3					
4					
5					
6					
7					
8					
9					
10					
11					
12					
13					
14					
15					
16					
17					
18					
19					
20					
21					
22					
23					
24					
25					
26					
27					
28					
29					
30					
31					

MONTHLY PLANNER

MONTH OF:

SUNDAY	MONDAY	TUESDAY	WEDNESDAY	THURSDAY	FRIDAY	SATURDAY
					1	2
3	4	5	6	7	8	9
10	11	12	13	14	15	16
17	18	19	20	21	22	23
24	25	26	27	28	29	30
31						

MONTH OF.

MONTHLY PLANNER

SUNDAY	MONDAY	TUESDAY	WEDNESDAY	THURSDAY	FRIDAY	SATURDAY
						1
2	3	4	5	6	7	8
9	10	11	12	13	14	15
16	17	18	19	20	21	22
23	24	25	26	27	28	29
30	31					

MONTHLY WORKSHEET

DATE																															
1																															
2																															
3																															
4																															
5																															
6																															
7																															
8																															
9																															
10																															
11																															
12																															
13																															
14																															
15																															
16																															
17																															
18																															
19																															
20																															
21																															
22																															
23																															
24																															
25																															
26																															
27																															
28																															
29																															
30																															
31																															

FIVE WEEK TRACKING

Monday					
Tuesday					
Wednesday					
Thursday					
Friday					
Monday					
Tuesday					
Wednesday					
Thursday					
Friday					
Monday					
Tuesday					
Wednesday					
Thursday					
Friday					
Monday					
Tuesday					
Wednesday					
Thursday					
Friday					
Monday					
Tuesday					
Wednesday					
Thursday					
Friday					

MONTH BY DAYS

Sunday	
Monday	
Tuesday	
Wednesday	
Thursday	
Friday	
Saturday	
Sunday	
Monday	
Tuesday	
Wednesday	
Thursday	
Friday	
Saturday	
Sunday	
Monday	
Tuesday	
Wednesday	
Thursday	
Friday	
Saturday	
Sunday	
Monday	
Tuesday	
Wednesday	
Thursday	
Friday	
Saturday	
Sunday	
Monday	
Tuesday	
Wednesday	
Thursday	
Friday	
Saturday	

MONTHLY TRACKING

1																			
2																			
3																			
4																			
5																			
6																			
7																			
8																			
9																			
10																			
11																			
12																			
13																			
14																			
15																			
16																			
17																			
18																			
19																			
20																			
21																			
22																			
23																			
24																			
25																			
26																			
27																			
28																			
29																			
30																			
31																			

THIS MONTH'S PLANS

SUNDAY	MONDAY	TUESDAY	WEDNESDAY	THURSDAY	FRIDAY	SATURDAY

THIS MONTH'S PLANS

1
2
3
4
5
6
7
8
9
10
11
12
13
14
15
16
17
18
19
20
21
22
23
24
25
26
27
28
29
30
31

THREE MONTH GOALS   PERIOD OF _____

	PRIORITY	GOAL	✔
1			
2			
3			
4			
5			
6			
7			
8			
9			
10			

	GOAL #	TASK	PRIORITY	TARGET DATE	✔
1					
2					
3					
4					
5					
6					
7					
8					
9					
10					
11					
12					
13					
14					
15					
16					
17					
18					
19					
20					
21					
22					
23					
24					

MONTHLY GOALS

MONTH _____

	PRIORITY	GOAL	✔
1			
2			
3			
4			
5			
6			
7			
8			
9			
10			

	GOAL #	TASK	PRIORITY	TARGET DATE	✔
1					
2					
3					
4					
5					
6					
7					
8					
9					
10					
11					
12					
13					
14					
15					
16					
17					
18					
19					
20					
21					
22					
23					
24					

FOUR MONTH PLANNER

MONTH OF:

SUNDAY	MONDAY	TUESDAY	WEDNESDAY	THURSDAY	FRIDAY	SATURDAY

MONTH OF:

SUNDAY	MONDAY	TUESDAY	WEDNESDAY	THURSDAY	FRIDAY	SATURDAY

MONTH OF:

SUNDAY	MONDAY	TUESDAY	WEDNESDAY	THURSDAY	FRIDAY	SATURDAY

MONTH OF:

SUNDAY	MONDAY	TUESDAY	WEDNESDAY	THURSDAY	FRIDAY	SATURDAY

THREE MONTH PLANNER

SUNDAY	MONDAY	TUESDAY	WEDNESDAY	THURSDAY	FRIDAY	SATURDAY

SUNDAY	MONDAY	TUESDAY	WEDNESDAY	THURSDAY	FRIDAY	SATURDAY

SUNDAY	MONDAY	TUESDAY	WEDNESDAY	THURSDAY	FRIDAY	SATURDAY

TWO MONTH PLANNER

SUNDAY	MONDAY	TUESDAY	WEDNESDAY	THURSDAY	FRIDAY	SATURDAY

SUNDAY	MONDAY	TUESDAY	WEDNESDAY	THURSDAY	FRIDAY	SATURDAY

TWO MONTH PLANNER

SUNDAY	MONDAY	TUESDAY	WEDNESDAY	THURSDAY	FRIDAY	SATURDAY

SUNDAY	MONDAY	TUESDAY	WEDNESDAY	THURSDAY	FRIDAY	SATURDAY

SIX MONTH GOALS

PERIOD OF _____

	PRIORITY	GOAL	✔
1			
2			
3			
4			
5			
6			
7			
8			
9			
10			

	GOAL #	TASK	PRIORITY	TARGET DATE	✔
1					
2					
3					
4					
5					
6					
7					
8					
9					
10					
11					
12					
13					
14					
15					
16					
17					
18					
19					
20					
21					
22					
23					
24					

MONTHLY PRIORITIES

DATE _____

	HIGH PRIORITY		
PRIORITY	ACTIVITY	✔	FOLLOW-UP
	LOW PRIORITY		
PRIORITY	ACTIVITY	✔	FOLLOW-UP
	ON HOLD		
PRIORITY	ACTIVITY	✔	FOLLOW-UP

SIX MONTH PLANNER

19___

JULY	AUGUST	SEPTEMBER

OCTOBER	NOVEMBER	DECEMBER

SIX MONTH PLANNER

19___

JANUARY	FEBRUARY	MARCH
APRIL	MAY	JUNE

THIS YEAR'S DEADLINES

YEAR _____

CHECK MONTH NEEDED												DATE NEEDED	TIME NEEDED		FOLLOW-UP	✔
J	F	M	A	M	J	J	A	S	O	N	D					

ANNUAL GOALS

YEAR _____

	PRIORITY	GOAL	✔
1			
2			
3			
4			
5			
6			
7			
8			
9			
10			

	GOAL #	TASK	PRIORITY	TARGET DATE	✔
1					
2					
3					
4					
5					
6					
7					
8					
9					
10					
11					
12					
13					
14					
15					
16					
17					
18					
19					
20					
21					
22					
23					
24					

QUARTERLY TRACKING

			27	28	29	30	31	32	33	34	35	36	37	38	39		40	41	42	43	44	45	46	47	48	49	50	51	52		
			1	2	3	4	5	6	7	8	9	10	11	12	13		14	15	16	17	18	19	20	21	22	23	24	25	26		

FOUR QUARTER WORKSHEET

WEEK																									
	SECOND QUARTER													**FIRST QUARTER**											
	26	25	24	23	22	21	20	19	18	17	16	15	14	13	12	11	10	9	8	7	6	5	4	3	2	1

WEEK																									
	FOURTH QUARTER													**THIRD QUARTER**											
	52	51	50	49	48	47	46	45	44	43	42	41	40	39	38	37	36	35	34	33	32	31	30	29	28	27

FOUR QUARTER WORKSHEET

WEEK	
FIRST QUARTER	1
	2
	3
	4
	5
	6
	7
	8
	9
	10
	11
	12
	13
SECOND QUARTER	14
	15
	16
	17
	18
	19
	20
	21
	22
	23
	24
	25
	26
THIRD QUARTER	27
	28
	29
	30
	31
	32
	33
	34
	35
	36
	37
	38
	39
FOURTH QUARTER	40
	41
	42
	43
	44
	45
	46
	47
	48
	49
	50
	51
	52

ONE QUARTER TRACKING

Week										
1										
2										
3										
4										
5										
6										
7										
8										
9										
10										
11										
12										
13										

YEARLY TRACKING _____

YEAR DIVIDED BY WEEK/QUARTER	SUBJECT
1	
2	
3	
4	
5	
6	
7	
8	
9	
10	
11	
12	
13	
1ST QUARTER	
14	
15	
16	
17	
18	
19	
20	
21	
22	
23	
24	
25	
26	
2ND QUARTER	
6 MONTHS	
27	
28	
29	
30	
31	
32	
33	
34	
35	
36	
37	
38	
39	
3RD QUARTER	
9 MONTHS	
40	
41	
42	
43	
44	
45	
46	
47	
48	
49	
50	
51	
52	
4TH QUARTER	
YEAR TOTAL	

52 WEEK TRACKING

1			
2			
3			
4			
5			
6			
7			
8			
9			
10			
11			
12			
13			
14			
15			
16			
17			
18			
19			
20			
21			
22			
23			
24			
25			
26			
27			
28			
29			
30			
31			
32			
33			
34			
35			
36			
37			
38			
39			
40			
41			
42			
43			
44			
45			
46			
47			
48			
49			
50			
51			
52			

ONE YEAR PROGRESS SHEET

Jan.											Jan.
Feb.											Feb.
Mar.											Mar.
Apr.											Apr.
May											May
Jun.											Jun.
Jul.											Jul.
Aug.											Aug.
Sept.											Sept.
Oct.											Oct.
Nov.											Nov.
Dec.											Dec.

ONE YEAR PROGRESS SHEET

Jan.		Jan.
Feb.		Feb.
Mar.		Mar.
Apr.		Apr.
May		May
Jun.		Jun.
Jul.		Jul.
Aug.		Aug.
Sept.		Sept.
Oct.		Oct.
Nov.		Nov.
Dec.		Dec.

TWELVE MONTH WORKSHEET

19___

DATE	JAN.	FEB.	MAR.	APR.	MAY	JUN.	JUL.	AUG.	SEP.	OCT.	NOV.	DEC.
1												
2												
3												
4												
5												
6												
7												
8												
9												
10												
11												
12												
13												
14												
15												
16												
17												
18												
19												
20												
21												
22												
23												
24												
25												
26												
27												
28												
29												
30												
31												

SIX MONTH WORKSHEET

DATE	MONTH OF	MONTH OF	MONTH OF	MONTH OF	MONTH OF	MONTH OF
1						
2						
3						
4						
5						
6						
7						
8						
9						
10						
11						
12						
13						
14						
15						
16						
17						
18						
19						
20						
21						
22						
23						
24						
25						
26						
27						
28						
29						
30						
31						

ONE YEAR CHECKLIST

Year:	J	F	M	A	M	J	J	A	S	O	N	D

52 WEEK CHECKLIST   YEAR _____

	1	2	3	4	5	6	7	8	9	10	11	12	13	14	15	16	17	18	19	20	21	22	23	24	25	26	27	28	29	30	31	32	33	34	35	36	37	38	39	40	41	42	43	44	45	46	47	48	49	50	51	52

52 WEEK WORKSHEET

WEEK	
1	
2	
3	
4	
5	
6	
7	
8	
9	
10	
11	
12	
13	
14	
15	
16	
17	
18	
19	
20	
21	
22	
23	
24	
25	
26	
27	
28	
29	
30	
31	
32	
33	
34	
35	
36	
37	
38	
39	
40	
41	
42	
43	
44	
45	
46	
47	
48	
49	
50	
51	
52	

ONE YEAR CHECKLIST

Year:	J	F	M	A	M	J	J	A	S	O	N	D

52 WEEK CHECKLIST

YEAR _____

	1	2	3	4	5	6	7	8	9	10	11	12	13	14	15	16	17	18	19	20	21	22	23	24	25	26	27	28	29	30	31	32	33	34	35	36	37	38	39	40	41	42	43	44	45	46	47	48	49	50	51	52

ONE YEAR PROGRESS SHEET

Jan.												Jan.
Feb.												Feb.
Mar.												Mar.
Apr.												Apr.
May												May
Jun.												Jun.
Jul.												Jul.
Aug.												Aug.
Sept.												Sept.
Oct.												Oct.
Nov.												Nov.
Dec.												Dec.

TWO YEARS BY MONTHS

YEAR:	
JAN	
FEB	
MAR	
APR	
MAY	
JUN	
JUL	
AUG	
SEP	
OCT	
NOV	
DEC	
YEAR:	
JAN	
FEB	
MAR	
APR	
MAY	
JUN	
JUL	
AUG	
SEP	
OCT	
NOV	
DEC	

TWO YEAR WORKSHEET

WEEK			WEEK
1			1
2			2
3			3
4			4
5			5
6			6
7			7
8			8
9			9
10			10
11			11
12			12
13			13
14			14
15			15
16			16
17			17
18			18
19			19
20			20
21			21
22			22
23			23
24			24
25			25
26			26
27			27
28			28
29			29
30			30
31			31
32			32
33			33
34			34
35			35
36			36
37			37
38			38
39			39
40			40
41			41
42			42
43			43
44			44
45			45
46			46
47			47
48			48
49			49
50			50
51			51
52			52

TWO YEAR CHECKLIST

		Years	J	F	M	A	M	J	J	A	S	O	N	D	Years

			J	F	M	A	M	J	J	A	S	O	N	D

TWO YEAR PROGRESS SHEET

Jan.							Jan.
Feb.							Feb.
Mar.							Mar.
Apr.							Apr.
May							May
Jun.							Jun.
Jul.							Jul.
Aug.							Aug.
Sept.							Sept.
Oct.							Oct.
Nov.							Nov.
Dec.							Dec.

Jan.							Jan.
Feb.							Feb.
Mar.							Mar.
Apr.							Apr.
May							May
Jun.							Jun.
Jul.							Jul.
Aug.							Aug.
Sept.							Sept.
Oct.							Oct.
Nov.							Nov.
Dec.							Dec.

TWO YEAR PROGRESS SHEET

Jan.		Jan.
Feb.		Feb.
Mar.		Mar.
Apr.		Apr.
May		May
Jun.		Jun.
Jul.		Jul.
Aug.		Aug.
Sept.		Sept.
Oct.		Oct.
Nov.		Nov.
Dec.		Dec.

Jan.		Jan.
Feb.		Feb.
Mar.		Mar.
Apr.		Apr.
May		May
Jun.		Jun.
Jul.		Jul.
Aug.		Aug.
Sept.		Sept.
Oct.		Oct.
Nov.		Nov.
Dec.		Dec.

THREE YEARS BY MONTHS

YEAR:	
JAN	
FEB	
MAR	
APR	
MAY	
JUN	
JUL	
AUG	
SEP	
OCT	
NOV	
DEC	
YEAR:	
JAN	
FEB	
MAR	
APR	
MAY	
JUN	
JUL	
AUG	
SEP	
OCT	
NOV	
DEC	
YEAR:	
JAN	
FEB	
MAR	
APR	
MAY	
JUN	
JUL	
AUG	
SEP	
OCT	
NOV	
DEC	

FOUR YEARS BY MONTHS

YEAR.													YEAR.												
	JAN	FEB	MAR	APR	MAY	JUN	JUL	AUG	SEP	OCT	NOV	DEC		JAN	FEB	MAR	APR	MAY	JUN	JUL	AUG	SEP	OCT	NOV	DEC
YEAR.													YEAR.												
	JAN	FEB	MAR	APR	MAY	JUN	JUL	AUG	SEP	OCT	NOV	DEC		JAN	FEB	MAR	APR	MAY	JUN	JUL	AUG	SEP	OCT	NOV	DEC

THREE YEAR CHECKLIST

Year:	J	F	M	A	M	J	J	A	S	O	N	D

Year:	J	F	M	A	M	J	J	A	S	O	N	D

Year:	J	F	M	A	M	J	J	A	S	O	N	D

FIVE YEAR TRACKING

Subject:

Years _____

Subject List: 1 2 3 4 5 6 7 8 9 10 11 12 13 — Sub-Total — Total

Columns: J F M A M J J A S O N D Total

Subject List: 1 2 3 4 5 6 7 8 9 10 11 12 13 — Sub-Total — Total

Years: 1 2 3 4 5 Total

FOUR YEAR CHECKLIST

	Year:	J F M A M J J A S O N D

	Year:	J F M A M J J A S O N D

	Year:	J F M A M J J A S O N D

	Year:	J F M A M J J A S O N D

LONG RANGE GOALS

DATE _____

	PRIORITY	GOAL	✔
1			
2			
3			
4			
5			
6			
7			
8			
9			
10			

	GOAL #	TASK	PRIORITY	TARGET DATE	✔
1					
2					
3					
4					
5					
6					
7					
8					
9					
10					
11					
12					
13					
14					
15					
16					
17					
18					
19					
20					
21					
22					
23					
24					

NATIONAL AREA CODE LISTING REFERENCE GUIDE

place	area code
ALABAMA	
All points	205
ALASKA	
All points	907
ARIZONA	
All points	602
ARKANSAS	
All points	501
CALIFORNIA	
Bakersfield	805
Beverly Hills	213
Burbank (L.A. County)	213
Fresno	209
Glendale	213
Inglewood	213
Long Beach	213
Los Angeles	213
Oakland	415
Palo Alto	415
Pomona	714
Sacramento	916
San Diego	714
San Francisco	415
San Jose	408
San Mateo	415
Santa Ana	714
Santa Rosa	707
Stockton	209
COLORADO	
All points	303
CONNECTICUT	
All points	203
DELAWARE	
All points	302
DIST. OF COLUMBIA	
Washington, D.C.	202
FLORIDA	
Clearwater	813
Daytona Beach	904
Fort Lauderdale	305
Fort Pierce	305
Gainesville	904
Hialeah	305
Jacksonville	904
Key West	305
Lakeland	813
Miami	305
Orlando	305
Pensacola	904
Pompano Beach	305
Sarasota	813
Tallahassee	904
West Palm Beach	305
GEORGIA	
Athens	404

place	area code
GEORGIA (Con't)	
Atlanta	404
Augusta	404
Columbus	404
Gainesville	404
Savannah	912
Macon	912
Rome	404
Valdosta	912
HAWAII	
All points	808
IDAHO	
All points	208
ILLINOIS	
Aurora	312
Bloomington	309
Chicago	312
Danville	217
Decatur	217
East St. Louis	618
Elgin	312
Joliet	815
La Grange	312
Highland Park	312
Peoria	309
Rockford	815
Springfield	217
INDIANA	
Elkhart	219
Evansville	812
Gary	219
Hammond	219
Indianapolis	317
Kokomo	317
Michigan City	219
Muncie	317
South Bend	219
IOWA	
Council Bluffs	712
Davenport	319
Des Moines	515
KANSAS	
Salina	913
Topeka	913
Wichita	316
KENTUCKY	
Ashland	606
Frankfort	502
Louisville	502
LOUISIANA	
Baton Rouge	504
New Orleans	504
Shreveport	318
MAINE	
All points	207

place	area code
MARYLAND	
All points	301
MASSACHUSETTS	
Amherst	413
Attleboro	617
Barnstable	617
Boston	617
Brockton	617
Cambridge	617
Chicopee	413
Fall River	617
Fitchburg	617
Framingham	617
Greenfield	413
Holyoke	413
Longmeadow	413
Lowell	617
Lynn	617
Marblehead	617
New Bedford	617
North Adams	413
Northampton	413
Pittsfield	413
Quincy	617
Roxbury	617
Salem	617
Springfield	413
Taunton	617
Westfield	413
Worcester	617
MICHIGAN	
Ann Arbor	313
Battle Creek	616
Benton Harbor	616
Dearborn	313
Detroit	313
Flint	313
Fort Lee	313
Grand Rapids	616
Jackson	517
Kalamazoo	616
Lansing	517
Marquette	906
Midland	517
Niles	616
Pontiac	313
Port Huron	313
Royal Oak	313
Saginaw	517
Wyandotte	313
MINNESOTA	
Duluth	218
Minneapolis	612
Rochester	507
St. Paul	612
MISSISSIPPI	
All points	601
MISSOURI	
Jefferson City	314
Kansas City	816
St. Joseph	816
St. Louis	314
Springfield	417

place	area code
MONTANA	
All points	406
NEBRASKA	
Lincoln	402
North Platte	308
Omaha	402
NEVADA	
All points	702
NEW HAMPSHIRE	
All points	603
NEW JERSEY	
Asbury Park	201
Atlantic City	609
Barnegat	609
Bayonne	201
Bound Brook	201
Bridgeton	609
Burlington	609
Camden	609
Carteret	201
Clifton	201
Cliffside Park	201
Collingswood	609
Dover	201
Eatontown	201
Elizabeth	201
Englewood	201
Ewing	609
Flemington	201
Fort Dix	609
Fort Lee	201
Garfield	201
Glassboro	609
Glen Ridge	201
Gloucester	609
Hackensack	201
Hackettstown	201
Haddonfield	609
Hasbrouck Heights	201
Hawthorne	201
Hoboken	201
Irvington	201
Jersey City	201
Kearny	201
Lakewood	201
Linden	201
Long Branch	201
Madison	201
Maplewood	201
Matawan	201
Mendham	201
Metuchen	201
Millburn	201
Montclair	201
Morristown	201
Mount Holly	609
New Brunswick	201
Newark	201
Nutley	201
Orange	201
Passaic	201
Paterson	201
Perth Amboy	201
Phillipsburg	201
NEW MEXICO	
All points	505

place	area code
NEW JERSEY (Con't)	
Plainfield	201
Pleasantville	609
Point Pleasant	201
Pompton Lakes	201
Princeton	609
Red Bank	201
Ridgefield	201
Ridgewood	201
Rutherford	201
Somerville	201
South Amboy	201
Summit	201
Teaneck	201
Trenton	609
Union City	201
Verona	201
Vineland	609
Weehawken	201
Westfield	201
Wildwood	609
Woodbridge	201
Woodbury	609
Wyckoff	201
NEW YORK	
Albany	518
Amagansett	516
Amityville	516
Amsterdam	518
Armonk Village	914
Auburn	315
Babylon	516
Baldwin	516
Bay Shore	516
Bedford Village	914
Binghamton	607
Brentwood	516
Brewster	914
Bridgehampton	516
Bronxville	914
Brookville	516
Buffalo	716
Callicoon	914
Carmel	914
Center Moriches	516
Central Islip	516
Cohoes	518
Cold Spring (Putnam Co.)	914
Congers	914
Corning	607
Cortland	607
Croton on Hudson	914
Deer Park	516
Dobbs Ferry	914
Dunkirk	716
East Hampton	516
Eastport	516
Ellenville	914
Elmsford	914
Elmira	607
Fairport	716
Farmingdale	516

place	area code
NEW YORK (Con't)	
Fire Island	516
Fishers Island	516
Freeport	516
Fulton	315
Garden City	516
Garrison	914
Glen Cove	516
Glens Falls	518
Gloversville	518
Great Neck	516
Hampton Bays	516
Harrison	914
Hastings-on-Hudson	914
Haverstraw	914
Hempstead	516
Hicksville	516
Hudson	518
Huntington	516
Hurleyville	914
Irvington	914
Islip	516
Ithaca	607
Jeffersonville	914
Katonah	914
Kenmore	716
Kingston	914
Lake Huntington	914
Lake Success	516
Larchmont	914
Liberty	914
Livingston Manor	914
Lockport	716
Lynbrook	516
Mahopac	914
Mamaroneck	914
Manhasset	516
Massapequa	516
Massena	315
Mineola	516
Monticello	914
Montauk Point	516
Mount Kisco	914
Mt. Vernon	914
Nanuet	914
Narrowsburg	914
Newark	315
Newburgh	914
New City	914
New Rochelle	914
New York City	212
Niagara Falls	716
Nyack	914
Norwich	607
Olean	716
Oneida	315
Oneonta	607
Ossining	914
Oswego	315
Oyster Bay	516
Patchogue	516
Pearl River	914
Peekskill	914
Pelham	914
Plattsburgh	518
Port Chester	914

place	area code
NEW YORK (Con't)	
Port Jefferson	516
Port Washington	516
Potsdam	315
Poughkeepsie	914
Riverhead	516
Rochester	716
Rockville Centre	516
Rome	315
Ronkonkoma	516
Roslyn	516
Rye	914
Sag Harbor	516
Sayville	516
Scarsdale	914
Schenectady	518
Shelter Island	516
Smithtown	516
Southampton	516
Spring Valley	914
Stony Point	914
Suffern (Rockland Co.)	914
Syracuse	315
Tarrytown	914
Ticonderoga	518
Tonawanda	716
Troy	518
Tuckahoe	914
Utica	315
Valley Stream	516
Wantagh	516
Watertown	315
Westbury	516
Westhampton (Westport Co.)	516
Wheatley Hills	516
White Lake	914
White Plains	914
Woodbourne	914
Woodmere	516
Woodridge	914
Woodstock	914
Yonkers	914
Yorktown Heights	914
NORTH CAROLINA	
Camp Le Jeune	919
Charlotte	704
Durham	919
Greensboro	919
Lexington	704
Raleigh	919
Salisbury	704
Sanford	919
Winston-Salem	919
NORTH DAKOTA	
All points	701
OHIO	
Akron	216
Canton	216
Cincinnati	513
Cleveland	216
Columbus	614
Dayton	513
East Liverpool	216

place	area code
OHIO (Con't)	
Findlay	419
Hamilton	513
Lancaster	614
Lima	419
Lorain	216
Mansfield	419
Marion	614
Middletown	513
Newark	614
Portsmouth	614
Springfield	513
Steubenville	614
Toledo	419
Warren	216
Youngstown	216
Zanesville	614
OKLAHOMA	
Oklahoma City	405
Tulsa	918
OREGON	
All points	503
PENNSYLVANIA	
Allentown (Lehigh Co.)	215
Altoona	814
Beaver Falls	412
Bethlehem	215
Bloomsburg	717
Bradford	814
Chambersburg	717
Du Bois	814
Easton	215
Erie	814
Greensburg	412
Harrisburg	717
Indiana	412
Lancaster	717
Levittown	215
Lock Haven	717
McKeesport	412
New Castle	412
Philadelphia	215
Pittsburgh	412
Pottstown	215
Pottsville	717
Reading	215
Scranton	717
Stroudsburg	717
State College	814
Sunbury	717
Uniontown (Indiana Co.)	412
Washington	412
Wayne	215
West Chester	215
Wilkes-Barre	717
Williamsport	717
RHODE ISLAND	
All points	401

place	area code
SOUTH CAROLINA	
All points	803
SOUTH DAKOTA	
All points	605
TENNESSEE	
Chattanooga	615
Memphis	901
Nashville	615
TEXAS	
Abilene	915
Amarillo	806
Austin	512
Brownsville	512
Corpus Christi	512
Dallas	214
Fort Worth	817
Galveston	713
Houston	713
San Antonio	512
Texas City — La Marque	713
UTAH	
All points	801
VERMONT	
All points	802
VIRGINIA	
Arlington	703
Charlottesville	804
Covington	703
Harrisonburg	703
Lynchburg	804
Norfolk	804
Richmond	804
Roanoke	703
WASHINGTON	
Olympia	206
Seattle	206
Spokane	509
Tacoma	206
Yakima	509
WEST VIRGINIA	
All points	304
WISCONSIN	
Appleton	414
Eau Claire	715
Green Bay	414
Madison	608
Milwaukee	414
Racine	414
WYOMING	
All points	307
WIDE AREA TEL. SERV	
All locations	800

place	area code
CANADA	
ALBERTA	
All points	403
BRITISH COLUMBIA	
All points	604
MANITOBA	
All points	204
NEW BRUNSWICK	
All points	506
NOVA SCOTIA	
All points	902
ONTARIO	
Fort William	807
London	519
North Bay	705
Ottawa	613
Toronto	416
QUEBEC	
Montreal	514
Quebec	418
Sherbrooke	819
SASKATCHEWAN	
All points	306
MEXICO	
All points	903
PUERTO RICO	
All points	809
VIRGIN ISLANDS	
All points	809

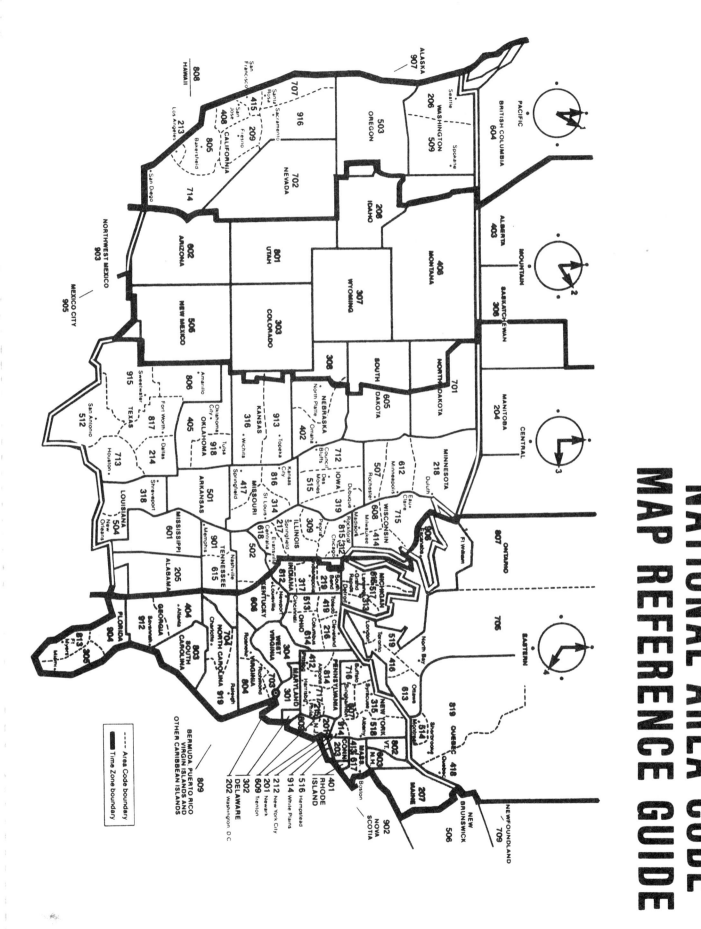

NATIONAL AREA CODE
MAP REFERENCE GUIDE

--- Area Code boundary
▬▬▬ Time Zone boundary

General Planners

1		
2		
3		
4		
5		
6		
7		
8		
9		
10		
11		
12		
13		
14		
15		
16		
17		
18		
19		
20		
21		
22		
23		
24		
25		
26		
27		
28		
29		
30		
31		
32		
33		
34		
35		
36		
37		
38		
39		
40		
41		
42		
43		
44		
45		
46		
47		
48		
49		
50		
51		
52		

1			
2			
3			
4			
5			
6			
7			
8			
9			
10			
11			
12			
13			
14			
15			
16			
17			
18			
19			
20			
21			
22			
23			
24			
25			
26			
27			
28			
29			
30			
31			
32			

B 113

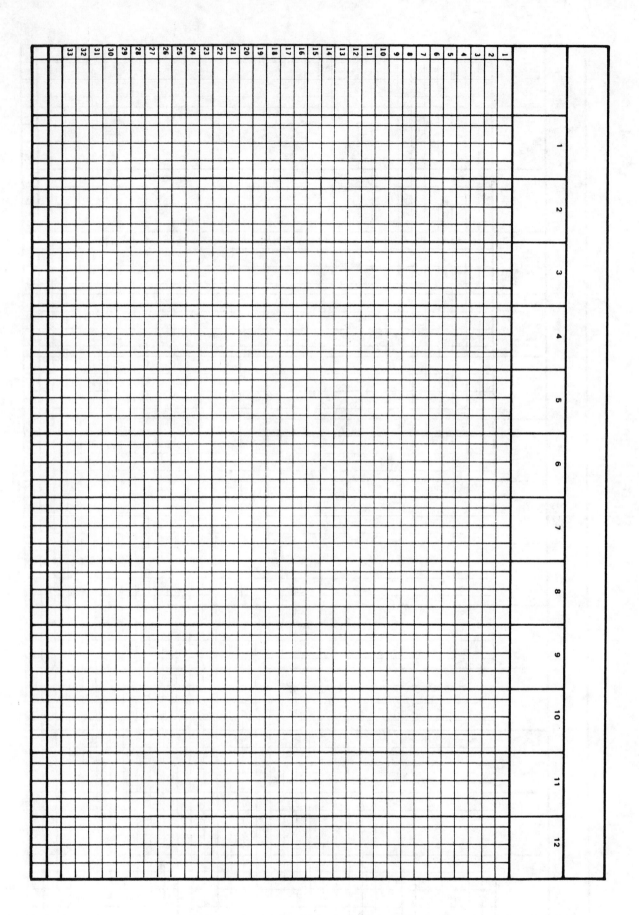

B 114

		33	32	31	30	29	28	27	26	25	24	23	22	21	20	19	18	17	16	15	14	13	12	11	10	9	8	7	6	5	4	3	2	1	
																																			1
																																			2
																																			3
																																			4
																																			5
																																			6
																																			7
																																			8
																																			9
																																			10

		1		2		3		4		5		6	
1													
2													
3													
4													
5													
6													
7													
8													
9													
10													
11													
12													
13													
14													
15													
16													
17													
18													
19													
20													
21													
22													
23													
24													
25													
26													
27													
28													
29													
30													
31													
32													
33													

			1			2			3			4		
1														
2														
3														
4														
5														
6														
7														
8														
9														
10														
11														
12														
13														
14														
15														
16														
17														
18														
19														
20														
21														
22														
23														
24														
25														
26														
27														
28														
29														
30														
31														
32														
33														

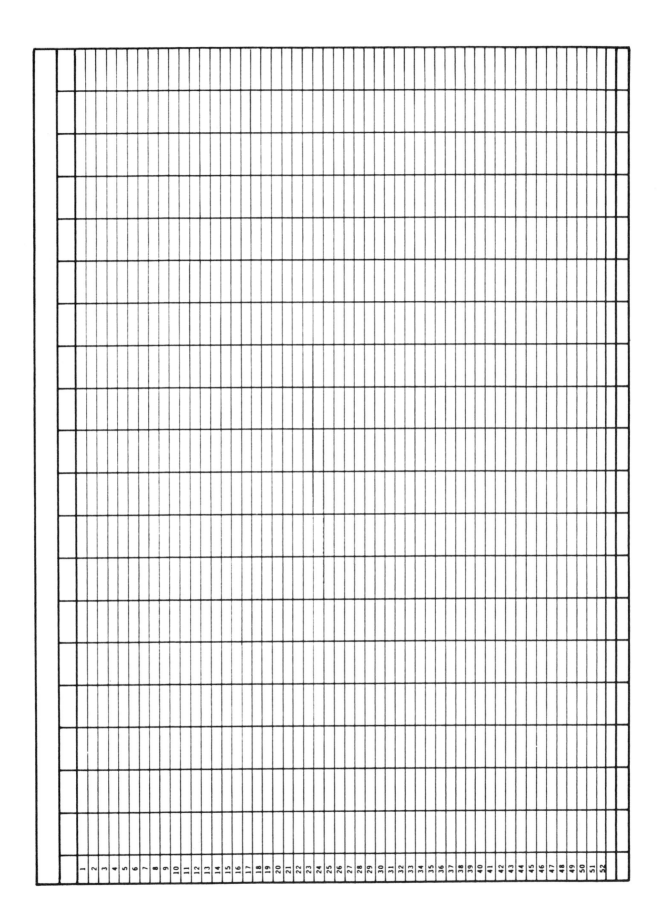

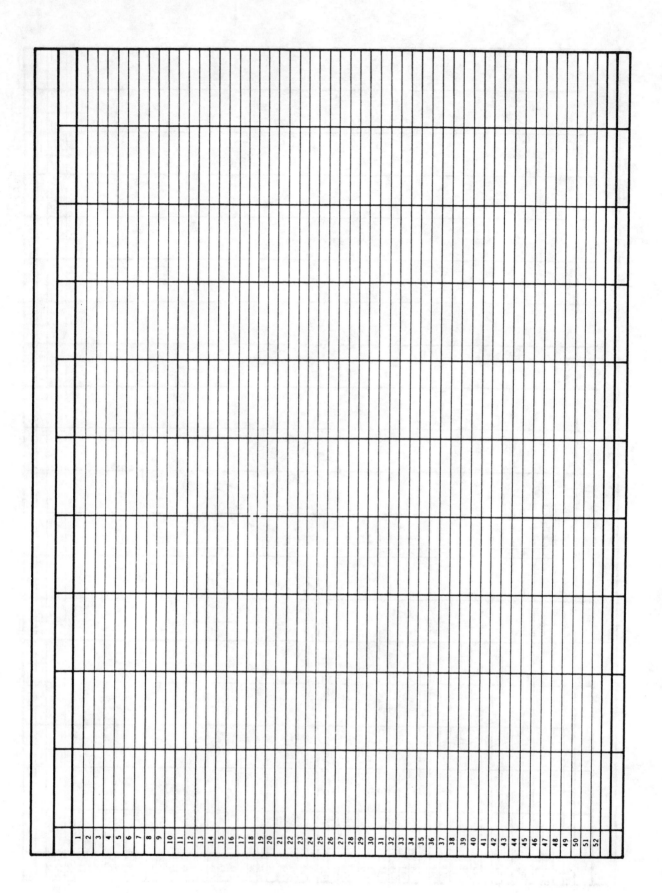

1 2 3 4 5 6 7 8 9 10 11 12 13 14 15 16 17 18 19 20 21 22 23 24 25 26 27 28 29 30 31 32 33 34 35 36 37 38 39 40 41 42 43 44 45 46 47 48 49 50 51 52

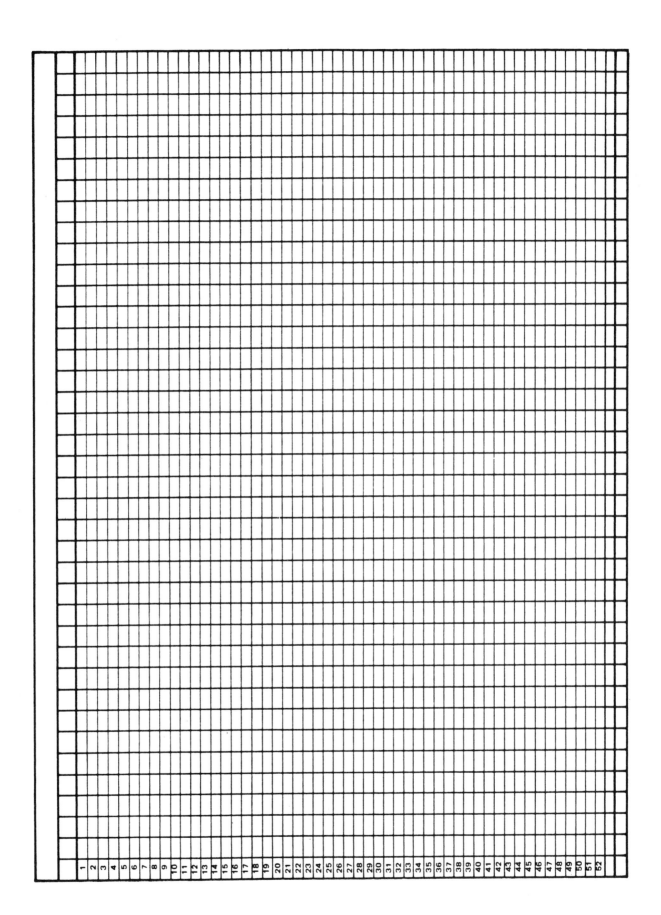

1 2 3 4 5 6 7 8 9 10 11 12 13 14 15 16 17 18 19 20 21 22 23 24 25 26 27 28 29 30 31 32 33 34 35 36 37 38 39 40 41 42 43 44 45 46 47 48 49 50 51 52

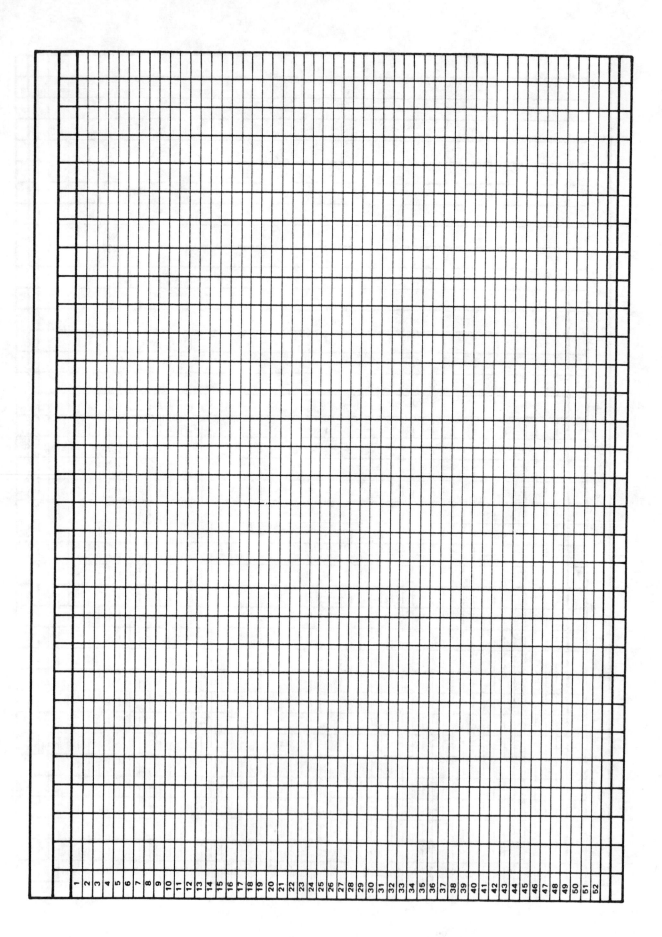

		1	2	3	4	5	6	7	8	9	10	11	12	13	14	15	16	17	18	19	20	21	22	23	24	25	26	27	28	29	30	31	32	33	34	35	36	37	38	39	40		

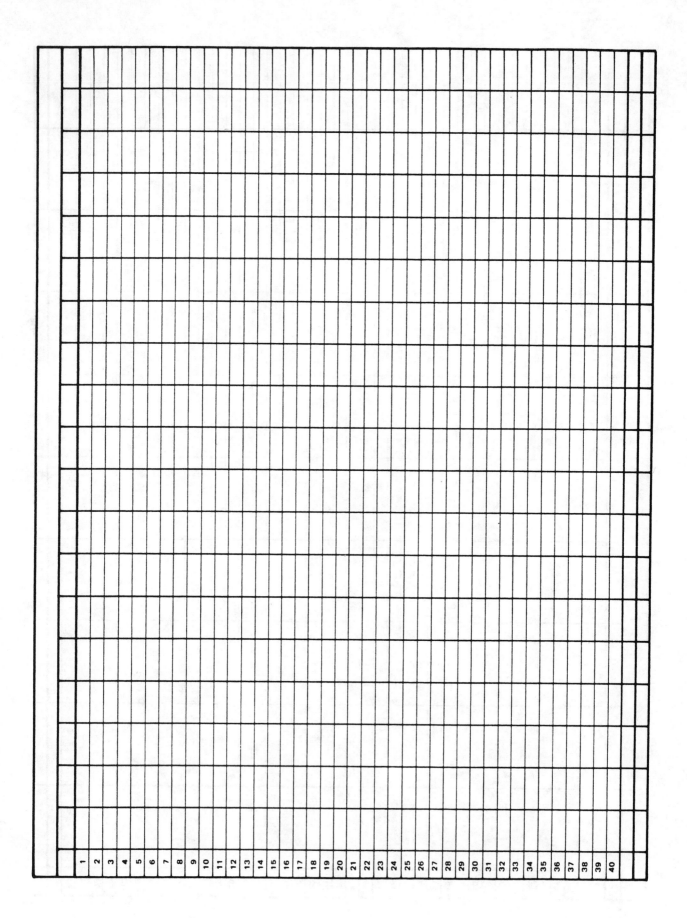

| | | 1 | 2 | 3 | 4 | 5 | 6 | 7 | 8 | 9 | 10 | 11 | 12 | 13 | 14 | 15 | 16 | 17 | 18 | 19 | 20 | 21 | 22 | 23 | 24 | 25 | 26 | 27 | 28 | 29 | 30 | 31 | 32 | 33 | 34 | 35 | 36 | 37 | 38 | 39 | 40 | | |

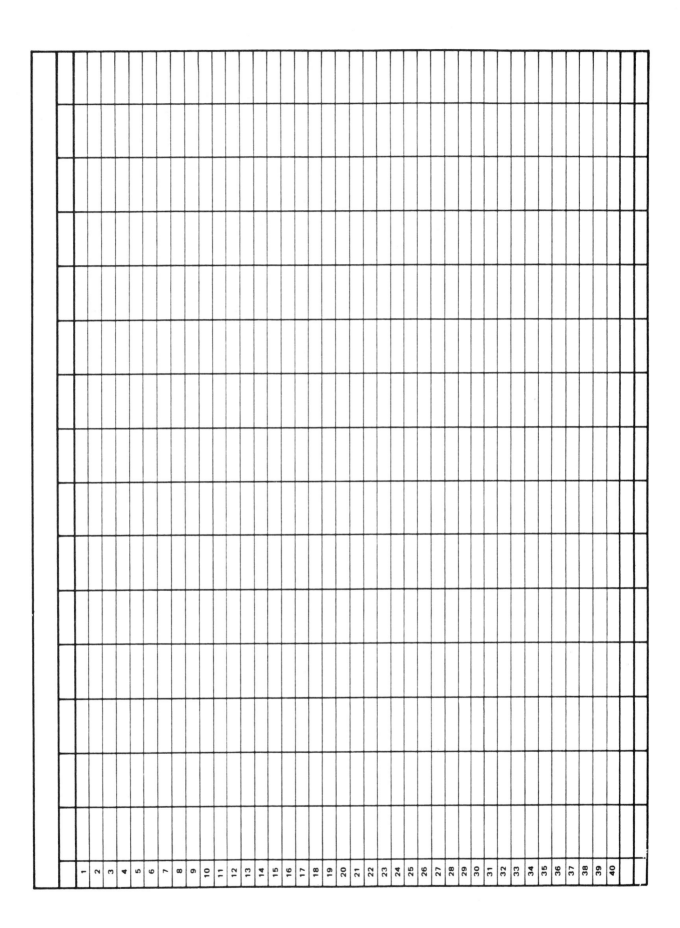

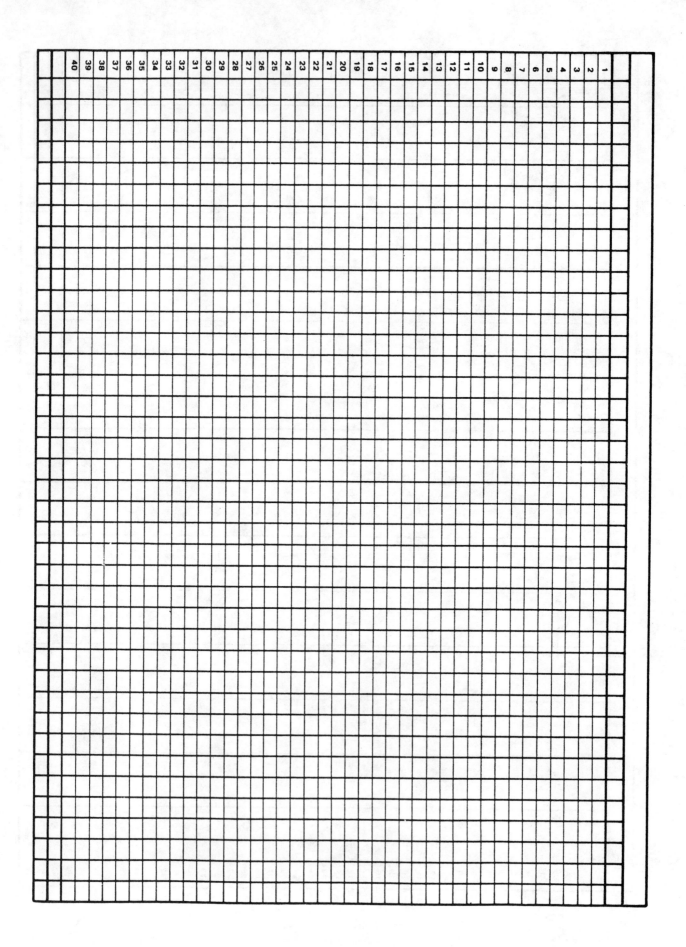

Projects

SEVEN DAY APPOINTMENTS

	SUNDAY	MONDAY	TUESDAY	WEDNESDAY	THURSDAY	FRIDAY	SATURDAY
8:00							
8:30							
9:00							
9:30							
10:00							
10:30							
11:00							
11:30							
12:00							
12:30							
1:00							
1:30							
2:00							
2:30							
3:00							
3:30							
4:00							
4:30							
5:00							
5:30							

WEEKLY PROJECTS

WEEK OF ———

CHECK DAY PLANNED								DATE NEEDED	FOLLOW-UP NEEDED	FOLLOW-UP DATE	✓
S	M	T	W	T	F	S					

B 130

MONTHLY PROJECT REVIEW

DATE _____

PLANNER DATE	GOAL NO.	TASK NO.	TASK	INITIAL TARGET DATE	REVISED TARGET DATE	FOLLOW-UP NEEDED	✔

DATE OF LAST REVIEW/UPDATE	DATE OF NEXT REVIEW/UPDATE

WEEKLY PROJECTS

WEEK OF _____

	CHECK DAY PLANNED					DATE NEEDED	FOLLOW-UP NEEDED	FOLLOW-UP DATE	✓
	M	T	W	T	F				

B 132

3 MONTH GOALS

For Period Ending: _____

Priority	Goal/Objective	Project Number	Completed (√)
_____	_____	_____	_____
_____	_____	_____	_____
_____	_____	_____	_____
_____	_____	_____	_____
_____	_____	_____	_____
_____	_____	_____	_____
_____	_____	_____	_____

PROJECTS TO COMPLETE GOALS

Project Number	Project	Assigned To	Target Date
_____	_____	_____	_____
_____	_____	_____	_____
_____	_____	_____	_____
_____	_____	_____	_____
_____	_____	_____	_____
_____	_____	_____	_____
_____	_____	_____	_____
_____	_____	_____	_____
_____	_____	_____	_____
_____	_____	_____	_____

KEY PROJECT CONTROL

Project No.	Project	Assigned To	Target Date	Last Review Date
_____	_____	_____	_____	_____
_____	_____	_____	_____	_____
_____	_____	_____	_____	_____
_____	_____	_____	_____	_____
_____	_____	_____	_____	_____
_____	_____	_____	_____	_____
_____	_____	_____	_____	_____
_____	_____	_____	_____	_____
_____	_____	_____	_____	_____
_____	_____	_____	_____	_____
_____	_____	_____	_____	_____
_____	_____	_____	_____	_____
_____	_____	_____	_____	_____
_____	_____	_____	_____	_____
_____	_____	_____	_____	_____
_____	_____	_____	_____	_____
_____	_____	_____	_____	_____
_____	_____	_____	_____	_____
_____	_____	_____	_____	_____
_____	_____	_____	_____	_____
_____	_____	_____	_____	_____
_____	_____	_____	_____	_____

6 MONTH GOALS

For Period Ending: _____

Priority	Goal/Objective	Project Number	Completed (√)
_____	_____	_____	_____
_____	_____	_____	_____
_____	_____	_____	_____
_____	_____	_____	_____
_____	_____	_____	_____
_____	_____	_____	_____
_____	_____	_____	_____

PROJECTS TO COMPLETE GOALS

Project Number	Project	Assigned To	Target Date
_____	_____	_____	_____
_____	_____	_____	_____
_____	_____	_____	_____
_____	_____	_____	_____
_____	_____	_____	_____
_____	_____	_____	_____
_____	_____	_____	_____
_____	_____	_____	_____
_____	_____	_____	_____
_____	_____	_____	_____

12 MONTH GOALS

For Period Ending: _____

Priority	Goal/Objective	Project Number	Completed (√)
_____	_____	_____	_____
_____	_____	_____	_____
_____	_____	_____	_____
_____	_____	_____	_____
_____	_____	_____	_____
_____	_____	_____	_____
_____	_____	_____	_____

PROJECTS TO COMPLETE GOALS

Project Number	Project	Assigned To	Target Date
_____	_____	_____	_____
_____	_____	_____	_____
_____	_____	_____	_____
_____	_____	_____	_____
_____	_____	_____	_____
_____	_____	_____	_____
_____	_____	_____	_____
_____	_____	_____	_____
_____	_____	_____	_____

PROJECT FOLLOW-UP

DATE _____

PRIORITY KEY:

1 - URGENT   2 - IMPORTANT   3 - LOW PRIORITY   4 - VERY LOW PRIORITY

PRIORITY		DATE NEEDED	FOLLOW-UP NEEDED	FOLLOW-UP DATE	✓

PROJECT DELAYS

ACTIVITY	REPORT DATE	REASON FOR DELAY	PERSON/DEPT. RESPONSIBLE	MARK YES OR NO: WILL AFFECT			ADDITIONAL COMMENTS
				START DATE?	FINISH DATE?	COMPLETION DATE?	

PROJECT COST SUMMARY

Appropriation Detail

Project Title _____   Plant/Mgr. _____   Purpose of Request _____

Project Number _____   Responsibility Center No. _____   Cost Distribution _____

Date of Request _____   Product Lines _____   Completion date _____

Project Description _____

_____

_____

Project Justification _____

_____

_____

Investment Summary	Projections					Actual		
	Start-up	1st Full Yr.	5-Yr. Total	10-Yr.Total	Proj. Total	Start-up	1st Full Yr.	5-Yr. Total
Capital Investment								
Working Capital								
Total Investment								
Sales								
Net Income								
Cash Flow								
Discounted ROI								
Payback in Yrs.								

Approvals

Requestor _____   (For request to $20,000)   (For request over $20,000)

V.P. Responsible _____   V.P.-Finance _____   Board of Directors _____

Date _____   President _____   By _____

Date _____   Date _____

PROJECT EXPENDITURE REVIEW

PROJECT: _____   REPORT NO.: _____   WEEK ENDING: _____   SIGNED: _____

Activity	Original Revised Activity Completion Cost	Actual Cost to Date	Percent Complete	Value	Overrun/(Underrun) This Week's	Overrun/(Underrun) Last Week's	Overrun/(Underrun) Difference	Previous Revised Activity Completion Cost	Current Revised Activity Completion Cost
TOTALS									

ONE YEAR PROJECT PROGRESS

PROJECT: _____   START DATE: _____

PHASE DESCRIPTION	PERSON/DEPT. RESPONSIBLE	Fill in 12 months, starting with first month of project											

SIX MONTH PROJECT PROGRESS

PROJECT: _____

START DATE _____

PHASE DESCRIPTION	PERSON/DEPT. RESPONSIBLE	WEEKS																						
		01	02	03	04	05	06	07	08	09	10	11	12	13	14	15	16	17	18	19	20	21	22	23	24

B 142

PROJECT REPORT

Project title: _____   Project no.: _____

Start date: _____   Priority: _____

Estimated completion date: _____

Total estimated project cost: _____

    Budget: 19 _____ $ _____
                 19 _____ $ _____

    To complete: $ _____

Review

Budget: Man-hours _____ $ _____   (year-to-date) $ _____   (as of)

Actual: Man-hours _____ $ _____ $ _____   _____

Accomplished to date (or since last review): _____

_____

_____

_____

_____

Current priority: _____   Action taken: _____

Remarks: _____

_____

_____

_____

_____

_____

Signed: _____   Review date: _____

PROJECT ASSIGNMENT RECORD

Date Assigned	Description of Assignment	Person Assigned To	Due Date	Notes:

PROJECT SCHEDULE

DATE _____

PROJECT	START DATE	TARGET DATE	PROGRESS TO DATE

PROJECT PLAN

FOR _____

SCHEDULED		ACTUAL			✔
Start	Finish	Start	Finish		

PROJECTS

DATE _____

PROJECT	PRIORITY	ACTIVITY	TIME NEEDED	✔	FOLLOW-UP

NOTES

KEY PROJECT CONTROL

Project No.	Project	Assigned To	Target Date	Last Review Date
_____	_____	_____	_____	_____
_____	_____	_____	_____	_____
_____	_____	_____	_____	_____
_____	_____	_____	_____	_____
_____	_____	_____	_____	_____
_____	_____	_____	_____	_____
_____	_____	_____	_____	_____
_____	_____	_____	_____	_____
_____	_____	_____	_____	_____
_____	_____	_____	_____	_____
_____	_____	_____	_____	_____
_____	_____	_____	_____	_____
_____	_____	_____	_____	_____
_____	_____	_____	_____	_____
_____	_____	_____	_____	_____
_____	_____	_____	_____	_____
_____	_____	_____	_____	_____
_____	_____	_____	_____	_____
_____	_____	_____	_____	_____
_____	_____	_____	_____	_____
_____	_____	_____	_____	_____
_____	_____	_____	_____	_____
_____	_____	_____	_____	_____

Executive
and
Administrative

MASTER FILE INDEX

*P = Permanent Direct Access   R = Rotational Consecutive

File Name	*	External Label	Internal Label	Shelf Number

FILE DESCRIPTION

Group Name

Data Element Name	Description	Origin	Size	Type Of Data	Volume	Frequency

Comments

FILE SHEET

Date: _____ Page _____ of _____

| Study: | Source: | Prepared by: |

File name: _____ File number: _____

| Location of file: | Stored in: |

Requirements of Access: _____

_____

Sequenced by: _____

_____

Content qualifications: _____

_____

Age: _____

_____

Retention: _____

_____

Labels: _____

_____

Comments: _____

Seq. No.	Message	Volume		Char. per Message	Char. per file	
		Avg.	Peak		Avg.	Peak

B 153

COMPUTER SOFTWARE RECORD

Software			Release Date	Date Received

Modification No.	Date Rec'd.	Updated	Comments

TELEPHONE INDEX

NAME AND ADDRESS	AREA CODE	TELEPHONE

TELEPHONE CALLS

DATE _____

PERSON TO CALL	COMPANY	TELEPHONE	PURPOSE	COM-PLETED ✓	CALL BACK ✓	WILL RETURN CALL ✓	COMMENTS

TELEPHONE LOG

| DATE | CALLER | | COMPANY/PERSON CALLED | | | AREA | TELEPHONE | COL- | PER. | CALLING | CHARGED | CHARGES |
	NAME	DEPT.	NAME	CITY	STATE	CODE	NUMBER	LECT	TO PER.	TIME	TO	
								✓	✓			

TELEPHONE LOG

TIME PERIOD _____

INSTRUCTIONS:
LOG ALL CALLS FOR A CERTAIN TIME PERIOD. AT THE END OF THE TIME PERIOD ANALYZE YOUR PHONE HABITS AND ELIMINATE WASTED TIME.

TIME	LENGTH OF CALL	CALLED ✓	RECEIVED ✓	SPOKE TO	REASON	PERSONAL ✓	BUSINESS ✓	RESULT

IN-OUT RECORD

DAY _____ DATE _____

NAME	EXT	IN ✓	OUT ✓	IN ✓	OUT ✓	IN ✓	OUT ✓	IN ✓	OUT ✓

MEMO

DATE:
TO:
FROM:
SUBJECT:

PERPETUAL INVENTORY CONTROL

Item: _____ Item number: _____ Sheet number: _____

Ordered			
Date	Order number	Quantity	Due date

Sold				
Date	Order number	Quantity	Balance	Comments

Received		
Date	Order number	Quantity

INVENTORY

		DATE _____ 19_____		
		SHEET NUMBER	FOLIO NUMBER	THIS SHEET COMPLETED-DATE/TIME
DEPARTMENT	LOCATION	PRICED BY		DATE
CALLED BY	DATE	EXTENDED BY		DATE
ENTERED BY	DATE	EXAMINED BY		DATE

ITEM NO.	DESCRIPTION	✔	QUANTITY	UNIT	PRICE	UNIT	EXTENSIONS
		Amount Forward					

OUT OF STOCK REPORT

Date: _____   Your order no: _____   Your order date: _____

To: _____

_____

_____

Item number	Description	Quantity

Your order cannot be filled because we are temporarily out of stock for the above. Please complete the form below and return to us. We apologize for any inconvenience.

Estimated shipping date: _____   Please return form to: _____

☐ Back order — ship as soon as possible   _____

☐ Substitute (specify) _____   _____

☐ Cancel   _____

Signed: _____   _____

STOCK BALANCE RECORD

ITEM_____

UNIT OF MEASURE_____ UNIT WEIGHT_____

LOCATION: BIN_____ SECTION_____

EXPEDITE POINT_____ REVIEW POINT_____

DATE	REFERENCE	ISSUED REC'D	USED MO. TO DATE	BALANCE	DATE	REFERENCE	ISSUED REC'D	USED MO. TO DATE	BALANCE

EMPLOYEE PRODUCTIVITY REPORT

(1) EMPLOYEE	ACTUAL HOURS WORKED				STANDARD HOURS PRODUCED		PRODUCTIVITY PERCENTAGE	
	(2) TOTAL	(3) WAGE INCENTIVE	(4) DAY WORK	(5) DELAYS	(6) WAGE INCENTIVE	(7) DAY WORK	(8) WAGE INCENTIVE (6) ÷ (3)	(9) DAY WORK (7) ÷ (4)
TOTALS								

PRODUCT CONTROL

PRODUCT	PRODUCT DESCRIPTION	SALES PRICE	STANDARD COST	UNIT OF MEASURE	INVENTORY ON ORDER	INVENTORY ON HAND	COMMITTED INVENTORY	LEAD TIME ON ORDERS

PRODUCTION REPORT

REPORT DATE: PERIOD OF ACTIVITY:

PRODUCT NUMBER	NUMBER OF ORDERS	OPEN ORDERS	% OF TOTAL PRODUCTION	REJECTS	REASON FOR REJECTS

DAILY PRODUCTION REPORT

WORK CENTER _____   SHIFT _____   DATE _____

PRODUCTION ORDER NO.	SCHEDULE				PRODUCTION					
	CUSTOMER	PRODUCT SIZE AND DESCRIPTION	ORDER QUANTITY	START	STOP	TOTAL HOURS	CHARGED WEIGHT	PRODUCT WEIGHT	SCRAP LOSS

DELAYS:

FROM	TO	EXPLANATIONS:

PREPARED BY: _____   APPROVED BY: _____

PRODUCTION ORDER

Customer code:_____   Production order no.:_____

Customer code:_____   Sales order no.:_____

Customer code:_____

Description of finished product:	Cost	Selling price	On hand

Required parts and materials	Product code no.	Standard cost	On hand	Out of stock	Lead time

Scheduled date of completion:

Planned shipping date:

Authorization signature upon completion_____

FACTORY ORDER

				ORDER NO.	LOT

PART NAME _____ PART NO. _____ ORDER QTY. _____

SHEET ____ OF ____

DATE SCHEDULED	RELEASE DATE	START DATE	DUE DATE	MOVE QUANTITY	ORDER MIN.

MATERIAL _____ QUANTITY PER 100 _____ LOT QUANTITY ____ BALANCE DUE ____

OPER. NO.	DEPT. NO.	OPERATION DESCRIPTION / PART NO. OR MAT.	MACHINE NO.	REPORT DATE		QUANTITY		INSP.
				SCHEDULE	ACTUAL	PASSED	REJECTED	

RECEIVED	BY	DATE	QUANTITY	ALLOCATED

SHOP ORDER

SYMBOL	MATERIAL	SCHEDULED		SHOP ORDER	PRIORITY
QUANTITY	QUANTITY	START	FINISH	NUMBER	
NUMBER	CODE	ACTUAL START		IN-PROCESS TIME	AUTHORIZED BY
DRAWING NUMBER	MATERIAL DESCRIPTION			UNIT	
				COST	
				SYMBOL DESCRIPTION	

OPR. NO	OPERATION	BASIC CODE CENTER	MACHINE NUMBER	PRODUCTION		LOAD HOURS		D.W. HRS PER 100	TOTAL LOAD HOURS	LOAD ASSIGN
				GOOD	DEFECT	SET UP	PER 100			

DEFECTIVE MATERIAL REPORT

No.

DEBIT
MEMO NO. _____

VENDOR

SHIPPING DATA

PURCHASE ORDER NO.	SHIPPING DATE	BILL OF LADING
RECEIVING SLIP NO.	VIA	QUANT.
SHOP JOB NO.	WGT.	CHGS.

PART NO.	MATERIAL DESCRIPTION	QUANT. REC'D	QUANT. REJ.	UNIT PRICE	VALUE

		REJ. IN DEPT.	DATE INSPECTED	INSPECTOR	INSPECTION AUTHORIZATION

REASONS FOR REJECTIONS

DISPOSITION		SIGN	DATE
RETURN	CHG. VENDOR		
REWORK	CHG. VENDOR		
SCRAP	CHG. VENDOR		
REWORK	OUR EXPENSE		
SCRAP	OUR EXPENSE		
REWORK ACCT. NO.			
OTHER DISPOSAL			

REMARKS:

DATE REWORKED	TOTAL PCS.	SIGN

REQUEST FOR REPAIR

Dept. _____   Date _____

Type of Mach. _____   Mach. No. _____

Maintenance required _____

_____

_____

_____

Signature _____

Maintenance Mechanic's Report

Name _____   Clock No. _____

Repairs made _____

_____

_____

_____

_____

Remarks _____

_____

_____

_____

_____

Leave Dept.		Leave Dept.		Leave Dept.	
Start		Start		Start	
Stop		Stop		Stop	
Return Dept.		Return Dept.		Return Dept.	

EQUIPMENT SERVICE RECORD

Equipment

Model Number	Serial Number	Our I.D. Number
Acquisition Date	Value at Acquisition	☐ New ☐ Used ☐ Recond.

Purchased From

Leased From	Lease Period	Rate

Condition of Equipment

Service Contract With		Phone

Date	Time	Service Performed	Parts Needed	Approved

EQUIPMENT SERVICE RECORD

Dept. _____   Location _____   Machine No. _____

DATE REPAIRED	REPAIRS OR PARTS REPLACED	CAUSE	REPAIRED BY	DATE NEXT INSPECTION

QUALITY CONTROL REPORT

STATION _____ PAGE # _____

PRODUCT _____ QTY PER SAMPLE _____

FREQUENCY/No. OF SAMPLES _____

REMARKS _____

WORKER'S NAME _____ FROM _____ TO _____

WORKER'S NAME _____ FROM _____ TO _____

WORKER'S NAME _____ FROM _____ TO _____

DATE	TIME	SAMPLE NUMBER	No. OF DEFECTS	+ √	− √	DATE	TIME	SAMPLE NUMBER	No. OF DEFECTS	+ √	− √

QUALITY CONTROL REPORT

PART NO.	ORDER NO.	DESCRIPTION	ORDER QUANTITY	QUANTITY REJECTED

DEPT.	WORKED		AT FAULT	EMPLOYEE NO.	SHIFT	INSPECTOR	DATE
	LAST OPN.	DEPT.	OPN.		1 2 3		

NATURE OF DEFECT	REJECTION DUE TO	(X)	DISPOSITION	(X)
	WORKMANSHIP		REWORK	
	RAW MATERIALS		SALVAGE	
	DESIGN		RETURN TO VENDOR	
	DESIGN CHANGE		SCRAP	
	MANUFACTURING EQUIPMENT		HOLD FOR SPECIAL INSTRUCTIONS	
	VENDOR			
	OTHER			

COST DEPARTMENT			PRODUCTION DEPARTMENT
COST	UNIT COST	EXTENSION	
Material			REWORK ORDER ISSUED
Labor			REPLACEMENT ORDER ISSUED
Burden			MATERIAL CONTROL POSTED
Total Cost			INVENTORY POSTED

SIGNED _____
FOREMAN OF DEPT. OR SHIFT CHARGED

SIGNED _____
CHIEF DIRECTOR

CUSTOMER FILE

CUSTOMER	BILLING NAME	BILLING ADDRESS	SHIPPING ADDRESS	INVOICE NO.	CUSTOMER TRADE CLASS	DISCOUNT CLASSIFICATION	CREDIT RATING	CREDIT LIMIT

MATERIAL REQUISITION REPORT

PROJECT: _____ LOCATION: _____ DATE: _____

HOW DELIVERED	INVOICE NO.	MATERIAL DESCRIPTION	DELIVERED BY	COST PER UNIT	QUANTITY	TAX	REMARKS

BALANCE-OF-STORES RECORD

DESCRIPTION

REQUIREMENTS												USED ON			PART NO.
MO.	QTY.	MO.	QTY.	MO.	QTY.	MO.	QTY.	MO.	QTY.	MO.	QTY.				
1		2		3		4		5		6					UNIT
7		8		9		10		11		12					CLASSIFICATION

DATE	ORDER NUMBER	QUANTITY	RECEIVED	BALANCE ON ORDER	ISSUED		STOCK BALANCE	ALLOCATED	AVAILABLE BALANCE
					T. S.	MFG.			

PARTS INVENTORY

Bin Number _____

Date _____

Page _____ Of _____

Part Number	Quan.	Unit Price		Extension		Part Number	Quan.	Unit Price		Extension	
							SUB-TOTAL				
							TOTAL				

DAILY TIME REPORT

Date: _____

JOB ARRIVAL	JOB DEPART.	DATE	JOB COMP. %	JOB ADDRESS	TYPE OF WORK	NUMBER OF HOURS

This form must be completed and turned in <u>daily</u>.

_____
Employee Signature

DAILY SCHEDULE

DATE: _____

TIME	NAME	ADDRESS	PHONE	SERVICE	C	PRICE	REMARKS	CO.

INVENTORY CONTROL

STORE RECORD OF USAGE FOR _____ DATE_____

DEPARTMENT_____

ITEM	DESCRIPTION	RETAIL	SOLD LAST SEASON	ON HAND	ON ORDER	TO ORDER	TOTAL	UNITS LEFT	UNITS SOLD	COVERAGE NEXT YEAR

DAILY TIME REPORT

CLOCK No. _____

NAME _____ DATE _____

ORDER No.	FOR	PART No.	OPERATION OR MACHINE No.	TIME STARTED	TIME STOPPED	ELAPSED TIME	QUANT TIME	RATE	FOR OFFICE USE		✔
									CHG.	NON-CHG.	

DEDUCTIONS

APPROVED _____

RUN RECORD

Machine				Machine No.	Date	
Time Run Started	Time Run Stopped		Subject		By	

WORK ASSIGNMENT SCHEDULE

For			Date	
Employee	Operation	Machine	From	To

MACHINE TIME RECORD

Date _____

Name	Employee Number	Operation Machine No.	Time Started	Time Stopped	Time Elapsed	

CUSTOMER LEDGER

Name & Address: _____

PURCHASE ORDER NO.	SALES ORDER		ACCT. NO.	QTY.	DESCRIPTION		SHIPPED		DATE BILLED
	NUMBER	DATE			PART NAME	PART NO.	VIA	DATE	

CUSTOMER ORDER FILE

CUSTOMER NAME/CODE NO.	CUSTOMER ORDER NO.	ORDER DATE	AVAILABLE INVENTORY	INVENTORY ALLOCATED TO ORDER	SPECIAL INSTRUCTIONS	SHIP DATE	SHIPPING LOCATION	PAYMENT TERMS	INVOICE AMOUNT	CUSTOMER DISCOUNT	NET INVOICE

INVENTORY LEDGER

Unit: _____ Minimum: _____

Article: _____ Location: _____

Date	Description	Received			Disbursed		Balance On Hand	
		Quantity	Amount	Unit Cost	Quantity	Amount	Quantity	Amount

INVENTORY DISCOUNT SCHEDULE

☐ Retail   ☐ Wholesale   Valid From:_____ To:_____

Item	Retail Price	Quantity	% – Amount Of Discount	Net Unit Price

SPEED MEMO

REFER TO ☐ YOUR ☐ MY ☐ BELOW ☐ ATTACHED
☐ LETTER ☐ PHONE CALL ☐ ORDER ☐ _____
☐ INQUIRY ☐ MEMO ☐ TELEGRAM _____
DATED _____ NO. _____

TO

FROM

SIGNATURE/TITLE/LOCATION/PHONE/DATE

REPLY

SIGNATURE/TITLE/LOCATION/PHONE/DATE

INTER-OFFICE MEMO

DATE:

TO:

FROM:

SUBJECT:

SIGNATURE/TITLE/LOCATION/PHONE/DATE

REPLY

SIGNATURE/TITLE/LOCATION/PHONE/DATE

B 194

INTER-OFFICE MEMO

DATE:

TO:

FROM:

SUBJECT:

SIGNATURE/TITLE/LOCATION/PHONE/DATE

ROUTING INSTRUCTIONS

DATE

ATTENTION

RE:

TO

PLEASE TAKE THE APPROPRIATE ACTION INDICATED BELOW:

☐ REVIEW & FILE
☐ REVIEW & RETURN
☐ REVIEW & RETURN WITH COMMENTS
☐ FOR YOUR APPROVAL
☐ FOR YOUR USE
☐ FOR YOUR SIGNATURE
☐ PREPARE FOR MY SIGNATURE
☐ PREPARE FOR _____
   SIGNATURE

☐ INVESTIGATE AND REPORT TO ME
☐ INVESTIGATE AND REPORT TO _____
☐ REWORK IN LINE WITH COMMENTS & DIRECTION
☐ RESUBMIT WITH _____ COPIES
☐ ATTACHED IS ☐ APPROVED ☐ REJECTED
☐ _____
   _____
☐ SEE ME ABOUT ☐ ATTACHED ☐ ABOVE ON
   _____ AT _____ AM/PM

COMMENTS

PREPARED BY		PREPARED FOR/APPROVED BY	
TITLE		TITLE	
LOCATION		LOCATION	
PHONE	DATE	PHONE	DATE

B 196

TRANSMITTAL LETTER

DATE	
ATTENTION	
RE	

TO

WE ARE SENDING ☐ ATTACHED   ☐ UNDER SEPARATE COVER VIA _____:

☐ SAMPLES	☐ SHOP DRAWINGS	☐ CONTRACTS
☐ LITERATURE	☐ ENGINEERING DRAWINGS	☐ OTHER _____
☐ PLANS	☐ CHANGE ORDERS	_____
☐ PRINTS	☐ LETTERS	_____

COPIES	DATE	NO	DESCRIPTION

THESE ARE BEING SENT:

☐ FOR YOUR APPROVAL	☐ APPROVED AS NOTED	☐ RESUBMIT _____ COPIES FOR APPROVAL
☐ FOR YOUR USE	☐ APPROVED AS SUBMITTED	☐ SUBMIT _____ COPIES FOR DISTRIBUTION
☐ FOR YOUR REVIEW	☐ APPROVED AS CHANGED	☐ RENEW _____ COPIES FOR
☐ FOR YOUR COMMENTS	☐ REJECTED AS NOTED	_____
☐ FOR YOUR SIGNATURE	☐ REJECTED AS CHANGED	☐ _____
☐ FOR YOUR _____	☐ RETURNED FOR CORRECTIONS	_____

NOTES _____

COPY TO	**SIGNATURE**
	TITLE / **DATE**

EXPENSE RECORD

NAME: _____ FOR WEEK ENDING:_____ DEPT._____

	SUNDAY	MONDAY	TUESDAY	WEDNESDAY	THURSDAY	FRIDAY	SATURDAY	TOTAL FOR WEEK
FROM								
TO								
TO								
TOTAL AUTO MILES								
MILEAGE MI.								
GAS—OIL—LUBE								
PARKING & TOLLS								
AUTO RENTAL								
LOCAL—CAB/LIMO								
AIR—RAIL—BUS								
LODGING								
BREAKFAST								
LUNCH								
DINNER								
LAUNDRY—CLEANING								
PHONE & TELEGRAM								
TIPS								
OTHER								
ENTERTAINMENT*								
TOTAL PER DAY								

*DETAILED ENTERTAINMENT RECORD

DATE	ITEM	PERSONS ENTERTAINED/ BUSINESS RELATIONSHIP	PLACE NAME & LOCATION	BUSINESS PURPOSE	AMOUNT

PURPOSE OF TRIP: _____

_____

REMARKS: _____

_____

DATE:_____ SIGNATURE: _____

SUMMARY

TOTAL EXPENSES	
LESS CASH ADVANCED	
LESS CHARGES TO CO.	
AMOUNT DUE ☐ ME ☐ CO.	

TURNOVER REPORT

DEPARTMENT				YEAR		

MONTH	FOR MONTH			YEAR TO DATE		
	No. Employees	Terminations	Turnover	No. Employees	Terminations	Turnover
YEAR TOTALS						

COMMENTS

APPROVED		APPROVED BY	

Accounting
and
Finance

COMMERCIAL CREDIT APPLICATION

T **NAME** _____ F **NAME** _____

O **ADDRESS** _____ R **ADDRESS** _____

CITY/STATE/ZIP _____ O **CITY/STATE/ZIP** _____

CREDIT MANAGER _____ M _____

PHONE NUMBER _____ **PHONE NUMBER** _____

BUSINESS TYPE: ☐ Sole Proprietorship ☐ Partnership ☐ Corporation - State of _____

Number of years in business _____ D and B Number _____

NAME AND ADDRESS OF INDIVIDUALS OR PARTNERS - NAME/TITLE/PHONE NUMBER OF CORPORATE OFFICERS

_____

_____

_____

NAME OF PERSON TO CONTACT REGARDING PURCHASE ORDERS AND INVOICE PAYMENTS, TITLE, ADDRESS AND PHONE NUMBER

_____ _____

_____ _____

_____ _____

_____ _____

BANK REFERENCE **BANK ACCOUNT NUMBER, CONTACT, TITLE AND PHONE NUMBER**

_____ _____

_____ _____

_____ _____

_____ _____

TRADE REFERENCES: COMPANY NAME, ADDRESS, CONTACT AND TITLE, AND PHONE NUMBER.

_____ _____ _____

_____ _____ _____

_____ _____ _____

_____ _____ _____

THE ABOVE INFORMATION IS HEREWITH SUBMITTED FOR THE PURPOSE OF OPENING AN ACCOUNT AND I DO HEREBY CERTIFY THIS INFORMATION TO BE TRUE.

SIGNED _____

TITLE _____

DATE _____

B 203

CREDIT INQUIRY

DATE _____

ON _____

ADDRESS _____

CITY, STATE, ZIP _____

CONTACT _____ PHONE No. _____

IN ORDER THAT WE MIGHT PROCESS A CREDIT APPLICATION THAT WE HAVE RECEIVED ON THE ABOVE ACCOUNT, WE WOULD APPRECIATE YOUR PROVIDING US WITH THE INFORMATION REQUESTED BELOW. PLEASE KNOW WE WILL TREAT YOUR RESPONSE WITH CONFIDENTIALITY.

DOLLAR SALES FROM _____ TO _____ TOTALED _____

TOTAL DOLLAR SALES IN YEAR _____ = $ _____ IN YEAR _____ = $ _____

TERMS _____ SPECIAL TERMS _____

LARGEST AMOUNT OWED _____ WHEN _____ CURRENT □ YES □ NO

TOTAL AMOUNT NOW OWED _____ CURRENT □ YES □ NO AMT. PAST DUE _____

RECENT TRENDS   □ PROMPTNESS   □ FULL TERM   □ SLIGHTLY SLOW   □ VERY SLOW

MAKES UNJUST CLAIMS _____

CREDIT □ HONORED □ REFUSED - EXPLAIN _____

☑ CHECK MANNER OF PAYMENT

□ PROMPT & TAKES DISCOUNTS	□ SLOW BUT COLLECTABLE	□ AN EXCELLENT ACCOUNT - BEST RECOMMENDATION
□ PROMPT & SATISFACTORY	□ SLOW AND UNSATISFACTORY	
□ PROMPT TO _____ DAYS SLOW	□ ACCEPTS C.O.D.'S PROMPTLY	□ WE DO NOT RECOMMEND EXTENDING CREDIT TO THIS ACCOUNT.
□ MAKES PARTIAL PAYMENTS	□ COLLECTED BY AN ATTORNEY	
□ ASK FOR ADDITIONAL TIME	□ IN HANDS OF AN ATTORNEY	

SPECIAL COMMENTS

WE WILL BE PLEASED TO SHARE ANY INFORMATION WE HAVE THAT WILL ASSIST IN YOUR CREDIT DECISIONS. THANK YOU FOR YOUR ASSISTANCE.

NAME _____

TITLE _____

CREDIT CONTROL LIST

Period From: _____ To: _____

Account Number	Account Name	Date Opened	Credit Line	Credit Available	Credit Used	Current	30	60	90
TOTALS									

OVERDUE ACCOUNT FILE

Name _____ Telephone _____

Address _____

_____

Spouse's name _____

Employer _____ Telephone _____

Address _____

_____

Guarantor _____ Telephone _____

Address _____

_____

Date account opened _____   Original balance due _____

Date delinquent file started _____

Date	Amount Paid	Balance Due	Date	Amount Paid	Balance Due

Date	History of Collection Efforts

CREDIT HISTORY

Name: _____   Spouse: _____

Address: _____

_____

_____

Telephone: _____

Business Name: _____   Business Name: _____

Business Address: _____   Business Address: _____

_____   _____

Business Telephone: _____   Business Telephone: _____

Date Approved	Credit Line	Payment Due Amount	Date	Payment Received Amount	Date	Balance	Date Notice Sent	Date 2nd Notice Sent

Collection Call: _____   Date To Attorney: _____

Disposition: _____

_____

ACCOUNTS RECEIVABLE RECAP REPORT

CUSTOMER	TOTAL BALANCE	MONTH OF	MONTH OF	MONTH OF	MONTH OF	PREVIOUS ITEMS DATE	AMOUNT
BALANCE BROUGHT FORWARD							

EXPENSE BUDGET

Month Of:_____

_____

	Estimate	Actual	Difference $	%
PERSONNEL: Office:				
Store:				
Salespeople:				
Others (List):				
OPERATING: Advertising:				
Bad Debts:				
Cash Discounts:				
Delivery Costs:				
Depreciation:				
Dues and Subscriptions:				
Employee Benefits:				
Insurance:				
Interest:				
Legal and Auditing:				
Maintenance and Repairs:				
Office Supplies:				
Postage:				
Rent or Mortgage:				
Sales Expenses:				
Shipping and Storage:				
Supplies:				
Taxes:				
Telephone:				
Utilities:				
Other (List):				
TOTAL:				

GENERAL AND ADMINISTRATIVE EXPENSE BUDGET

	Month Ending _____ 19 _____			Year to Date		
	Budget	Actual	Variance	Budget	Actual	Variance
Fixed						
Exec. salaries						
Office salaries						
Employee benefits						
Payroll taxes						
Pensions						
Travel and entertainment						
Directors' fees & expenses						
Insurance						
Rent						
Depreciation						
Taxes						
Legal						
Audit						
Telephone and telegraph						
Utilities						
Contributions						
Postage						
Dues						
Sundry						
Variable						
Office salaries						
Employee benefits						
Payroll taxes						
Travel and entertainment						
Telephone and telegraph						
Stationery and office supplies						
Bad debts						
Postage						
Contributions						
Sundry						
TOTAL						

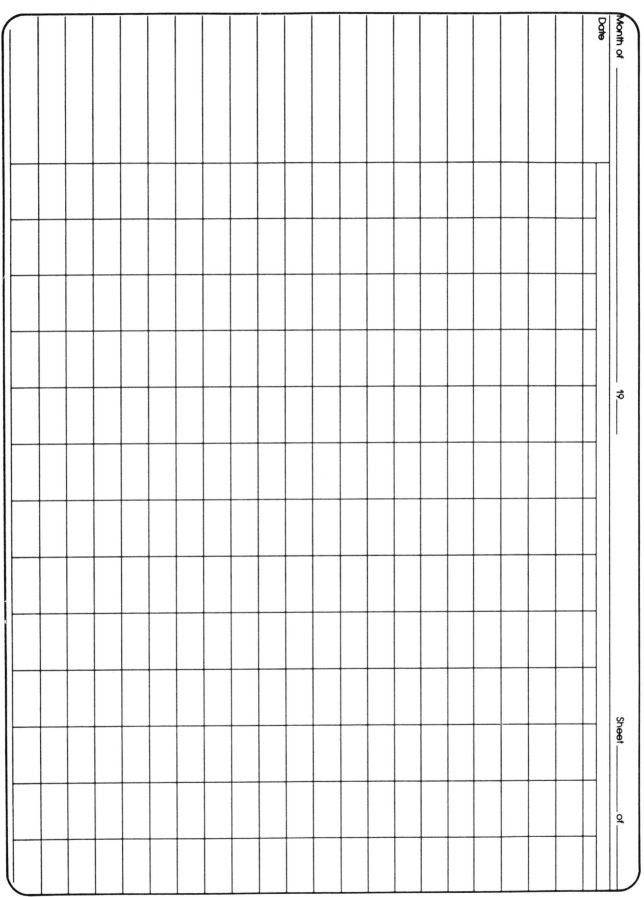

EXPENSE DISTRIBUTION ANALYSIS

Month of _____ 19 _____   Sheet _____ of _____

Date

MONTHLY CASH FLOW PROJECTIONS

Year: _____ Month: _____

	Estimate		Actual		Estimate		Actual	
	$	% of total	$	% of total	$	% of total	$	% of total
Cash on hand, first of month:								
Cash receipts, total:								
Cash sales:								
Collections:								
Loans:								
Total cash available								
Cash paid out Salaries and wages:								
Payroll taxes:								
Rent/Mortgage:								
Health insurance:								
Business insurance:								
Office supplies:								
Utilities:								
Telephone:								
Repairs and maintenance:								
Operating supplies:								
Taxes, licenses:								
Professional fees:								
Commissions:								
Travel:								
Entertainment:								
Purchases:								
Advertising:								
Transportation:								
Subtotal								
Loan payment with interest:								
Capital purchases:								
Owner's withdrawal:								
Total cash paid out								
Cash position								

CASH FLOW BUDGET

Year: _____

	Jan.	Feb.	Mar.	April	May	June	July	Aug.	Sept.	Oct.	Nov.	Dec.	Cumula-tive
Cash balance - beginning													
Cash from operations													
Total Available Cash													
Less:													
Capital expenditures													
Interest													
Dividends													
Debt retirement													
Other													
Total Cash Disbursements													
Cash Balance or (deficit)													
Add:													
Short-term loans													
Long-term loans													
Capital stock issues													
Cash Balance - end													

INCOME STATEMENT

For _____ (month) and year to date ended _____ , 19_____
($000)

	Current Month		Year to Date	
	Amount	% of Sales	Amount	% of Sales
REVENUE				
Gross Sales	_____		_____	
Less sales returns and allowances	_____		_____	
Net Sales	_____	100	_____	100
Cost of Sales	_____	_____	_____	_____
Beginning inventory	_____	_____	_____	_____
Plus purchases (retailer) or	_____	_____	_____	_____
Plus cost of goods				
manufatured (manufacturer)	_____	_____	_____	_____
Total Goods Available	_____	_____	_____	_____
Less ending inventory	_____	_____	_____	_____
Total Cost of Goods Sold	_____	_____	_____	_____
Gross Profit (Gross Margin)	_____	_____	_____	_____
OPERATING EXPENSES				
Selling				
Salaries and wages	_____	_____	_____	_____
Commissions	_____	_____	_____	_____
Advertising	_____	_____	_____	_____
Depreciation (e.g., on delivery vans)	_____	_____	_____	_____
Others (detail)	_____	_____	_____	_____
Total Selling Expenses	_____	_____	_____	_____
General/Administrative				
Salaries and wages	_____	_____	_____	_____
Employee benefits	_____	_____	_____	_____
Insurance	_____	_____	_____	_____
Depreciation (e.g., on equipment)	_____	_____	_____	_____
Total General/Administrative Expenses	_____	_____	_____	_____
Total Operating Expenses	_____	_____	_____	_____
Other Operating Income	_____	_____	_____	_____
Other Revenue and Expenses	_____	_____	_____	_____
Net Income before Taxes	_____	_____	_____	_____
Taxes on Income	_____	_____	_____	_____
Net Income after Taxes	_____	_____	_____	_____
Extraordinary Gain or Loss	_____	_____	_____	_____
Income tax on extraordinary gain	_____	_____	_____	_____
NET INCOME (NET PROFIT)	_____	_____	_____	_____

Company Name

BALANCE SHEET

Year Ending _____ , 19 _____

($000)

ASSETS		LIABILITIES	
Current Assets		**Current Liabilities**	
Cash	_____	Accounts payable	_____
Accounts receivable_____		Short-term notes	_____
less allowance		Current portion	
doubtful accounts _____		of long-term notes	_____
Net realizable value	_____	Interest payable	_____
Inventory	_____	Taxes payable	_____
Temporary investment	_____	Accrued payroll	_____
Prepaid expenses	_____	**Total Current Liabilities**	_____
Total Current Assets	_____		
		Equity	_____
Long-Term Investments	_____	Total owner's equity	_____
		(proprietorship)	
Fixed Assets			
Land	_____	or	
Buildings _____ at			
cost, less accumulated		(Name's) equity	_____
depreciation of _____		(Name's) equity	_____
Net book value	_____	(partnership)	
Equipment _____ at		Total Partner's equity	_____
cost, less accumulated		Shareholder's equity	
depreciation of _____		(corporation)	
Net book value	_____	Capital stock	_____
Furniture/Fixtures _____ at		Capital paid-in in	
cost, less accumulated		excess of par	_____
depreciation of _____		Retained earnings	_____
Net book value	_____	Total shareholder's	
		equity	_____
Total Net Fixed Assets	_____	**TOTAL LIABILITIES**	
		AND EQUITY	_____
Other Assets	_____		
TOTAL ASSETS	_____		

CHART OF MONTHLY SALES

_____, 19_____ to _____, 19_____

1st	2nd	3rd	4th	5th	6th	7th	8th	9th	10th	11th	12th

Month by month, 19 _____

PRO-FORMA BALANCE SHEET

Item	19 ____	19 ____	19 ____	19 ____
Current Assets				
Cash				
Accounts receivable less allowance for doubtful accounts				
Net accounts receivable				
Notes receivable				
Inventory				
Prepaid expenses				
Other				
Total Current Assets				
Fixed Assets				
Land				
Buildings				
Equipment				
Total Net Fixed Assets				
Other assets				
Total Assets				
Current Liabilities				
Accounts payable				
Notes payable				
Accrued payroll				
Taxes payable				
Other				
Total Current Liabilities				
Long-term liabilities				
Equity				
Withdrawals				
Net equity				
Total Liability & Equity				

PRO-FORMA INCOME STATEMENTS

Item				
Revenues				
Sales allowances				
Net Revenues				
Cost of goods sold				
Gross Margin				
Expenses				
Selling				
Salaries				
Advertising				
Other				
General/Administrative				
Salaries				
Employee benefits				
Professional services				
Rent				
Insurance				
Depreciation				
Amortization				
Office supplies				
Interest				
Utilities				
Bad debt/doubtful accounts				
Other				
TOTAL EXPENSES				
Net Income before Taxes				
Provision for taxes				
Net Income after Taxes				
Prior period adjustments				
Net Increase/(Decrease) to Retained Earnings				

FINANCIAL PERFORMANCE TRENDS

Key Indicators	19 _____	19 _____	19 _____	19 _____
Income data				
Net sales				
Cost of goods sold				
Gross profit				
Net profit before taxes				
Net profit after taxes				
Asset/liability data				
Accounts receivable				
Inventory				
Total assets				
Accounts payable				
Short term debt				
Long term debt				
Total liabilities				
Net worth				
Ratios (see Industry Analysis section for definitions)				
Current				
Total debt to total assets				
Collection period				
Net sales to inventory				
Net profit margin after taxes				
Return on net worth				

FINANCIAL COMPARISON ANALYSIS

		Industry				Company	
	19 ____	19 ____	19 ____	19 ____	19 ____	19 ____
Assets:						
Accts & notes receivable						
Inventory						
Total current						
Fixed assets (net)						
TOTAL ASSETS						
Liabilities						
Accts & note payable						
Total current						
Long-term debt						
Net worth						
TOTAL LIABILITIES						
& NET WORTH						
Income Data						
Net sales						
Cost of goods sold						
Gross profit						
Operating expenses						
Operating profit						
All other expenses (net)						
PROFIT BEFORE TAXES						
Ratios						
Current						
Total debt/total Assets						
Total debt/tangible net worth						
Collection period days						
Net sales/inventory						
Total assets turnover						
Gross profit margin						
Operating profit margin						
Return on net worth						

MONTHLY SALES RECORD

Month Of _____

Daily Receipts _____

Day	Amount
1	_____
2	_____
3	_____
4	_____
5	_____
6	_____
7	_____
8	_____
9	_____
10	_____
11	_____
12	_____
13	_____
14	_____
15	_____
16	_____
17	_____
18	_____
19	_____
20	_____
21	_____
22	_____
23	_____
24	_____
25	_____
26	_____
27	_____
28	_____
29	_____
30	_____
31	_____
Total Month	_____
Total Year to Date	_____

Comments:

_____

Prepared by:

Month Of _____

Daily Receipts _____

Day	Amount
1	_____
2	_____
3	_____
4	_____
5	_____
6	_____
7	_____
8	_____
9	_____
10	_____
11	_____
12	_____
13	_____
14	_____
15	_____
16	_____
17	_____
18	_____
19	_____
20	_____
21	_____
22	_____
23	_____
24	_____
25	_____
26	_____
27	_____
28	_____
29	_____
30	_____
31	_____
Total Month	_____
Total Year to Date	_____

Comments:

_____

Prepared by:

Month Of _____

Daily Receipts _____

Day	Amount
1	_____
2	_____
3	_____
4	_____
5	_____
6	_____
7	_____
8	_____
9	_____
10	_____
11	_____
12	_____
13	_____
14	_____
15	_____
16	_____
17	_____
18	_____
19	_____
20	_____
21	_____
22	_____
23	_____
24	_____
25	_____
26	_____
27	_____
28	_____
29	_____
30	_____
31	_____
Total Month	_____
Total Year to Date	_____

Comments:

_____

Prepared by:

PAYMENT RECORD

Period From: _____ To: _____

Date	To	For	Charge Account	Amount
____	___	___	_____	_____
____	___	___	_____	_____
____	___	___	_____	_____
____	___	___	_____	_____
____	___	___	_____	_____
____	___	___	_____	_____
____	___	___	_____	_____
____	___	___	_____	_____
____	___	___	_____	_____
____	___	___	_____	_____
____	___	___	_____	_____
____	___	___	_____	_____
____	___	___	_____	_____
____	___	___	_____	_____
____	___	___	_____	_____
____	___	___	_____	_____
____	___	___	_____	_____
____	___	___	_____	_____
____	___	___	_____	_____
____	___	___	_____	_____
____	___	___	_____	_____
____	___	___	_____	_____
____	___	___	_____	_____
____	___	___	_____	_____
____	___	___	_____	_____
____	___	___	_____	_____
____	___	___	_____	_____
____	___	___	_____	_____
____	___	___	_____	_____

_____   _____
        Audited By   Approved By

_____   _____
          Date   Date

B 222

VENDOR PAYMENT RECORD

Period From: _____   To: _____

DUE _____ _____ _____

Month of: _____ _____ _____ _____

Account Number	Invoice Number	Vendor	Description	30	60	90 +	Total
				TOTAL			

INVOICE CONTROL

Month of _____

Sheet _____ of _____

Date Of Invoice	Invoice Number	Credit Accounts Payable	Description	General Accounts Name of Account	Amount	Date Paid	Check Number
			Amount Forwarded				

DAILY CASH REPORT

CHECKS — PAID OUT TO:		
TOTAL		

CASH — PAID OUT TO:		
TOTAL		

REPORT DATE _____		
RECEIPTS FROM		
RECEIPTS FROM		
RECEIPTS FROM		
TOTAL RECEIPTS		
—CASH PAID OUT	—	
+ CASH WORKING FUND		
BALANCE		
OVER OR SHORT		
BANK DEPOSIT		
DEPOSIT NUMBER		
DEPOSIT DATE		
DEPOSIT MADE BY		
SIGNATURE		

B 225

PETTY CASH REPORT

PROJECT _____

DATE _____   AMOUNT OF PETTY CASH $ _____

MANAGER _____

DATE	PAID TO	PURPOSE	COST	BALANCE ON HAND

TOTAL _____

Amount to be reimbursed $ _____

Approved by _____

B 226

PETTY CASH RECONCILIATION

Department: _____ Section: _____

Petty cash check: _____ Supervisor: _____

Last audit date: _____ Audited by: _____

Date	Paid to or received from	For	Cash received Cash disbursed	Balance
	Balance from last page			

Audit/review date _____ by _____

P.C. reimbursement: date _____ amount _____

by _____ ck. no. _____

_____
Audited/reconciled by

_____
Supervisor approval

Summary

Cash on hand _____

Petty cash slips _____

Total _____

☐ Over _____   ☐ Short _____

Disposition: _____   Disposition: _____

_____   _____

DAILY CASH BALANCE

Date _____

CASH ON HAND . . . . $ _____

CASH SALES - Counter . . . . $ _____

CASH SALES - C.O.D. . . . . $ _____

COLLECTIONS . . . . $ _____

LESS: Deposits . . . . $ _____

_____ . . . . $ _____

      BALANCE . . . . $ _____

CASH . . . . $ _____

CHECKS . . . . $ _____

CASH PAYOUTS . . . . $ _____

OUT TICKETS . . . . $ _____

_____ . . . . $ _____

      BALANCE . . . . $ _____

REMARKS: _____

_____

_____

CASH REGISTER RECONCILIATION

NAME

SHIFT_____ DATE _____

OPENING - CASH		
OPENING - F/S		
REGISTER READING		
EXTRA CASH		
REBATES		
TOTAL		
	TWENTIES	
	TENS	
	FIVES	
	ONES	
	HALVES	
	QUARTERS	
	DIMES	
	NICKELS	
	PENNIES	
	CHECKS	
	ENDING - CASH	
	ENDING - F/S	
	PAYOUTS	
	DEPOSITS	
	REFUND	

TOTAL   _____

OVER _____   SHORT _____

B 229

BANK RECONCILIATION

Name _____ Month of _____ 19____

Bank _____ Prepared by_____

GENERAL LEDGER ACCOUNT BALANCE			$		

GENERAL LEDGER ACCOUNT BALANCE .... $ _____

ADD DEBITS $ _____
....
....
....
....
Total Dr .... $ _____
      Total .... $ _____

LESS CREDITS: $ _____
....
....
....
....
Total Cr .... $ _____
BANK BALANCE — Per General Ledger .... $ _____

BALANCE PER BANK STATEMENT $ _____
AS OF .... 19......

ADD DEPOSITS IN TRANSIT $ _____
....
....
....
....
....
Total in Transit .... $ _____
      Total .... $ _____

LESS CHECKS OUTSTANDING: $ _____
(See list below) ....
....
....
....
Total .... $ _____
BANK BALANCE — Per Reconciliation .... $ _____

CHECKS OUTSTANDING

NUMBER	AMOUNT	NUMBER	AMOUNT	NUMBER	AMOUNT	NUMBER	AMOUNT
					TOTAL	$

GENERAL LEDGER

Account Number _____

Account Name _____

Address _____

Sheet _____ of _____

Date	Description	Charges	Credits	Balance Charges	Credits
	Amount Brought Forward				

B 231

JOURNAL

Number: _____   Month of: _____

		General Ledger			Date	Description			Credits	General Ledger			
Charges Accounts Receivable	Accounts Payable	Acct. No.	Amount							Acct. No.	Amount	Accounts Payable	Acc Rece

Amount Brought Forward

EMPLOYER TAX DEPOSIT RECORD

	January	February	March	
Number of Employees:				
Total Wages Paid:				
Withholding Tax:				
Employer's Social Security Contribution:				TOTAL FOR
Employee's Social Security Contribution:				QUARTER
TOTAL DEPOSIT:				

	April	May	June	
Number of Employees:				
Total Wages Paid:				
Withholding Tax:				
Employer's Social Security Contribution:				TOTAL FOR
Employee's Social Security Contribution:				QUARTER
TOTAL DEPOSIT:				

	July	August	September	
Number of Employees:				
Total Wages Paid:				
Withholding Tax:				
Employer's Social Security Contribution:				TOTAL FOR
Employee's Social Security Contribution:				QUARTER
TOTAL DEPOSIT:				

	October	November	December	
Number of Employees:				
Total Wages Paid:				
Withholding Tax:				
Employer's Social Security Contribution:				TOTAL FOR
Employee's Social Security Contribution:				QUARTER
TOTAL DEPOSIT:				

TOTAL
FOR YEAR _____

EXPENSE RECORD

MONTH OF _____

SALES _____

ADDRESS _____

CITY _____

STATE _____ ZIP _____

TERRITORY NO.	BRANCH/REGION OR ZONE	PRODUCT LINE/SALES GROUP	COMPANY CHARGE CARD NO.
			☐ TELEPHONE _____
			☐ OTHER _____

DATE	TRANS.	PARKING/ TOLLS	HOTEL	MEALS	ENTERTAINMENT		MISC.	PAYMENT METHOD			DAILY TOTALS
					PURPOSE	AMOUNT		COMPANY CHARGE	EMPLOYEE CHARGE	CASH	
TOTALS											

IF SUBMITTED AS AN EXPENSE REPORT - SIGN BELOW		MONTHLY AUTO EXPENSE RECORD	
PREPARER SIGNATURE/TITLE	DATE	LESS CASH ADVANCE	
		LESS CHARGES TO COMPANY	
APPROVAL SIGNATURE/TITLE	DATE	BALANCE DUE ☐ COMPANY ☐ EMPLOYEE	

B 234

MONTHLY EXPENSE RECORD

MONTH OF _____

SALES _____

ADDRESS_____

CITY _____

STATE _____ ZIP_____

TERRITORY NO.	BRANCH/REGION OR ZONE	PRODUCT LINE/SALES GROUP	COMPANY CHARGE CARD NO.
			☐ TELEPHONE _____ ☐ OTHER _____

DATE	TRANS.	PARKING/ TOLLS	HOTEL	MEALS	ENTERTAINMENT		MISC.	PAYMENT METHOD			DAILY TOTALS
					PURPOSE	AMOUNT		COMPANY CHARGE	EMPLOYEE CHARGE	CASH	
TOTALS											

MONTHLY AUTO EXPENSE RECORD	
LESS CASH ADVANCE	
LESS CHARGES TO COMPANY	
☐ COMPANY	
BALANCE DUE ☐ EMPLOYEE	

IF SUBMITTED AS AN EXPENSE REPORT - SIGN BELOW	
PREPARER SIGNATURE/TITLE	DATE
APPROVAL SIGNATURE/TITLE	DATE

B 235

AUTO EXPENSE RECORD

MONTH OF _____

SALES _____

ADDRESS _____

CITY _____

STATE _____ ZIP _____

TERRITORY NO.	BRANCH/REGION OR ZONE	PRODUCT LINE/SALES GROUP	COMPANY CHARGE CARD NO.
			☐ _____ # _____
			☐ _____ # _____

DATE	ODOMETER READING		MILEAGE	GAS/OIL	PARKING TOLLS	MISC	PAYMENT METHOD			DAILY TOTALS
	START	STOP					COMPANY CHARGE	EMPLOYEE CHARGE	CASH	
TOTALS										

MONTHLY AUTO EXPENSE RECORD	
LESS CASH ADVANCE	
LESS CHARGES TO COMPANY	
BALANCE DUE ☐ COMPANY ☐ EMPLOYEE	

IF SUBMITTED AS AN EXPENSE REPORT - SIGN BELOW	
PREPARER SIGNATURE/TITLE	DATE
APPROVAL SIGNATURE/TITLE	DATE

B 236

ASSET DEPRECIATION SCHEDULE

Prepared By: _____ Date: _____

	Date of Purchase	Item	Total Cost	No. Yrs. Useful Lifetime	Salvage Value	Total Depreciation	Annual Depreciation	Depreciation Years From	To
1									
2									
3									
4									
5									
6									
7									
8									
9									
10									
11									
12									
13									
14									
15									
16									
17									
18									
19									
20									

TOTAL
ANNUAL FIXED ASSETS
DEPRECIATION: _____

ANNUAL EXPENSE SUMMARY

FOR YEAR _____

MONTH	PHONE	MEALS	TRAVEL	HOTEL	ENTERTAINMENT	MISC.	MONTHLY TOTAL
JANUARY							
FEBRUARY							
MARCH							
1st QUARTER TOTAL							
APRIL							
MAY							
JUNE							
2nd QUARTER TOTAL							
JULY							
AUGUST							
SEPTEMBER							
3rd QUARTER TOTAL							
OCTOBER							
NOVEMBER							
DECEMBER							
4th QUARTER TOTAL							
YEARLY TOTAL							

NOTES _____
_____
_____
_____
_____

COMPANY CREDIT CARD SUMMARY

☐ _____ # _____
☐ _____ # _____
☐ _____ # _____
☐ _____ # _____

MONTHLY FINANCIALS

			1				2		
1									
2									
3									
4									
5									
6									
7									
8									
9									
10									
11									
12									
13									
14									
15									
16									
17									
18									
19									
20									
21									
22									
23									
24									
25									
26									
27									
28									
29									
30									
31									
32									
33									

Purchasing
and
Shipping

VENDOR MASTER FILE

Vendor's Name _____   Address _____

Contact _____   Phone _____

Capacity _____   Credit Rating _____   Our Rating _____

Delivery time:
    Freight _____   Express _____   Truck _____

Date	Purchase Order No.	Material	Symbol	Quantity	Remarks

STOCK RECORD CARD

ITEM						SIZE		BIN		MINIMUM		STOCK NO.
						UNIT		SHELF		MAXIMUM		

RECEIVED			RELEASED			BALANCE	RECEIVED			RELEASED			BALANCE
DATE	ORDER	QUANTITY	DATE	ORDER	QUANTITY	ON HAND	DATE	ORDER	QUANTITY	DATE	ORDER	QUANTITY	ON HAND

B 244

PURCHASE ORDER REQUISITION

Date: _____

PURCHASING DEPARTMENT: Please purchase the following items:

For _____ Department

Purpose Or Use: _____

Source: _____

Remarks: _____

Requisition No.: _____

Notify: _____

Charge To: _____

Ship Via: _____

Quantity	Unit	Stock Number	Description	Date Needed	Estimated Cost

Requested By: _____

Departmental Approval: _____

For Purchasing Department Use:

Approved: _____

Ordered From: _____

P.O. No. _____ Date: _____

MATERIAL REQUISITION

REQ. DATE	REQUISITIONED BY	MUST HAVE BY	CHARGE TO ACCT.	DELIVER TO

ITEM	QTY.	UNIT	DESCRIPTION	ESTIMATED COST	PURCHASING USE ONLY	
					UNIT PRICE	EXTENDED

CERTIFICATION ☐ YES ☐ NO	SHIP VIA	APPROVED BY	DATE	TOTAL	TOTAL

SUGGESTED VENDORS

1

2

3

PURCHASING USE ONLY

VENDOR	VENDORS PROMISED SHIP DATE
ADDRESS	☐ RESALE ☐ TAXABLE
	TERMS / P.O. NUMBER
CONTACT TELEPHONE	BUYER / P.A. APPROVAL

PURCHASE REQUISITION INDEX

Requisition No.	Date Received	Article	Symbol	Quantity	Buyer	Bids Re-quired	Purchase Order No.	Order Date	Vendor	Invoice Received	Invoice Passed

REQUEST FOR QUOTATION

NUMBER _____

The above NUMBER MUST APPEAR on all QUOTATIONS and related CORRESPONDENCE.
THIS IS NOT AN ORDER!

DATE	DATE DELIVERY REQUIRED	REPLY NOT LATER THAN	REQUISITION NO.	JOB NO.

VENDOR

- •
- •
- •

- •
- •
- •

SUMMARY OF QUOTATIONS

ITEM	QUANTITY	VENDOR NO. 1	VENDOR NO. 2
TERMS			
F.O.B.			
DELIVERY			

1. TERMS	2. F.O.B.	3. SHIPMENT VIA	4. SHIPPING WEIGHT	5. DATE SHIPMENT CAN BE MADE

ITEM	QUANTITY	DESCRIPTION	6. UNIT PRICE	7. AMOUNT

REASON ORDER PLACED WITH SUCCESSFUL VENDOR

Lowest Price	Quality	Best Del'y	Service	Only Source	Best Design
☐	☐	☐	☐	☐	☐

BUYER _____

P. O. No. _____ DATE _____ 19 _____

REQUEST FOR QUOTATION

THIS IS
NOT AN ORDER

DATE

DELIVERY POINT

PLEASE QUOTE YOUR BEST PRICE AND DELIVERY ON THE ITEMS LISTED BELOW:

PRICES QUOTED F.O.B.	TERMS	TO BE SHIPPED VIA	EARLIEST SHIPPING DATE

QUANTITY	DESCRIPTION	PRICE	AMOUNT

BY _____

B 249

QUOTATION RECORD

Material Name _____

Description _____ Specification No. _____

Unit _____

Date	Purchase Order No.	Quantity Purchased	List Price	Discount	Net Price	Freight	Total Cost	Unit Cost	Vendor	Remarks

B 250

QUOTATION EVALUATION

Date: _____

Job Number: _____

Job: _____

Job Description: _____

Firm	Contact	Item	Quantity	Delivery Schedule	Terms	Total Price	Unit Price	Delivery Charge	Net Price	Remarks

Notes:

VENDOR PRICE ANALYSIS

Product:

Vendor	Quantity						Lead time	Est del $	Other Factors Terms
	25 ea.	50 ea.	75 ea.	100 ea.	150 ea.				
1									
2									
3									
4									
5									
6									
7									
8									
9									
10									
11									
12									
13									
14									

Operating Unit: Prepared By: Date:

REQUEST FOR SAMPLE

Date:_____

Name: _____ Title:_____ Address: _____

Company: _____ City: _____

Telephone: _____ State: _____ Zip:_____

☐ New Account   ☐ Previous Customer   ☐ Charge   ☐ No Charge

Quantity	Description	Total

Ship Via: _____

Signed: _____ Authorized: _____

B 253

PURCHASE REQUISITION

☐ Send Confirmation
  Verbal Order Placed

Purchased From _____   Purchase Order No. _____

_____   Date _____ 19 ____

For Dept. _____   To Be Used For _____

For Shop Order No. _____   When Wanted _____   Classification _____

F. O. B. Point _____   Terms _____   Ship Via _____

QUANTITY	FULL DESCRIPTION	PRICE		UNIT

Signed _____   Approved _____   Authorized _____

DEPT. HEAD   PURCHASING AGENT

B 254

PURCHASE ORDER

P.O. NUMBER	
DATE	DATE REQUIRED
TERMS	
SHIP VIA	
F.O.B.	

TO

SHIP TO

QTY.	UNIT	PLEASE SUPPLY ITEMS BELOW	UNIT PRICE	AMOUNT

IMPORTANT
This Purchase Order Number must appear on all invoices, acknowledgments, bills of lading, correspondence and shipping cartons.

Please notify us immediately if you are unable to ship complete order by date specified.

STATE RESALE NUMBER

☐ RESALE   ☐ USE

Please send _____ copies of your invoice

AUTHORIZED SIGNATURE

PURCHASE ORDER

DATE _____ 19 ____

TO

SHIP TO

SHIP TO ABOVE UNLESS OTHERWISE INDICATED HERE

SHIP VIA	F.O.B.	TERMS	DELIVERY REQUIRED	JOB OR REQ. NO.

QUANTITY		DESCRIPTION	PRICE	UNIT	AMOUNT
ORDERED	RECEIVED				

IMPORTANT

Above Order Number must appear on all correspondence, invoices, packages and shipping papers. Notify us immediately if you are unable to ship complete order by date specified. Your acceptance of this order is your warranty to us that you are complying with the U. S. Fair Labor Standard: Act of 1938, as amended, and we reserve the right to refuse merchandise act in strict accordance with this order.

BY _____

B 256

PURCHASE ORDER

P.O. NUMBER	
DATE	DATE REQUIRED
TERMS	
SHIP VIA	
F.O.B.	

TO _____

SHIP TO _____

QTY.	UNIT	PLEASE SUPPLY ITEMS BELOW	UNIT PRICE	AMOUNT

IMPORTANT

This Purchase Order Number must appear on all invoices, acknowledgments, bills of lading, correspondence and shipping cartons.

Please notify us immediately if you are unable to ship complete order by date specified.

STATE RESALE NUMBER

_____

☐ RESALE ☐ USE

Please send _____ copies of your invoice

AUTHORIZED SIGNATURE

B 257

PURCHASE ORDER FOLLOW-UP

DATE _____ 19 _____

THIS IS OUR _____ REQUEST
PLEASE ANSWER IMMEDIATELY

REPLY TO ITEMS
CHECKED BELOW BY

THIS FORM ☐   WIRE ☐   PHONE ☐

OUR PURCHASE ORDER NO.	REQUEST FOR QUOTATION NO.	YOUR INVOICE NO.	DATE	AMOUNT	YOUR REFERENCE

☐ 1. Rush shipment. Advise earliest date.
☐ 2. When will shipment be made? If shipped, advise method.
☐ 3. Please trace shipment.
☐ 4. If shipment has been made, mail invoice, today.
☐ 5. Please mail receipted freight bill.
☐ 6. Why did you not ship as promised? Advise when you will ship?
☐ 7. Will you ship on date shown on purchase order?
☐ 8. Realease shipments as shown under remarks.
☐ 9. Please mail us acceptance copy of our purchase order.
☐ 10. Please acknowledge our order.
☐ 11. Please make your date more specific.
☐ 12. When will balance of order be shipped?
☐ 13. When will price be submitted? Please rush.
☐ 14. Please mail shipping notice.
☐ 15. Please indicate our purchase order number on papers referred to, or attached.

☐ 16. We have no record of transaction covered by your invoice. Advise date of shipment, name of person placing order and furnish signed delivery receipt copy.
☐ 17. Invoice returned herewith.
☐ 18. Invoice is required in _____ copies.
☐ 19. Price or discount is not in accordance with quotation.
☐ 20. Terms on invoice are not in accordance with the purchase order.
☐ 21. Enclosed invoice sent to us in error.
☐ 22. Difference in quantity.
☐ 23. Unit price incorrect.
☐ 24. Extension incorrect.
☐ 25. Purchase order lacking or incorrect.
☐ 26. Sales tax does not apply.
☐ 27. Should be billed F. O. B. destination.
☐ 28. Have you considered this order complete?
☐

REPLY OR REMARKS

DATE _____ 19 _____

VENDOR _____

BY _____   BY _____

DAILY RECEIVING REPORT

REPORTING PERIOD: FROM _____ AM/PM TO _____ AM/PM

DATE _____ SHIFT _____ PAGE _____ OF _____ PAGES

TIME AM/PM	RECEIVED FROM	DESCRIPTION OF CARTONS & CONTENTS	OUR ORDER NUMBER	COMPLETE OR PARTIAL	CARRIER & FT. BILL NO.	PREPAID OR COLLECT	# OF CTNS	WEIGHT	RECEIVED/ CHECKED BY

COMPLETE THE INFORMATION BELOW ON THE LAST SHEET OF REPORT

RECEIVING STAFF THIS SHIFT

☐ ☐ ☐ ☐ ☐

ASST. SUPERVISOR THIS SHIFT

SUPERVISOR THIS SHIFT

FOR OFFICE USE ONLY

REVIEWED BY

AUDIT/APPROVED BY

CLERK

CLERK

TITLE   DATE

TITLE   DATE

RECEIVING REPORT

DATE _____ SHIFT _____

RECEIVED FROM _____
ADDRESS _____
CITY/ST/ZIP _____
SHIPPED FROM _____
_____
_____

CARRIER NAME: _____
- ☐ UPS   ☐ SHIPPER'S TRUCK
- ☐ P. POST ☐ AIR EXPRESS
- ☐ TRUCK   ☐ EXPRESS MAIL
- ☐ RAIL   ☐ _____

☐ PREPAID ☐ COLLECT $ _____

OUR ORDER NUMBER	DATE SHIPPED	SHIPPED TO ATTENTION OF	LOCATION	PHONE

QUANTITY	DESCRIPTION	NUMBER OF CARTONS	WEIGHT EACH	WEIGHT TOTAL	CARTON CONDITION	REC. BY INITIALS

SHIPMENT:
☐ COMPLETE ☐ PARTIAL

TOTAL NUMBER OF CARTONS

TOTAL WEIGHT

NUMBER ITEMS
☐ REC. OK _____
☐ REC. DAMAGED _____

RECEIVED BY	DATE	RECEIVED IN OFFICE BY	DATE
CHECKED BY	DATE	AUDITED BY	DATE

INSPECTION REPORT

DATE _____ SHIFT _____

RECEIVED FROM _____
ADDRESS _____
CITY/STATE/ZIP _____
SHIPPED FROM _____
_____
_____

CARRIER NAME _____
☐ UPS   ☐ SHIPPER'S TRUCK
☐ P.POST   ☐ AIR EXPRESS
☐ TRUCK   ☐ EXPRESS MAIL
☐ RAIL   ☐ _____

INSPECTED ☐ ON DOCK ☐ IN QUAL. CONTROL

QUANTITY RECEIVED	QUANTITY ACCEPTED	QUANTITY REJECTED

ITEM	DESCRIPTION	INSPECTION ACTION			
		APPROVED	REJECTED	REASON	DISPOSITION RECOMMENDED
1					
2					
3					
4					
5					
6					
7					
8					
9					
10					
11					
12					
13					
14					
15					
16					
16					
17					
18					
19					
20					
21					
22					
23					

INSPECTED BY	DATE	RECEIVED IN OFFICE BY	DATE	OUR PURCHASE ORDER NO.
CHECKED BY	DATE	AUDITED BY	DATE	DISPOSITION CODES FOR ABOVE ☐ RETURN TO SUPPLIER ☐ REWORK & BILL SUPPLIER
APPROVED BY	DATE	ACCOUNTING DISPOSITION BY	DATE	☐ SCRAP ☐ _____

BACKORDER CONTROL

Period From:_____ To:_____

Item Number	Description	Qty. On Order	Qty. On B.O.	TOTAL	Date Ordered	Due	Received

Signed: _____

INVOICE CHECK

Date received _____   Purchase order no. _____

Discount date _____   Invoice no. _____

Date passed _____   Voucher no. _____

Terms OK _____

F.O.B. point OK _____

Unit price OK _____

Discounts OK _____

Extensions OK _____

Quantity OK _____

Amount of invoice ....$ _____

Deductions:

   Cash discount ....$ _____

   Rejections ....$ _____

   Other deductions ....$ _____

   Total deductions ....$ _____

Net payable ....$ _____

Nature of deductions _____

_____

_____

_____

OK for payment _____
                                       Invoice Clerk

Passed for payment _____
                                       Purchasing Agent

INVOICE RECORD

Company _____

Address _____

Order No.	Invoice No.	Invoice Date	Date Received	Amount	Deduc- tions	Net Passed	Discount Date	Date Passed	By	Remarks

PROPOSAL

FROM

Proposal No.

Sheet No.

Date

Proposal Submitted To	Work To Be Performed At
Name_____	Street _____
Street _____	City_____ State _____
City_____	Date of Plans_____
State _____ Zip _____	Architect _____
Telephone Number_____	

We hereby propose to furnish all the materials and perform all the labor necessary for the completion of

_____

_____

_____

_____

_____

_____

_____

_____

_____

_____

_____

All material is guaranteed to be as specified, and the above work to be performed in accordance with the drawings and specifications submitted for above work and completed in a substantial workmanlike manner for the sum of_____

_____ Dollars ($_____),

with payments to be made as follows: _____

_____

_____

Any alteration or deviation from above specifications involving extra costs, will be executed only upon written orders, and will become an extra charge over and above the estimate. All agreements contingent upon strikes, accidents or delays beyond our control. Owner to carry fire, tornado and other necessary insurance upon above work. Workmen's Compensation and Public Liability Insurance on above work to be taken out by _____

Respectfully submitted _____

Per _____

NOTE — This proposal may be withdrawn by us if not accepted within _____ days.

ACCEPTANCE OF PROPOSAL

The above prices, specifications and conditions are satisfactory and are hereby accepted. You are authorized to do the work as specified. Payment will be made as outlined above.

_____

Accepted _____ Signature _____

Date _____ Signature ,_____

QUOTATION

DATE:

F.O.B.

TO

TERMS:

DELIVERY:

GENTLEMEN: THANK YOU FOR YOUR INQUIRY OF _____ NO. _____

WE ARE PLEASED TO QUOTE YOU AS FOLLOWS:

QUANTITY	DESCRIPTION	PRICE

We shall be pleased to supply any further information you may desire and trust that you
will decide to favor us with this order which will receive our prompt and careful attention.

Per _____

B 266

SALES ORDER

DATE REQUIRED _____

SHIP VIA _____

DATE _____ 19 _____

Charge to _____ ☐ WILL CONFIRM

_____

Ship to _____

_____

Customer Order No. _____ Order taken by _____ OPEN ☐

Ordered by Mr. _____ COMPLETE ☐

UPS	PP	Air PP	Spec. Del.	Spec. Hand.	Ry. Ex.	Air Ex.	Rail Fgt.	Rail	Motor Truck	Messenger	Our Del.	Pick-Up
☐	☐	☐	☐	☐	☐	☐	☐	☐	☐	☐	☐	☐

PREPAID ☐   COLLECT ☐   C.O.D. ☐   SALESMAN _____

B 267

TELEPHONE SALES ORDER

Sold To: _____   Customer no: _____

_____   Terms: _____

_____   Sales: _____

_____   Ship week of: _____

Ship To: _____   Ship via: _____

_____   FOB: _____

_____   Routing: _____

_____   Interest will be charged at   % per month
This equals an   % annual rate.

Your order no:		Order date:		Our order no:			
Item	Quantity Ordered	Description	Date Needed	Unit Count	Unit Price	Amount

Telephone Sales Order Number: _____   Total: _____

Purchaser Signature: _____   Salesman Signature: _____

Title: _____   Date: _____

Date: _____

TELEPHONE ORDER

Date: _____

Sold To:

Company: _____   Order no: _____

Address: _____   Attention: _____

City: _____   State: _____   Zip code: _____

Ship To:

Company: _____   Order no: _____

Address: _____   Attention: _____

City: _____   State: _____   Zip code: _____

Called in or placed by: _____

Taken by: _____   Time: _____

Item No.	Quantity	Description	Unit Price

Special instructions: _____

_____

_____

_____

LAYAWAY ORDER

Sold To: _____   Date: _____

_____   Salesperson: _____

_____   ☐ To be picked up   ☐ Delivered

Item/description	Quantity	Unit price	Amount

Payment plan

_____ payments   Total _____

$ _____ each   Sales tax _____

$ _____ final payment   Total due _____

                                                          Deposit _____

Date: _____ Amount due: _____ Payment: _____   Balance _____

B 270

JOB ESTIMATE

Estimate Number _____

Date of Estimate _____

Prepared By _____

RE: ☐ Day Work   ☐ Contract   ☐ Extra

Explanation _____

Job Name/Number _____

Job Location _____

Job Phone _____ Exten. _____

Start Date _____ End Date _____

#	MATERIAL	QTY	PRICE EACH	TOTAL PRICE	#	LABOR	RATE	HRS.	TOTAL AMOUNT
1					1				
2					2				
3					3				
4					4				
5					5				
6					6				
7					7				
8					8				
9					9				
10					10				
11					11				
12									
13					#	MISC. OTHER ITEMS			TOTAL AMOUNT
14					1				
15					2				
16					3				
17					4				
18					5				
19						OVERHEAD			
20						TOTAL LABOR			
21						TOTAL MISC.			
22						TOTAL MATERIALS			

ESTIMATE APPROVED BY _____

TOTAL BID	
TOTAL COST	
TOTAL PROFIT	

Signature Approval for Quotation Release

WORK ORDER

DATE _____   CUST. ORDER NO. _____

CUSTOMER _____

PART NO. AND DESCRIPTION _____

_____

QUANTITY _____ PRINT NO. _____ DEL. DATE _____

DESCRIPTION OF OPERATION

_____

_____

_____

MATERIAL	COST	OUTSIDE WORK	AMOUNT

TOTALS

MATERIAL COST		
DIRECT LABOR		
OUTSIDE WORK		
BURDEN		
TOTAL COST		
SELLING PRICE		
PROFIT		

B 272

JOB ORDER

No. _____ .

Page _____ of _____ Pages

CUSTOMER	DATE
NAME	JOB NAME
STREET	JOB LOCATION
CITY	
STATE, ZIP	JOB PHONE
PHONE	

Location	Stock No.	Description	Size	Area	FOR OFFICE USE ONLY:
					Material in stock ☐
					Material to be ordered ☐
					Date ordered:
					_____
					Date received:
					_____

Job assigned to _____

Date to start _____ A.M. ☐   P.M. ☐

Date started _____

Date completed _____

Job completed by _____

Signature

Remarks if any:

JOB INSPECTED AND FOUND SATISFACTORY BY:

_____

Customer's Signature

B 273

JOB ORDER CHANGE

Estimate Number ______________________
Date of Estimate ______________________
Prepared By ______________________
RE: ☐ Day Work ☐ Contract ☐ Extra
Explanation ______________________
Job Name/Number ______________________
Job Location ______________________
Job Phone ______________ Exten. ________
Start Date ____________ End Date ________

ADDITIONAL WORK AUTHORIZATION

#	MATERIAL	QTY	PRICE EACH	TOTAL PRICE
1				
2				
3				
4				
5				
6				
7				
8				
9				
10				
11				
12				
13				
14				
15				
16				

#	LABOR	RATE	HRS.	TOTAL AMOUNT
1				
2				
3				
4				
5				
6				
7				
8				
9				

#	MISC. OTHER ITEMS	TOTAL AMOUNT
1		
2		
3		
4		
5		

Your Order No. ____________ Date ____________
Work Ordered By ______________________
Explanation ______________________

ADDITIONAL WORK SUMMARY
TOTAL MATERIALS
TOTAL LABOR
TOTAL MISC.
TOTAL TAX/PERMIT/INS.

Estimate Approved By ______________________

TOTAL COST	
TAX	
TOTAL BILLING	

____
Signature Approval For Quotation Release

CHANGE ORDER

NO. _____

PROJECT _____ DATE _____

SUB-CONTRACTOR:

Our Job No. _____

Type of Work _____

YOU ARE HEREBY AUTHORIZED TO MAKE THE FOLLOWING CHANGES IN YOUR WORK ON THE ABOVE NAMED PROJECT, IT BEING MUTUALLY UNDERSTOOD THAT THESE CHANGES ARE TO BE EXECUTED UNDER THE TERMS OF AND CONDITIONS IN OUR CONTRACT.

| | Original Contract Price | $ |
| | This Change Order | $ |

DESCRIPTION OF ADDED OR DELETED CONTRACT ITEMS	INCREASE	DECREASE
	$	$
	$	$
Revised Contract Price Through Change Order		$

ACCEPTED:

FOR _____

BY _____

DATE _____

BY _____

TITLE _____

B 275

CHANGE ORDER

CHANGE ORDER
NO.

ADDRESSEE:

JOB:

REFERENCE:

THE ABOVE SUBJECT AGREEMENT IS HEREBY CHANGED AS FOLLOWS:

ITEM NO.	DESCRIPTION OF CHANGE	ADD	DEDUCT

PREVIOUS AMOUNT	THIS CHANGE ORDER		REVISED AMOUNT
	ADD	DEDUCT	

EXCEPT AS MODIFIED BY THIS CHANGE ORDER (AND PREVIOUS CHANGE ORDERS, IF ANY) THE SUBJECT AGREEMENT
REMAINS UNCHANGED AND CONTINUES IN FULL FORCE AND EFFECT.

PLEASE SIGN AND RETURN THE ORIGINAL OF THIS CHANGE ORDER.

BY: _____

TITLE: _____

DATE: _____

BY: _____

DATE: _____

B 276

SERVICE INVOICE

Sold To: Service At:

_____   _____

_____   _____

_____   _____

Make of Equipment	Model No.	Serial No.	Date Repaired

–:– PARTS USED –:–

Quantity	DESCRIPTION	Price	Amount

Date	No. Hours	Rate/Hour	Amount	Total	
				Tax	
				Total Labor	
				TOTAL BILL	
				GUARANTEED FOR 30 DAYS AGAINST FAULTY LABOR AND MATERIALS ONLY.	
		TOTAL			

Comments:

_____

_____

_____

_____

Service Man: _____   Signed: _____

B 277

TIME AND MATERIAL REPORT

JOB NO. _____

NAME _____ DATE _____

SCALE:　　Straight Time_____　　　Overtime _____

No. Hours　　　　　　　_____　　　　　　_____

WAGES　　_____　　　　　_____　　TOTAL WAGES _____

MATERIAL

QUANTITY	DESCRIPTION	PRICE PER UNIT	TOTAL PRICE	QUANTITY	DESCRIPTION	PRICE PER UNIT	TOTAL PRICE
	TOTAL					TOTAL	

DESCRIPTION OF WORK

Residence　New ( )　　　Old ( )

Commercial New ( )　　　Old ( )

REMARKS

SUMMARY		
MATERIAL		
PERMIT		
LABOR		
JOB COST		
PROFIT		
OVERHEAD		
PRICE OF JOB		
GAIN		
LOSS		

WORK AUTHORIZATION

NAME		DATE	PHONE
ADDRESS		DATE PROMISED	DATE COMPLETED
CITY		SERIAL NO.	MODEL NO.

COMPLAINT:

AMT.	NAME OF PART & NUMBER	AMOUNT		DESCRIPTION OF WORK	AMOUNT	
				LABOR ONLY		
				PARTS		
	PARTS			TOTAL		
	TAX			TAX		
	TOTAL AMOUNT			TOTAL AMOUNT		

CUSTOMER'S SIGNATURE

RETURN AUTHORIZATION

SOLD TO

CUSTOMER NO _____

TERMS _____

SALES _____

APP. RTN SHIP WEEK _____

COMPLETE FOR RETURN SHIPMENT AND INCLUDE A COPY OF THIS FORM AS PACKING LIST
DATE SHIPPED
FOB
ROUTING

SHIP TO

YOUR ORDER NO.	ORDER DATE	OUR ORDER NO.

ITEM	QUANTITY	DESCRIPTION	QUANTITY RECEIVED	UNIT PRICE	AMOUNT

RETURN AUTHORIZATION
THIS FORM AUTHORIZES YOUR RETURN OF THE ABOVE ITEMS

DATE	TOTAL RETURN OF	
	ITEMS	DOLLAR AMOUNT

DATE	APPROVED BY	DATE	ITEMS RECEIVED OUR PLANT BY
DATE	APPROVED BY	DATE	ITEMS RECEIVED OUR PLANT BY

STATEMENT

DATE _____

NUMBER _____ TERMS _____

AMOUNT REMITTED

$ _____

DATE	INVOICE NO/DESCRIPTION	CHARGE	CREDIT	BALANCE
PREVIOUS BALANCE BROUGHT FORWARD				

THANK YOU FOR YOUR BUSINESS PLEASE PAY THIS AMOUNT ▶

B 281

CREDIT MEMO

SOLD TO

CUSTOMER NO _____

TERMS _____

SALES _____

RECEIVED OUR PLANT _____

SHIPPED TO

REASON FOR CREDIT	
APPROVED BY	APPROVED BY
DATE	DATE

YOUR ORDER NO	ORDER DATE	OUR ORDER NO

ITEM	QUANTITY	INVOICE NO/DESCRIPTION	UNIT PRICE	AMOUNT

CREDIT MEMO

CREDIT MEMO ISSUED DATE	TOTAL CREDIT MEMO AMOUNT $

B 282

DEBIT MEMO

SOLD TO

CUSTOMER NO _____

TERMS _____

SALES_____

RECEIVED OUR PLANT_____

SHIPPED TO

REASON FOR DEBIT	
APPROVED BY	APPROVED BY
DATE	DATE

YOUR ORDER NO.	ORDER DATE	OUR ORDER NO.

ITEM	QUANTITY	INVOICE NO/DESCRIPTION	UNIT PRICE	AMOUNT

DEBIT MEMO

DEBIT MEMO ISSUED DATE	TOTAL DEBIT MEMO AMOUNT $

ESTIMATE OF REPAIR COSTS

NAME			ADDRESS				PHONE NO.	PHONE EXT.	DATE
MAKE OF CAR			TYPE	STATE	LICENSE NUMBER			JOB NO.	INSPECTOR
YEAR	MILEAGE	MOTOR NO.	SERIAL NO.		INSURANCE		ASSURED		ADJUSTER

QUAN.	WORK TO BE DONE	PARTS NO.	PARTS		LABOR	

The above is an estimate based on our inspection and does not cover any additional parts or labor which may be required after the work has been opened up. Occasionally after the work has started, worn or damaged parts are discovered which are not evident on the first inspection. Because of this the above prices are not guaranteed, and are for immediate acceptance only.

TOTAL LABOR		
TOTAL PARTS		
TAX ON PARTS		
TOTAL OF ESTIMATE		

CONTRACTOR'S INVOICE

	DATE
	CUSTOMER ORDER NO.
	ORDER TAKEN BY
JOB ADDRESS	STARTING DATE
JOB PHONE	
BILL TO	☐ DAY WORK
ADDRESS	☐ CONTRACT
PHONE	☐ EXTRA
DESCRIPTION OF WORK	INSPECTION
	☐ PERMIT
	☐ FINAL
	☐ COVER
	BUILDING PERMIT

SIGNATURE

☐ I HEREBY AUTHORIZE THE ABOVE DESCRIBED WORK TO BE PERFORMED.

☐ AT OUR REGULAR RATES   ☐ C.O.D.

☐ FOR THE AMOUNT OF   ☐ INVOICE

WORK ORDERED BY   TIME STARTED

☐ COMPLETE   TIME FINISHED

☐ JOB INCOMPLETE   TRAVEL TIME

DATE	HOURS	TOTAL MATERIAL		
MECHANIC		TOTAL LABOR		
		PERMIT		
HELPER		MISC.		
		TOTAL AMOUNT		

B 285

SERVICE CONTRACT

Customer's Name _____

Address _____

Phone _____

Date _____

ADDRESS(ES) OF WORK TO BE PERFORMED	ESTIMATE 1ST JOB	MAINTAINING PRICE(S)

Services to Be Performed _____

_____

_____

_____

_____

_____

Terms _____

_____

_____
CUSTOMER'S SIGNATURE

_____
DATE

INVOICE

SOLD TO _____   DATE _____ 19 _____

_____   TERMS _____

SHIP TO _____   ORDER NO._____

_____   DEPT. _____

_____   SHIP VIA_____

SALESMAN _____

QUANTITY	STYLE NO.	DESCRIPTION	PRICE		TOTAL	

B 287

INVOICE

			INVOICE DATE	
			OUR ORDER NO.	
			YOUR ORDER NO.	
			TERMS	F.O.B.
			SALESMAN	

SHIPPED TO		SHIPPED VIA	PPD. or COLL.

QUANTITY	DESCRIPTION	PRICE	AMOUNT

INVOICE

SHIPPED TO

SOLD
TO

OUR ORDER NO.	YOUR ORDER NO.	DATE	TERMS	SHIPPED VIA	PPD. or COLL.
QUANTITY	D E S C R I P T I O N			PRICE	AMOUNT

"SELLER REPRESENTS THAT WITH RESPECT TO THE PRODUCTION OF THE ARTICLES AND/OR THE SERVICES COVERED BY THIS INVOICE,
IT HAS FULLY COMPLIED WITH THE PROVISIONS OF THE FAIR LABOR STANDARDS ACT OF 1938, AS AMENDED."

B 289

SERVICE INVOICE

QUAN.	DESCRIPTION	PRICE

RECEIVED | PROMISED | MECHANIC

PERSON CALLING | AUTHORIZED BY

NAME:

PHONE NUMBER:

STREET:

CITY:　　　　STATE　　　　ZIP

☐ OFFICE　　☐ HOME

WORK TO BE DONE:

☐ WARRANTY - REASON -　　MODEL　　SERIAL NUMBER

☐ NORMAL　　☐ SERVICE CONTRACT　　☐ TIME & MATERIAL ☐

DATE

DESCRIPTION OF WORK PERFORMED

UPON INSPECTION, OUR TRAINED SERVICE PERSONNEL
RECOMMEND THE FOLLOWING:

SERVICE CHARGE

MATERIAL

TAX

TOTAL DUE | $

I HAVE AUTHORITY TO ORDER THE WORK WHICH HAS
BEEN SATISFACTORILY PERFORMED, AS OUTLINED A-
BOVE. IT IS AGREED THAT THE SELLER WILL RETAIN
TITLE TO ANY EQUIPMENT OR MATERIAL THAT MAY BE
FURNISHED UNTIL FINAL PAYMENT IS MADE, AND IF
SETTLEMENT IS NOT MADE AS AGREED, THE SELLER
SHALL HAVE THE RIGHT TO REMOVE SAME AND THE
SELLER WILL BE HELD HARMLESS FOR ANY DAMAGES
RESULTING FROM THE REMOVAL THEREOF.

CUSTOMER'S SIGNATURE

SERVICE WORK STRICTLY CASH

B 290

RECEIPT FOR GOODS

DATE _____ 19 _____

OUR P. O. NO. _____

CHARGES
PREPAID $ _____

CHARGES
COLLECT $ _____

RECEIVED FROM _____

ADDRESS _____

FOR DEPT. _____

DELIVERED BY (NAME OF CARRIER) | B/L NUMBER | FREIGHT BILL NO.

JOB NO. _____ REQ. NO. _____

☐ FREIGHT	☐ AIR FREIGHT	☐ EXPRESS	☐ AIR EXPRESS	☐ LOCAL DELIVERY	
☐ P. P.	☐ AIR P. P.	☐ PICK-UP	☐ MESSENGER	☐	

FOR OFFICE USE

CASES	CARTONS	PACKAGES	CRATES	BUNDLES	DRUMS	BAGS	OTHER

INVOICE NO. _____

TOTAL NO. OF PACKAGES	TOTAL WEIGHT	PARTIAL	COMPLETE	

INVOICE DATE _____

	QUANTITY	DESCRIPTION	CONDITION	WEIGHT	ENTERED
1					
2					
3					
4					
5					
6					
7					
8					
9					
10					
11					
12					
13					
14					
15					
16					
17					
18					
19					
20					
21					
22					
23					
24					

REMARKS:

RECEIVED BY	CHECKED BY

BE SURE TO MAKE THIS RECORD
ACCURATE AND COMPLETE.

B 291

STATEMENT

DATE_____ 19 _____

_____

_____

_____

TAX EXEMPT RESALE CERTIFICATE

To: _____

_____

_____

_____

(Vendor)

The undersigned hereby certifies that all tangible personal property hereafter purchased by him/her is for the purpose of resale. Purchaser assumes liability for payment of Retailers Occupation Tax, Service Occupation Tax, or Use Tax with respect to receipts from resale of this property.

This certificate shall be considered part of each transaction between Vendor and Purchaser unless otherwise specified.

Purchaser: _____ Date: _____

Address: _____ Signature of Purchaser or Authorizing Agent: _____

City: _____ Certificate of Registration No. of Vendor: _____

To: _____

_____

_____

_____

(Vendor)

The undersigned hereby certifies that all tangible personal property hereafter purchased by him/her is for the purpose of resale. Purchaser assumes liability for payment of Retailers Occupation Tax, Service Occupation Tax, or Use Tax with respect to receipts from resale of this property.

This certificate shall be considered part of each transaction between Vendor and Purchaser unless otherwise specified.

Purchaser: _____ Date: _____

Address: _____ Signature of Purchaser or Authorizing Agent: _____

City: _____ Certificate of Registration No. of Vendor: _____

RETURN BOTH CERTIFICATES, EACH PROPERLY FILLED OUT, TO THE VENDOR.
ONE IS FOR THE STATE DEPARTMENT OF REVENUE, THE OTHER IS FOR OUR RECORDS.

B 293

SHIPPING ORDER

SOLD TO

SHIP TO

CUSTOMER NO. _____

TERMS _____

SALES _____

APP. SHIP WEEK _____

DATE SHIPPED _____

FOB _____

ROUTING _____

INTEREST WILL BE CHARGED AT _____ % PER MONTH
THIS EQUALS AN _____ % ANNUAL RATE.

YOUR ORDER NO.	ORDER DATE	OUR ORDER NO.

ITEM	QUANTITY ORDERED	DESCRIPTION

QUANTITY SHIPPED	NO. OF CARTONS	TOTAL WEIGHT	PACKED BY (Initials)

INSTRUCTIONS

1) PACK AND SHIP THE ABOVE PRODUCTS TO THE CUSTOMER'S SHIP TO ADDRESS PROVIDED ABOVE.
2) PLACE PACKING LIST IN WITH SHIPMENT.
3) RETURN ONE COPY OF THIS FORM TO OFFICE ON THE DAY OF SHIPMENT.

TOTALS	QUANTITY	CARTONS	TOTAL WEIGHT
PACKED BY			DATE
CHECKED BY			DATE

B 294

SHIPPING ORDER

Deliver to:

Date

Cust. Order No.

Our Order No.

QUANTITY ORDERED	QUANTITY SHIPPED	ITEMS

Received by _____ Per _____ Date _____ 19 _____

B 295

Sales
and
Marketing

SALES PROSPECT FILE

New ☐   Update ☐   Follow-up date: _____

Company name: _____

Contact: _____ Title: _____

Address: _____

_____

Telephone: _____

Market segment: _____

Call-in ☐   Referral ☐   Referred by: _____

Current supplier: _____

Approximate volume (monthly): _____

Form letters sent: _____

Material sent: _____

Sales calls (date and summary): _____

_____

_____

_____

Date and summary of last discussion: _____

_____

_____

Desirability as client: Very high ☐   High ☐   Medium ☐   Low ☐

Possibility of closing   100% ☐   90% ☐   70% ☐   50% ☐   30% ☐   None ☐

General comments: _____

_____

_____

SALES LEAD

APPOINTMENT DATE

Day _____ Time _____ ☐ a.m. ☐ p.m.

SOURCE OF LEAD

Date _____

Name _____

Address _____

Phone No. _____

Interested in _____

_____

_____

_____

Remarks: _____

_____

_____

_____

SALES LEAD

APPOINTMENT DATE

Day _____ Time _____ ☐ a.m. ☐ p.m.

SOURCE OF LEAD

Date _____

Name _____

Address _____

Phone No. _____

Interested in _____

_____

_____

_____

Remarks: _____

_____

_____

_____

SALES PROJECTIONS WORKSHEET

	NEW BUSINESS			REORDERS			TOTAL		
	GOAL	ACTUAL	VARIANCE	GOAL	ACTUAL	VARIANCE	GOAL	ACTUAL	VARIANCE

MONTHLY SALES PROJECTIONS

SALESPERSON OR DEPARTMENT _____ DATE _____

	NEW BUSINESS			REORDERS			TOTAL		
	GOAL	ACTUAL	VARIANCE	GOAL	ACTUAL	VARIANCE	GOAL	ACTUAL	VARIANCE
JAN									
FEB									
MAR									
APR									
MAY									
JUN									
JUL									
AUG									
SEP									
OCT									
NOV									
DEC									
YEAR									

PREPARED BY _____

CHART OF MONTHLY SALES

_____, 19____ to _____, 19____

1st	2nd	3rd	4th	5th	6th	7th	8th	9th	10th	11th	12th

Month by month, 19____

SALES FORECAST

SALESPERSON _____ TERRITORY _____ DATE _____

ACCOUNT NAME & ADDRESS	STATUS			PURCHASES ($)	
	PAST ✓	EXIST'G ✓	POTEN. ✓	PAST YEAR	FORECAST

THREE YEAR SALES FORECAST

SALESPERSON OR DEPARTMENT _____ DATE _____

		NEW BUSINESS			REORDERS			TOTAL		
		GOAL	ACTUAL	VARIANCE	GOAL	ACTUAL	VARIANCE	GOAL	ACTUAL	VARIANCE
19	1									
	2									
	3									
	4									
19	1									
	2									
	3									
	4									
19	1									
	2									
	3									
	4									
TOTAL										

PREPARED BY _____

B 305

SALES/PROFIT PROJECTIONS

DATE _____

SALES		MONTH			YTD			ESTIMATED YR. END		
		FORECAST	ACTUAL	VARIANCE	FORECAST	ACTUAL	VARIANCE	FORECAST	ACTUAL	VARIANCE
TOTAL										
PROFIT(LOSS)										

SALES ACTIVITY ANALYSIS

SALESPERSON_____ TERRITORY_____ DATE_____

		FORECAST	ACTUAL
SALES & PROFIT	Gross Sales		
	Gross Profit		
	% Gross Profit to Gross Sales		
	Net Profit		
	% Net Profit to Gross Sales		
SELLING COST	Salary		
	Commission		
	Expense: Auto		
	Travel		
	Telephone		
	Entertainment		
	Other		
ACTIVITY	Total Days Worked		
	Number of Calls Made		
	Avg. No. Calls per Day		
ACCT. INFO.	No. New Accounts		
	No. of Accts. Lost		
	No. of Accts. at Period End		
	No. of Potential Accts.		

PREPARED BY _____

MONTHLY SALES ACTIVITY ANALYSIS

SALESPERSON _____ TERRITORY _____ PREPARED BY _____ DATE _____

	JAN	FEB	MAR	APR	MAY	JUN	JUL	AUG	SEP	OCT	NOV	DEC	YEAR
PROFIT													
Gross Sales													
Gross Profit													
% Gross Profit to Gross Sales													
Net Profit													
% Net Profit to Gross Sales													
SALES COST													
Salary													
Commission													
Expense: Auto													
Travel													
Telephone													
Entertainment													
Other													
ACCT. INFO.													
Total Days Worked													
No. Calls Made													
Avg. No. Calls per Day													
ACTIVITY													
No. New Accounts													
No. of Accts. Lost													
No. of Accts. at Month End													
No. of Potential Accts.													

B 308

MONTHLY RECORD OF AD RECEIPTS

Product		Selling Price		Key	
Publication		Circulation		Issue	On Sale
Cost		Size of Ad		Monthly Profit	Monthly Loss

Projection: Total Number of Orders			Total Cash		
Month_____ Day of Month	Daily Number of Orders	Total Number of Orders	Daily Receipts	Total Receipts	
1					
2					
3					
4					
5					
6					
7					
8					
9					
10					
11					
12					
13					
14					
15					
16					
17					
18					
19					
20					
21					
22					
23					
24					
25					
26					
27					
28					
29					
30					
31					
Total					

Comments _____

_____

QUARTERLY SALES ACTIVITY ANALYSIS

SALESPERSON _____ TERRITORY _____ DATE _____

		1		2		3		4		YEAR	
		Forecast	Actual	Forecast	Actual	Forecast	Actual	Forecast	Actual	Forecast	Actual
SALES & PROFIT	Gross Sales										
	Gross Profit										
	% Gross Profit to Gross Sales										
	Net Profit										
	% Net Profit to Gross Sales										
SELLING COST	Salary										
	Commission										
	Expense: Auto										
	Travel										
	Telephone										
	Entertainment										
	Other										
ACTIVITY	Total Days Worked										
	Number of Calls Made										
	Avg. No. Calls per Day										
ACCT. INFO.	No. New Accounts										
	No. of Accts. Lost										
	No. of Accts. at Qtr. End										
	No. of Potential Accts.										

PREPARED BY _____

B 310

MONTHLY SALES TREND ANALYSIS

	$ LAST YEAR	$ GOAL THIS YR	$ ACTUAL THIS YR	%	$ LAST YEAR	$ GOAL THIS YR	$ ACTUAL THIS YR	%	TOTAL $ LAST YEAR	$ GOAL THIS YR	$ ACTUAL THIS YR	%
JAN												
FEB												
MAR												
APR												
MAY												
JUN												
JUL												
AUG												
SEP												
OCT												
NOV												
DEC												
YEAR												

PREPARED BY _____

B 311

PRODUCT SALES TREND ANALYSIS   19___

	LAST YEAR $	GOAL THIS YR $	% CHANGE	LAST YEAR $	GOAL THIS YR $	% CHANGE	LAST YEAR $	GOAL THIS YR $	% CHANGE	LAST YEAR $	GOAL THIS YR $	% CHANGE	TOTAL LAST YEAR $	TOTAL GOAL THIS YR $	TOTAL % CHANGE
JAN															
FEB															
MAR															
APR															
MAY															
JUN															
JUL															
AUG															
SEP															
OCT															
NOV															
DEC															
TOTAL															

PREPARED BY _____   DATE _____

MEDIA FORECAST

19___

	TELEVISION		RADIO		MAGAZINE		NEWSPAPER		DIRECT MAIL		BILLBOARD		TOTAL	
MEDIA	FORECAST	ACTUAL	FORECAST	ACTUAL	FORECAST	ACTUAL	FORECAST	ACTUAL	FORECAST	ACTUAL	FORECAST	ACTUAL	FORECAST	ACTUAL
JANUARY														
FEBRUARY														
MARCH														
APRIL														
MAY														
JUNE														
JULY														
AUGUST														
SEPTEMBER														
OCTOBER														
NOVEMBER														
DECEMBER														
YEAR														

B 313

ADVERTISING ANALYSIS

MEDIA

19___

		COST	SALES	COST	SALES	COST	SALES	COST	SALES	COST	SALES	COST	SALES	COST	SALES	COST	SALES	COST	SALES
JANUARY																				
FEBRUARY																				
MARCH																				
APRIL																				
MAY																				
JUNE																				
JULY																				
AUGUST																				
SEPTEMBER																				
OCTOBER																				
NOVEMBER																				
DECEMBER																				
YEAR																				

PROFITABILITY ANALYSIS

	SALES				COSTS				EARNINGS			
	FORECAST		ACTUAL		FORECAST		ACTUAL		FORECAST		ACTUAL	
	MO.	YTD	MO.	YTD	MO.	YTD	MO.	YTD	MO.	YTD	MO.	YTD
JANUARY												
FEBRUARY												
MARCH												
APRIL												
MAY												
JUNE												
JULY												
AUGUST												
SEPTEMBER												
OCTOBER												
NOVEMBER												
DECEMBER												

PREPARED BY _____   DATE _____

DIRECT MAIL ANALYSIS

PROMOTION _____ DATE _____

PRODUCT		PROMOTION	
1. SELLING PRICE		16. CIRCULARS	
2. ADD: SERVICE CHARGE		17. INSERTS	
3. TOTAL SELLING PRICE		18. LETTERS	
4. LESS: MERCHANDISE COST		19. ENVELOPES	
5. SHIPPING/DELIVERY		20. ORDER FORMS	
6. ORDER PROCESSING		21. LIST RENTAL	
7. COST OF RETURNS		22. INSERTING	
8. BAD DEBT		23. ADDRESSING	
9.		24. MAILING	
10.		25. POSTAGE	
11.		26. MISCELLANEOUS	
12.		27. TOTAL CIRCULATION COST	
13.		28. ADD: FIXED OVERHEAD PER M	
14. TOTAL COST		29. TOTAL COST(C)	
15. UNIT PROFIT(P)		30. BREAK EVEN SALES PER M (C ÷ P)	

NET PROFIT

FORECASTED NET SALES PER M (In Units)	
LESS: BREAK EVEN SALES-LINE 30 (In Units)	−
UNIT SALES PER M EARNING TOTAL PROFIT	
UNIT PROFIT - LINE 15	x
NET PROFIT PER M	$
M CIRCULARS MAILED	x
TOTAL NET PROFIT	

PREPARED BY _____

PROMOTION BUDGET

DATE_____

FIXED COSTS

ITEMS	REQUIRED BY	COST
	TOTAL (A)	

VARIABLE COSTS

ITEMS	REQUIRED BY	COST
	TOTAL (B)	

TOTAL DIRECT COST (A + B)	
DIVISIONAL COSTS	
ADMINISTRATIVE COSTS	
TOTAL PROMOTIONAL COSTS	

COMPARATIVE ADVERTISING PLAN

DATE _____

MEDIA

	TELEVISION		RADIO		MAGAZINE		NEWSPAPER		DIRECT MAIL		BILLBOARD		TOTAL	
	SPENT LAST YEAR	FORECAST THIS YEAR	SPENT LAST YEAR	FORECAST THIS YEAR	SPENT LAST YEAR	FORECAST THIS YEAR	SPENT LAST YEAR	FORECAST THIS YEAR	SPENT LAST YEAR	FORECAST THIS YEAR	SPENT LAST YEAR	FORECAST THIS YEAR	SPENT LAST YEAR	FORECAST THIS YEAR
JANUARY														
FEBRUARY														
MARCH														
APRIL														
MAY														
JUNE														
JULY														
AUGUST														
SEPTEMBER														
OCTOBER														
NOVEMBER														
DECEMBER														
YEAR														

ANNUAL ADVERTISING FORECAST   19___

MEDIA

	FORECAST	ACTUAL	FORECAST	ACTUAL	FORECAST	ACTUAL	FORECAST	ACTUAL	FORECAST	ACTUAL	FORECAST	ACTUAL
JANUARY												
FEBRUARY												
MARCH												
APRIL												
MAY												
JUNE												
JULY												
AUGUST												
SEPTEMBER												
OCTOBER												
NOVEMBER												
DECEMBER												
YEAR												

MAILING LIST UPDATE

	Date Added To List	Customer Number	Name	Address	Mailing Sent	Maintain	Drop
1							
2							
3							
4							
5							
6							
7							
8							
9							
10							
11							
12							
13							
14							
15							
16							
17							
18							
19							
20							
21							
22							
23							
24							
25							
26							

B 320

COMMISSION REPORT

Name: _____   Period From: _____ To: _____

Order Date	Order Number	Account	Invoice Amount	Commission Rate	Amount

Total Sales _____

Total Commission Earned _____

Less Advance/Credit _____

Commission Payable _____

_____   _____
Signed   Date

DAILY TELEPHONE SALES REPORT

SALES

ADDRESS

CITY/STATE/ZIP

PRODUCT LINE

TERRITORY NO

BRANCH/REGION OR ZONE

DATE

REPORTING PERIOD } FROM

TO

DATE SUBMITTED

REPORT NO.

PAGE _____ OF _____ PAGES

FIRM NAME AND ADDRESS	PARTY INTERVIEWED AND TITLE	PRODUCTS PRESENTED/SOLD/REMARKS

SIGNATURE

TITLE

COMMISSION INCOME JOURNAL

MONTH _____
YEAR _____

ORDER NO.	CUSTOMER/ SUPPLIER	P. ORDER NO/DATE	P. ORDER AMOUNT	COMMISSION DUE			SHIPPING/INVOICE INFORMATION			COMMISSIONS PAID			DEPOSIT # & DATE
				%	AMOUNT	DATE	REQ. SHIP DT.	ACTUAL SHIP DT.	ACTUAL INV. AMT.	DATE	CK. #	AMOUNT	
PAGE TOTALS			$		$				$			$	

TELEMARKETING PROSPECT SHEET

Date: _____

Prospect: _____

Address: _____

Business telephone: _____

Delivery instructions: _____

Preferred contact:

   Time: _____

   Place: _____

.   .   .

Objectives of this call: _____

Previous purchase (if any): _____

Current sale: _____

Future potential: _____

Potential reference: _____

.   .   .

Comments: _____

_____

_____

_____

_____

_____

To be followed up: _____

_____

Signature of caller: _____

TELEMARKETING CALLBACK WORKSHEET

Telemarketing representative: _____   Date: _____

Call frequency: _____

Account/prospect: _____

Mailing address: _____

Delivery address: _____

Delivery instructions: _____

Business telephone: _____

Contact: _____

   Time: _____

   Place: _____

Objective(s) of this call: _____

Objective(s) of last call: _____

Last purchase: _____

Current sales potential: _____

Future sales potential: _____

"Prospect" referral potential: _____

SUMMARY:

_____

_____

_____

_____

_____

_____

Next follow-up date: _____

B 325

TELEMARKETING REPORT

PROGRESS REPORT FOR WEEK OF: _____

	NUMBER OF CALLS COMPLETED			NUMBER OF ORDERS PLACED		
	TO CLIENTS	TO PROSPECTS	GOAL	FROM CLIENTS	FROM PROSPECTS	GOAL
MONDAY						
TUESDAY						
WEDNESDAY						
THURSDAY						
FRIDAY						
THIS WEEK'S TOTAL						
LAST WEEK'S TOTAL						
NEXT WEEK'S TOTAL						

Notes: _____

_____

_____

_____

_____

_____

_____

_____

_____

_____

_____

TELEPHONE SALES ANALYSIS

Date: _____

PROSPECT NAME	TELEPHONE NO.	OBJECTIONS/COMMENTS	

Personnel

PERSONNEL ACTIVITY REPORT

Month of:_____

Date prepared:_____

Prepared by:_____

	Salaried	Hourly	P/T
No. employees at beginning			
No. employees at end			
No. positions open			
No. applicants interviewed			
No. applicants hired			
% hires to interviews			
No. employees terminated			
No. employees resigned			
No. openings at beginning			
No. openings at end			
Total requisitions to be filled			
Requisitions received			
Requisitions filled			
Requisitions unfilled			
Turnover rate			

Comments:

AFFIRMATIVE ACTION SUMMARY

Date	Applicants for Hire	New Hires	Applicants for Promotion	Promotions	Terminations
MALE					
White					
Black					
Hispanic					
Asian					
American Indian					
FEMALE					
White					
Black					
Hispanic					
Asian					
American Indian					

Selection procedures used to fill vacancies during the year were as follows:

_____

REQUEST FOR APPROVAL
TO HIRE

Requisition No._____Date_____

Applicant_____

Title/Job Classification_____

_____

_____

P/T_____ F/T_____ Perm._____ Temp._____

Starting Salary $_____

Reports To_____

Replacement_____New Position_____

Department_____Budget_____

Description of Duties_____

_____

_____

_____

Relocation Authorization_____

_____

_____

_____

Exceptions To Policy_____

_____

_____

Starting Date_____

_____
Requested By

EMPLOYMENT REQUISITION

JOB TITLE _____

DEPARTMENT _____ LOCATION _____ SUPERVISOR _____ EXT. _____

Date Wanted	Shift	Addition ☐ Replacement ☐	If Replacement, For whom? _____	Desired Starting Rate:

JOB DUTIES: _____

_____

_____

_____

EXPERIENCE REQUIREMENTS: _____

_____

SIGNED _____ DATE _____ APPROVED _____ DATE _____

FOR EMPLOYMENT OFFICE USE ONLY

DATE RECEIVED _____

DATE	SPECIAL INSTRUCTIONS	DATE	SPECIAL INSTRUCTIONS

Position filled by	Starting Date	Starting Rate	Remarks

Job Code _____ Rate Range _____

Signed _____ Date _____

EMPLOYMENT APPLICATION

PERSONAL INFORMATION:

Date _____   Social Security Number _____

Name _____
Last   First   Middle

Present Address _____
Street   City   State   Zip

Permanent Address _____
Street   City   State   Zip

Phone No. _____   Height _____   Weight _____

State Name and Department of Any Relatives, Other Than Spouse, Already Employed By This Company _____

Referred by _____

EMPLOYMENT DESIRED:

Position _____   Date You Can Start _____   Salary Desired _____

Are You Employed Now? _____   If So—May We Inquire of Your Present Employer? _____

Ever Applied to this Company Before? _____   Where _____   When _____

Last

First

Middle

EDUCATION:

	Name and Location of School	Circle Last Year Completed	Did You Graduate?	Subjects Studied and Degree(s) Received
Grammar School		1 2 3 4	☐ Yes ☐ No	
High School		1 2 3 4	☐ Yes ☐ No	
College		1 2 3 4	☐ Yes ☐ No	
Trade, Business or Correspondence School		1 2 3 4	☐ Yes ☐ No	

Subjects of Special Study or Research Work: _____

What Foreign Languages Do You Speak Fluently? _____

Read? _____   Write? _____

List Activities Other Than Religious (Civic, Athletic, etc.) _____

EXCLUDE ORGANIZATIONS—THE NAME OR CHARACTER OF WHICH INDICATES THE RACE, CREED, COLOR OR NATIONAL ORIGIN OF ITS MEMBERS.

(Continued on Reverse Side)

FORMER EMPLOYERS: *List Below the Last Four Employers—Starting with Last One First*

Date Month and Year	Name and Address of Employer	Salary	Position	Reason for Leaving
From				
To				
From				
To				
From				
To				
From				
To				

REFERENCES: *List Below the Names of Three Persons, Not Related To You, Whom You Have Known At Least One Year.*

	Name	Address	Business	Years Acquainted
1				
2				
3				

PHYSICAL RECORD: *Do you have any physical condition which may limit your ability to perform the job applied for?*

In Case of Emergency Notify

Name   Address   Phone No.

I authorize investigation of all statements contained in this application. I understand that misrepresentation or omission of facts called for is cause for dismissal. Further, I understand and agree that my employment is for no definite period and may, regardless of the date of payment of my wages and salary, be terminated at any time without any previous notice.

Date   Signature

DO NOT WRITE BELOW THIS LINE

Interviewed By   Date

REMARKS:

Neatness		Character	
Personality		Ability	

Hired   For Dept.   Position   Will Report   Salary Wages

Approved: 1.   2.   3.

Employment Manager   Department Head   General Manager

EMPLOYMENT ELIGIBILITY VERIFICATION

1 **EMPLOYEE INFORMATION AND VERIFICATION:** (To be completed and signed by employee.)

Name: (Print or Type) Last	First	Middle	Maiden
Address: Street Name and Number	City	State	ZIP Code
Date of Birth (Month/Day/Year)		Social Security Number	

I attest, under penalty of perjury, that I am (check a box):

- ☐ A citizen or national of the United States.
- ☐ An alien lawfully admitted for permanent residence (Alien Number A_____).
- ☐ An alien authorized by the Immigration and Naturalization Service to work in the United States (Alien Number A_____, or Admission Number _____, expiration of employment authorization, if any _____).

I attest, under penalty of perjury, the documents that I have presented as evidence of identity and employment eligibility are genuine and relate to me. I am aware that federal law provides for imprisonment and/or fine for any false statements or use of false documents in connection with this certificate.

Signature	Date (Month/Day/Year)

PREPARER TRANSLATOR CERTIFICATION (If prepared by other than the individual). I attest, under penalty of perjury, that the above was prepared by me at the request of the named individual and is based on all information of which I have any knowledge.

Signature	Name (Print or Type)		
Address (Street Name and Number)	City	State	Zip Code

2 **EMPLOYER REVIEW AND VERIFICATION:** (To be completed and signed by employer.)

Examine one document from those in List A and check the correct box, _or_ examine one document from List B _and_ one from List C and check the correct boxes. Provide the *Document Identification Number* and *Expiration Date*, for the document checked in that column.

List A Identity and Employment Eligibility	List B Identity	and	List C Employment Eligibility
☐ United States Passport ☐ Certificate of United States Citizenship ☐ Certificate of Naturalization ☐ Unexpired foreign passport with attached Employment Authorization ☐ Alien Registration Card with photograph	☐ A State issued driver's license or I.D. card with a photograph, or information, including name, sex, date of birth, height, weight, and color of eyes. (Specify State_____) ☐ U.S. Military Card ☐ Other (Specify document and issuing authority) _____		☐ Original Social Security Number Card (other than a card stating it is not valid for employment) ☐ A birth certificate issued by State, county, or municipal authority bearing a seal or other certification. ☐ Unexpired INS Employment Authorization Specify form #_____
Document Identification #_____	*Document Identification* #_____		*Document Identification* #_____
Expiration Date (if any) _____	*Expiration Date (if any)* _____		*Expiration Date (if any)* _____

CERTIFICATION: I attest, under penalty of perjury, that I have examined the documents presented by the above individual, that they appear to be genuine, relate to the individual named, and that the individual, to the best of my knowledge, is authorized to work in the United States.

Signature	Name (Print or Type)	Title
Employer Name	Address	Date

Form 1-9 (03/20/87)
OMB No. 1115-0136

U.S. Department of Justice
Immigration and Naturalization Service

B 337

Employment Eligibility Verification

Section 1.   Employee's/Preparer's instructions for completing this form.

Instructions for the employee.

All employees, upon being hired, must complete Section 1 of this form. Any person hired after November 6, 1986 must complete this form. (For the purpose of completion of this form the term "hired" applies to those employed, recruited or referred for a fee.)

All employees must print or type their complete name, address, date of birth, and Social Security Number. The block which correctly indicates the employee's immigration status must be checked. If the second block is checked, the employee's Alien Registration Number must be provided. If the third block is checked, the employee's Alien Registration Number *or* Admission Number must be provided, as well as the date of expiration of that status, if it expires.

All employees must sign and date the form.

Instructions for the preparer of the form, if not the employee.

If the employee is assisted with completing this form, the person assisting must certify the form by signing it, and printing or typing his or her complete name and address.

Section 2.   Employer's instructions for completing this form.

(For the purpose of completion of this form, the term "employer" applies to employers and those who recruit or refer for a fee.)

Employers must complete this section by examining evidence of identity and employment authorization, and:
- checking the appropriate box in List A *or* boxes in both Lists B and C;
- recording the document identification number and expiration date (if any);
- recording the type of form if not specifically identified in the list;
- signing the certification section.

NOTE: Employers are responsible for reverifying employment eligibility of aliens upon expiration of any employment authorization documents, should they desire to continue the alien's employment.

Copies of documentation presented by an individual for the purpose of establishing identity and employment eligibility may be copied and retained for the purpose of complying with the requirements of this form and no other purpose. Any copies of documentation made for this purpose should be maintained with this form.

Employers may photocopy or reprint this form, as necessary, for their use.

RETENTION OF RECORDS.

After completion of this form, it must be retained by the employer during the period beginning on the date of hiring and ending:
- three years after the date of such hiring, or;
- one year after the date the individual's employment is terminated, whichever is later.

U.S. Department of Justice
Immigration and Naturalization Service

OMB #1115-0136
Form 1-9 (03 20 87)

TEMPORARY
EMPLOYMENT REQUISITION

Date:_____

Position/Duties_____

Department_____

Supervisor_____

Dates Required:_____ To_____

Shift Required:_____ To_____

Reasons for Requisition_____

_____

_____

_____

_____

Estimated Expense:_____

Budget No:_____

Funds Budgeted:_____yes _____no

_____

Signed By

Date:_____   _____

Approved By

TEMPORARY PERSONNEL ARE NOT ALLOWED
EMPLOYMENT BEYOND APPROVED PERIOD OR
FOR AN AMOUNT IN EXCESS OF ESTIMATED
EXPENSE UNLESS APPROVED IN ADVANCE

INTERVIEW SCHEDULE

Time	Applicant	Position	Tests	Comments	Date

INTERVIEW SUMMARY

Date:

Applicant_____

Position_____

Date Interviewed_____

Date Available to Start Employment_____

Salary Requested_____

EVALUATION

	Good	Fair	Poor
Appearance	____	____	____
Experience	____	____	____
Education	____	____	____
Skills Required	____	____	____
Enthusiasm	____	____	____
Attitude	____	____	____
Other:	____	____	____
	____	____	____
	____	____	____

Comments:

_____

_____

Recommendations:

_____

_____

_____
Interviewers Signature

B 341

TELEPHONE REFERENCE REPORT

Applicant's Name	Position

Name of Company	Telephone No.

Reference	Title

Relationship to Applicant	Years Known

Employment Dates From To	Starting Salary	Leaving Salary

Position	Reason for Leaving	

Duties

	Good	Fair	Poor	Comments
Overall Performance				
Productivity				
Work Quality				
Attitude				
Ability to work with others				
Ability to work with little supervision				

Strong Points

Weak Points

Supervisory Experience	How many People	How Long

Overall Evaluation

Comments

Signature	Date

NEW EMPLOYEE RECORD CHART

Employee_____Date_____

Department_____Date Employed_____

The above new employee must have
checked item(s) in file.

Document	Required	Completed
Employment Application	_____	_____
Personal Data Sheet	_____	_____
Employee Verification Checklist	_____	_____
W-4 Document	_____	_____
Fidelity Bond	_____	_____
Physical/Medical Report	_____	_____
Employment Contract	_____	_____
Non-Compete Agreement	_____	_____
Trade Secret Agreement	_____	_____
Conflict of Interest Declaration	_____	_____
Indemnity Agreement	_____	_____
Security Clearance	_____	_____
Other:		
_____	_____	_____
_____	_____	_____
_____	_____	_____
_____	_____	_____

_____
Supervisor

EMPLOYEE PERSONNEL FILE

EMPLOYEE NAME: _____

POSITION HISTORY

| DATE | | POSITION AND DEPARTMENT | PAY RATE | |
FROM	TO		AMOUNT	PER

ADDRESS _____

	City	State	Zip	Telephone
	City	State	Zip	Telephone
	City	State	Zip	Telephone

SOCIAL SECURITY NO. _____ DATE OF BIRTH _____ SEX: ☐ M ☐ F

CITIZEN OF: _____

MARITAL STATUS: ☐ SINGLE ☐ MARRIED ☐ SEPARATED ☐ WIDOWED ☐ DIVORCED

NAME OF SPOUSE _____ NO. OF DEPENDENTS _____

IN EMERGENCY NOTIFY _____ RELATIONSHIP _____

ADDRESS _____ TELEPHONE _____

RELATIVES WORKING FOR US: NAME _____ RELATIONSHIP _____

EDUCATION: ELEMENTARY _____ HIGH _____ COLLEGE _____ GRADUATE _____

OTHER _____

UNION MEMBER: ☐ YES ☐ NO   UNION (Local) NAME _____

| NAME | DATES | |
	Eligible	Enrolled
PENSION PLAN		
PROFIT SHARING		
CREDIT UNION		

| NAME | DATES | |
	Eligible	Enrolled
GROUP INSURANCE		

COMPANY TRAINING AND SPECIAL SKILLS _____

SECURITY CLEARANCE _____

TERMINATION INFORMATION

DATE TERMINATED _____ WOULD WE REHIRE? YES ☐ NO ☐

REASON FOR TERMINATION: _____

CONFIDENTIAL EMPLOYEE
HISTORY

EMPLOYEE NAME		EMPLOYMENT DATE	STATUS ☐ REGULAR ☐ PART TIME ☐ TEMPORARY

YEARS OF SERVICE	1	2	3	4	5	6	7	8	9	10	11	12	13	14	15	16	17	18	19	20	21	22	23	24	25	26		SECURITY CLEARANCE	LEVEL	DATE GRANTED

PAYROLL DATA

BIRTHDATE	SEX	SOCIAL SECURITY NO.	MARITAL STATUS	NAME OF SPOUSE	NO. OF CHILDREN

FEDERAL WITHHOLDING:	EXEMPTIONS CLAIMED										
	ADDITIONAL AMOUNT WITHHELD										

	DATE ELIGIBLE	DATE JOINED	DATE WITHDRAWN	INSURANCE	DATE ELIGIBLE	DATE JOINED	DATE WITHDRAWN
UNION STATUS				LIFE			
PENSION PLAN				MEDICAL - SELF			
CREDIT UNION				DEP.			
				MAJ. MED. - SELF			
				DEP.			

GENERAL INFORMATION

ADDRESS	CITY	STATE	ZIP	PHONE
ADDRESS	CITY	STATE	ZIP	PHONE
ADDRESS	CITY	STATE	ZIP	PHONE
ADDRESS	CITY	STATE	ZIP	PHONE

IN EMERGENCY NOTIFY	RELATIONSHIP	CITY	STATE	ZIP	PHONE
	RELATIONSHIP	CITY	STATE	ZIP	PHONE

RELATIVES OR FRIENDS EMPLOYED BY THIS CO.	NAMES	RELATIONSHIP	NAMES	RELATIONSHIP

EDUCATION	ELEM. _____ J H S _____ S H S _____	SPECIAL SKILLS OR TRAINING	
	COLLEGE 1 2 3 4 MAJOR _____		
	OTHER _____		

TERMINATION RECORD

☐ RESIGNATION DATE_____	REASON
☐ DISMISSAL DATE_____	REASON
RECOMMENDED FOR RE-EMPLOYMENT ☐ YES ☐ NO	REASON

EMPLOYEE HEALTH RECORD

NAME		ADDRESS		PHONE

SEX	AGE	DATE OF PRE-EMPLOYMENT EXAM	PERSONAL PHYSICIAN	PHONE

DATE EMPLOYED	JOB TITLE	DEPARTMENT	SUPERVISOR

IN CASE OF EMERGENCY, NOTIFY:		RELATIONSHIP	ADDRESS	PHONE

PERTINENT MEDICAL HISTORY (ALLERGIES, RESTRICTIONS, ETC.)

DATE	TIME	REASON FOR VISIT	TREATMENT	SIGNED BY (Med. Personnel)

SUPERVISORS ORIENTATION CHECKLIST

Employee_____ Department _____

Employment Date_____

Position_____

<u>Items Reviewed</u>

Department Function/Goals   _____

Schedule of Hours   _____

Co-Employee Introduction   _____

Locker/Desk/Office   _____

Supplies & Storage   _____

Department Safety Procedures   _____

Equipment & Tools   _____

Record Keeping Procedures   _____

Job Training   _____

Overtime Policy   _____

Other:

_____   _____

_____   _____

_____   _____

Date:

     I acknowledge the above checked information has been discussed to my satisfaction and understanding

_____   _____
           Employee   Supervisor

RECEIPT FOR COMPANY PROPERTY

Employee_____

ID No._____

Department/Section_____

    I acknowledge receipt of the company-owned equipment listed below. I agree to maintain the equipment in good condition and to return it when I cease working for the company, or earlier on request. I promise to report any loss or damage immediately. I further agree to use said property only for work-related purposes.

	Receipt			*Return*	
Item	*Quantity*	*Serial No.*	*Returned to*	*Date*
_____	____	_____	_____	_____
_____	____	_____	_____	_____
_____	____	_____	_____	_____
_____	____	_____	_____	_____
_____	____	_____	_____	_____
_____	____	_____	_____	_____
_____	____	_____	_____	_____
_____	____	_____	_____	_____

_____
Signature

_____
Date

Issued By:_____

PAYROLL SUMMARY

For week/month ending _____

Employee	Salary Rate	Total Hours	Regular Hours	Straight Overtime	Premium Overtime	Sick Leave	Vacation	Comp. Time	Holiday	Excused Absence	Earnings
Total Hours.............										
Total Dollars............										
Total Adjustments........										
Grand Totals.............										

DEPARTMENT OVERTIME LIST

Department			Time period	
Employee	Date	Overtime hrs.	Overtime $ paid	% of payroll

Prepared by: Approved by:

OVERTIME PERMIT

Name_____Date_____

Department_____Clock No._____

    Is approved and authorized to work overtime for a maximum of   hours

between the dates of   to   , for the purpose of:

    The overtime rate shall be paid in accordance with company policy.

Comments/Conditions For Approval

_____

_____

_____

_____

_____

Requested By_____

Approved By_____

USE REVERSE SIDE FOR OVERTIME APPROVAL
BEYOND MAXIMUM HOURS, ALLOWED DATES
OR PERMITTED OVERTIME WAGES

B 351

OVERTIME SUMMARY

Department		Date

Pay Period	Total O.T. hours	Total O.T. $. paid	% of payroll

Prepared by: Approved by:

EMPLOYEE STATUS CHANGE

Employee_____Date_____

Department_____I.D. No._____

Effective Date_____

1. Pay Rate Change:

    From_____ To_____

2. Job Title Change:

    From_____ To_____

3. Job Classification Change:

    From_____ To_____

4. Shift Change:

    From_____ To_____

5. Full-Time/Part-Time Change:

    From_____ To_____

6. Temporary/Permanent Change:

    From_____ To_____

7. Other: (Describe)

    _____

    _____

_____   _____
        Prepared By   Approved By

B 353

CONSENT TO RELEASE OF INFORMATION

Date:_____

To:_____(Employee)

From: Office of Personnel

A request for verification of employment information has been received from:_____
_____

Please check below those items for which information may be released.

_____ Salary

_____ Position

_____ Department.

_____ Supervisor.

_____ Dates of employment.

_____ Part-time/Full-time.

_____ Whether you worked under a maiden name.

_____ Garnishes, if any.

_____ Reason for separation.

_____ Other.

_____   _____

Employee Signature   Date

PLEASE RETURN THIS FORM TO THE OFFICE OF PERSONNEL AS
SOON AS POSSIBLE IN ORDER THAT WE MAY RESPOND TO THE
REQUEST FOR INFORMATION.
YOUR CONSENT ON THIS OCCASION WILL NOT CONSTITUTE A
CONSENT TO RELEASE ON FUTURE OCCASIONS.

DAILY ATTENDANCE REPORT

NUMBER	NAME	1	2	3	4	5	6	7	8	9	10	11	12	13	14	15	16	17	18	19	20	21	22	23	24	25	26	27	28	29	30	31	TOTAL	LATE HRS	LATE MIN	DAYS ABSENT SICK	DAYS ABSENT EXC	DAYS ABSENT INEXC

19___

JAN. · FEB. · MARCH · APRIL · MAY · JUNE · JULY · AUG. · SEPT. · OCT. · NOV. · DEC.

19___

JAN. · FEB. · MARCH · APRIL · MAY · JUNE · JULY · AUG. · SEPT. · OCT. · NOV. · DEC.

TOTAL

CODE:

I – INEXCUSED ABSENCE	V – VACATION	L – LATE (SHOW NO. OF MINUTES LATE)
E – EXCUSED ABSENCE	S – SICK	J – JURY DUTY

NOTES:

B 355

JOB TIME RECORD

Employee				Employee Number	

Date	Department	Job Title	Rate	Per	Comments

EMPLOYEE TIME SHEET

Employee_____ Period ending_____

Department_____

Date	Time started a.m.	Time finished p.m.	Overtime	Total

Authorized Signature	Title	Date

B 357

DAILY TIME SHEET

Date _____

Day					
Employee	Began Work	End Work	Over Time	Comments	

Supervisor _____

WEEKLY SCHEDULE

WEEK OF_____

EMPLOYEE	HOURS						
	SUN	MON	TUE	WED	THU	FRI	SAT

WEEKLY TIME SHEETS

For week ending _____

Employee	Mon	Tues	Wed	Thurs	Fri	Sat	Sun	Total	Gross Pay	Ded	Net Pay
Totals											

PAYROLL REGISTER

DATE: _____

YEAR-TO-DATE EARNINGS	WITH TAX	EMPLOYEE DEPT	NUMBER	NAME OF EMPLOYEE	HOURS WORKED	BASE RATE	EARNINGS REGULAR	OT PREM	OTHER	TOTAL	DEDUCTIONS FICA	WITH TAX	MISC.	NET PAY

WEEKLY PAYROLL SUMMARY

DEPARTMENT

WEEK ENDING

EMPLOYEE NAME	HOURS WORK'D	RATE	TOTALS			DEDUCTIONS						NET PAY	CHECK NO.
			REG. WAGES	O.T. WAGES	GROSS WAGES	FED. TAXES	STATE TAXES	FICA	INS.	DUES			

EMPLOYEE EARNINGS RECORD

EMPLOYEE		EMP. No.		SOCIAL SECURITY No.	DEPENDENTS	SALARY/WAGES

FIRST QUARTER

WEEK ENDING	HOURS		DEDUCTIONS				NET PAY
	Reg.	O.T.	Fed. W.H.	St. W.H.	FICA		
TOTAL 1st QUARTER							
TOTAL 3 MONTHS							

THIRD QUARTER

WEEK ENDING	HOURS		DEDUCTIONS				NET PAY
	Reg.	O.T.	Fed. W.H.	St. W.H.	FICA		
TOTAL 3rd QUARTER							
TOTAL 9 MONTHS							

SECOND QUARTER

WEEK ENDING	HOURS		DEDUCTIONS				NET PAY
	Reg.	O.T.	Fed. W.H.	St. W.H.	FICA		
TOTAL 2nd QUARTER							
TOTAL 6 MONTHS							

FOURTH QUARTER

WEEK ENDING	HOURS		DEDUCTIONS				NET PAY
	Reg.	O.T.	Fed. W.H.	St. W.H.	FICA		
TOTAL 4th QUARTER							
TOTAL 12 MONTHS							

EMPLOYEE FLEXTIME SCHEDULE

Employee

Week of:

Day	A.M. Time In	Lunch Out	Lunch In	P.M. Time Out	Evening In	Evening Out	Hours for Day	Cumulative Total
Monday								
Tuesday								
Wednesday								
Thursday								
Friday								
Saturday								
Sunday								

VACATION SCHEDULE

Department _____

EMPLOYEE ON VACATION	ALTERNATE TO COVER JOB	WEEK BEGINNING:					OTHER WEEKS
		APRIL	MAY	JUNE	JULY	AUGUST	

INJURY REPORT

Name: _____   Social Security No.: _____

Home address: _____

_____

Age: _____   Sex: Male ☐   Female ☐

Shift _____   Clock/Emp. No.: _____

Dept.: _____   Foreman: _____

Is injury or illness related to employment?   Yes ☐   No ☐

Date of injury or initial diagnosis: _____   Time of injury: _____

Describe the illness or injury in detail and indicate the part of body affected, e.g., amputation of right index finger at second joint; fracture of ribs; lead poisoning; dermatitis of left hand; etc.

_____

_____

_____

Did employee return to work?   Yes ☐   No ☐

If employee did not return to work, indicate last day worked: _____

Name and address of physician: _____

_____

If hospitalized, name and address of hospital: _____

_____

Names of witnesses: _____

_____

Comments: _____

_____

Signature of employee: _____

Signature of nurse or first aid person: _____

Date: _____

PHYSICIANS REPORT

Doctor_____ Date_____

Address_____

                                     Re:_____

Dear Doctor:

       The above employee has been absent from duty on the days noted on the reverse side of this letter and we have been advised that our employee has been under your care. As it is our policy to verify protracted medical absences, we would appreciate your completing the form below and returning it for our records.

       Sincerely,

_____

_____

Physicians Report

       I certify that   has been under my medical care and that the absences listed were medically necessary or reasonable based on the medical condition.

Dated:_____   _____
                                             Physicians Signature

VACATION/LEAVE
REQUEST

Employee_____ Employee No._____

Department_____Position_____

1. Date(s) Requested:

    From_____To_____

2. Alternate Dates Acceptable:

    From_____ To_____, or
    From_____ To_____

3. Reasons (For Leave of Absence):

    _____
    _____
    _____
    _____

4. Non-Vacation Leave Time To Be:

    ____With Pay ____Without Pay ____Make-Up ____Partial Pay

Date of Request:

                              _____
                              Employee

Approved By   Approval Date

_____   _____

B 368

ABSENCE REQUEST

EMPLOYEE	DATE	DEPARTMENT

DATE(S) REQUESTED	HOUR(S) REQUESTED
FROM TO	FROM TO

___WITH PAY   ___WITHOUT PAY   ___MAKEUP

REMARKS

EMPLOYEE SIGNATURE

APPROVED BY	DATE(S) APPROVED

ABSENCE REPORT

Employee	Date	Department

Date(s) absent	Date return	Day(s) missed

Did employee notify company

_____Yes   _____No

Notified_____

TITLE_____

Was absence approved ?

____yes   ____no

Reason for absence

Reason verified

ACTION TAKEN

____   NONE

____   DEDUCT PAY

____   MAKE-UP

____   OTHER _____

Comments

SIGNED	TITLE	DATE

LATE REPORT

EMPLOYEE	DATE	DEPARTMENT

TIME DUE AT WORK	ACTUAL ARRIVAL TIME	TIME MISSED

DID EMPLOYEE NOTIFY COMPANY

____YES   ____NO

NOTIFIED_____

TITLE_____

COMMENTS

ACTION TAKEN

____   NONE

____   DEDUCT PAY

____   MAKE-UP

____   OTHER _____

SIGNED	TITLE	DATE

MEDICAL SUMMARY

Date _____   Period ending _____   Completed by: _____

Employee Name	Attended by	Time	Injury/Illness	Treatment

Comments:

B 372

SALARY REVIEW FORM

PAYROLL NO.	NAME	EFFECTIVE DATE

JOB TITLE

DEPT.

USE FIGURES TO MATCH RANGE.

DIV. DEPT. CODE	EMPLOYMENT DATE

RANGE_____ TO_____

PRESENT
SALARY_____

TIME IN PRESENT JOB	AGE	☐ MALE ☐ FEMALE

RECOMMENDED
INCREASE_____

RECOMMENDED
NEW SALARY _____

ATTENDANCE PAST 12 MONTHS

PAID ABS.	NON-PAID ABS.	LATE

STATUS AFTER INCREASE

☐ EXEMPT   ☐ NON-EXEMPT

EXPLAIN ANY PERIOD OF ABSENCE BELOW.

☐ PROMOTION – SHOW QUALIFICATIONS UNDER REASON

DATE PROMOTED	FORMER JOB TITLE AND DEPT.
FORMER SALARY RANGE	

☐ MERIT –

REASON

FOR INCENTIVE JOBS: RECOMMENDING DEPARTMENT HEAD MUST NOTIFY THE INCENTIVE OFFICE THAT THERE HAS BEEN A CHANGE IN RATE FOR THE EMPLOYEE.

SALARY COMMITTEE ACTION

☐ S/M ☐ HRLY.	FOR SAL. ADMIN. AND PAYROLL USE			NON-EXEMPT
PRESENT RATE ANNUAL	NEW RATE ANNUAL	S/M INCREASE	ANNUAL INCREASE	HRLY. RATE

REQUEST FOR TRANSFER

NAME		EMPLOYEE NO.	SHIFT
DEPARTMENT			DEPT. NO.
PRESENT JOB			ANNIVERSARY DATE
JOB REQUESTED			

RELATED EXPERIENCE

REASON FOR TRANSFER REQUEST

EMPLOYEE'S SIGNATURE	DATE	EXTENSION

SUPERVISOR'S COMMENTS

EVALUATION IN PRESENT JOB

SUPERVISOR'S SIGNATURE	DATE	EXTENSION

PLEASE FORWARD TRANSFER REQUEST TO EMPLOYEE RELATIONS PROMPTLY

EMPLOYEE RELATIONS

DATE RECEIVED	DATE INTERVIEWED	TIME INTERVIEWED

COMMENTS

ACTION

DATE EMPLOYEE NOTIFIED	INTERVIEWER'S SIGNATURE	DATE

EMPLOYEE PERFORMANCE
CHECKFORM

Employee_____ Date_____

Department_____ Last Check Date_____

Reviewer_____

Checklist

	Excellent	Good	Fair	Poor
Honest y	____	____	____	____
Productivity	____	____	____	____
Work Quality	____	____	____	____
Technical Skills	____	____	____	____
Work Consistency	____	____	____	____
Enthusiasm	____	____	____	____
Cooperation	____	____	____	____
Attitude	____	____	____	____
Initiative	____	____	____	____
Working Relations	____	____	____	____
Originality	____	____	____	____
Punctuality	____	____	____	____
Attendance	____	____	____	____
Dependability	____	____	____	____
Appearance	____	____	____	____
Other:				
_____	____	____	____	____
_____	____	____	____	____

_____

Reviewer

EMPLOYEE SELF-EVALUATION

CONFIDENTIAL	Name of employee	Completed by:	Date

List most successful job accomplishments since last performance period:

A._____

B._____

C._____

D._____

List least successful job accomplishments since last performance period:

A._____

B._____

C._____

List key strengths:

A._____

B._____

C._____

List what performance areas need improvement:

A._____

B._____

What action we will take where improvement is desired:

_____

_____

_____

_____

INCIDENT/GRIEVANCE
REPORT

Date:_____

Employee_____

Department_____

Date of Incident_____

1.   Nature of Incident/Grievance_____

      _____

      _____

      _____

2.   Action Taken_____

      _____

      _____

      _____

3.   Witnesses:

          Name   Address

      _____   _____

      _____   _____

      _____   _____

      _____   _____

4.   Reported To:

          Person   Date

      _____   _____

      _____   _____

      _____   _____

      _____   _____

                         _____

                               Completed By

USE REVERSE SIDE FOR
ADDITIONAL REMARKS

B 377

FIRST WARNING NOTICE

Employee _____   Clock # _____

Shift _____   Time _____ a.m. / p.m.   Date of Warning _____

Date of violation _____

Time of violation _____

Location violation occurred _____

Nature of Violation

___ Substandard work   ___ Conduct   ___ Tardiness

___ Carelessness   ___ Disobedient   ___ Absenteeism

___ Ringing out ahead of time   ___ Ringing out wrong time card ___ Intoxication or drinking

___ Other _____

Additional Remarks

_____
_____
_____
_____
_____

Employee Comments

_____
_____
_____
_____

Signatures

_____   _____   _____
Employee   Supervisor   Personnel Manager

DISCIPLINARY REPORT

Employee		Date	Department

Nature of offense

Date of offense	Location		Time

Reported by		Title	Department

Witnesses

Comments

Supervisor's Signature	Employee's Signature

Offense Number	Date of last Offense

Action Taken

Recommendations

The above offense(s) have been noted and have been recorded as part of the above employee's personnel file.

Personnel Dept. Sign. _____ Date_____

NOTICE OF DISMISSAL

Date:

To:

We regret to inform you that your employment with the firm shall be terminated on

_____, 19___, for the following reasons:

_____

_____

_____

_____

_____

_____

Severance pay shall be in accordance with company policy. Within 30 days of termination we shall issue to you a statement of accrued benefits. Any insurance benefits shall continue in accordance with applicable law and/or the provisions of our personnel policy. Please contact _____, at your earliest convenience, who will explain each of these items and arrange with you for the return of any company property.

We sincerely regret this action is necessary.

Very truly,

Copies to:

B 380

SEPARATION REPORT

Employee_____Date_____

Department_____Classification_____

Supervisor_____

1.   Termination Date:_____Pay Thru:_____

2.   Reason for Termination:_____

_____

_____

3.   Unemployment Compensation Eligibility:_____

_____

_____

4.   Continued Benefits Eligibility:_____

_____

_____

5.   Overall Assessment of Employee:_____

_____

_____

6.   Would Company Rehire?_____

_____

_____

7.   Comments:_____

_____

_____

_____

Supervisor

USE REVERSE SIDE IF NECESSARY

B 381

CHECKOUT RECORD

Employee_____ Department_____

Termination Date_____

Each of the below items (as applicable)
must be returned or completed upon
termination and before issuance of
final pay check.

<u>Return</u>		<u>Complete</u>	
Company Tools	_____	Exit Interview	_____
ID Badge	_____	Expense Reports	_____
Security Statement	_____	Terminations Form	_____
Air Travel Cards	_____	Confidentiality Report	_____
Credit Cards	_____	Other:	
Petty Cash Advances	_____	_____	_____
Expense Accounts	_____	_____	_____
Desk/File Keys	_____	_____	_____
Keys to Premises	_____		
Catalog & Sales Items	_____		
Sample Products	_____		
Automobile	_____		
Company Documents	_____		
Customer Lists	_____		
Other:			
_____	_____		
_____	_____		
_____	_____		

_____
Supervisor

TELEPHONE LOG

DATE	CALLER		COMPANY/PERSON CALLED			AREA CODE	TELEPHONE NUMBER	COL- LECT ✓	PER. TO PER. ✓	CALLING TIME	CHARGED TO	CHARGES
	NAME	DEPT.	NAME	CITY	STATE							

EMPLOYEE PROFIT-SHARING RECORD

NAME_____   ☐ MALE   ☐ SINGLE

ADDRESS_____   ☐ FEMALE   ☐ MARRIED

_____

DATE OF BIRTH_____

DATE ENTERED PLAN_____

AGE AT ENTRY_____

DATE EMPLOYED_____

NORMAL RETIREMENT DATE_____

PARTICIPATION TERMINATION: DATE_____

☐ RETIREMENT   ☐ DEATH   ☐ DISABILITY   ☐ SEVERANCE   ☐ OTHER _____

CHANGE OF ADDRESS:

DATE	NEW ADDRESS	DATE	NEW ADDRESS

BENEFICIARIES:

NAME	ADDRESS	RELATIONSHIP	DATE DESIGNATED

SPECIAL NOTES:

Date: _____

PROFIT-SHARING PLAN RECORD

EMPLOYEE'S NAME	ANNIVERSARY DATE	SHARE OF INCREASE (OR DECREASE) IN VALUE OF FUND	SHARE OF FORFEITURES	SHARE OF CONTRIBUTIONS	WITHDRAWALS	BALANCE	PERCENT VESTING	VESTED INTEREST

STATEMENT OF
ACCRUED BENEFITS

Date of Issue:_____

Employee_____ Department_____

Benefits Accrued As Of:_____

Accrued Vacation Days   _____

Accrued Vacation Pay $_____

Accrued Sick Days   _____

Accrued Sick Pay $_____

Profit-Sharing - Non-Vested $_____

Profit-Sharing Vested $_____

Stock Dividend Value $_____

Company Shares Held   _____

Vested Pension $_____

Non-Vested Pension $_____

Cash Value Life Insurance $_____

Credit Union Balance $_____

Severance Pay $_____

Accrued Expenses $_____

Other:

_____   _____

_____   _____

_____   _____

This is an interim _____ final _____ statement.

SUBJECT TO CORRECTION

_____
Signed

EXIT INTERVIEW REPORT

Employee's Name_____I.D. No._____

Department_____Position_____

Dates of Employment: From_____ To_____

Supervisor_____

Reason For Leaving Company_____

Return of:

      _____ keys   _____ company documents   _____ uniform

      _____ ID card   _____ safety equipment   _____ tools

      _____credit card   _____ other company property   _____ company auto

Employee informed of restrictions on:

      _____ trade secrets   _____ employment with competitor (if applicable)

      _____ patents   _____ removing company documents

      _____ other data   _____ other_____

Employee exit questions:

1.   Did management adequately recognize employee contributions?_____

_____

2.   Do you feel that you have had the support of management on the job?_____

_____

3.   Were you adequately trained for your job?_____

_____

4.   Did you find your work rewarding?_____

_____

5.   Do you feel you were fairly treated by the company?_____

_____

6. Were you paid an adequate salary for the work you did?_____

_____

7. Were you content with your working condition?_____

_____

8. Do you feel your supervision was adequate?_____

_____

9. Did you understand company policies and the reasons for them?_____

_____

10. Have you observed incidences of theft of company property?_____

_____

11. How can the company improve security?_____

_____

12. How can the company improve working conditions?_____

_____

13. What are the company's strengths?_____

_____

14. What are the company's weaknesses?_____

_____

15. Other comments:_____

_____

_____

_____

USE ADDITIONAL SHEETS FOR FURTHER COMMENTS.

ALL ANSWERS ARE HELD STRICTLY CONFIDENTIAL.

TELEPHONE REFERENCE LOG

Date:_____ Time:_____

Reference on employee:_____

Person inquiring:_____

Company:_____

Address:_____

Reason for inquiry:_____

_____

Reference Summary:

_____

_____

_____

_____

_____

_____

_____

_____

Specific Questions/Replies:

_____

Issued By

Graphs and Charts

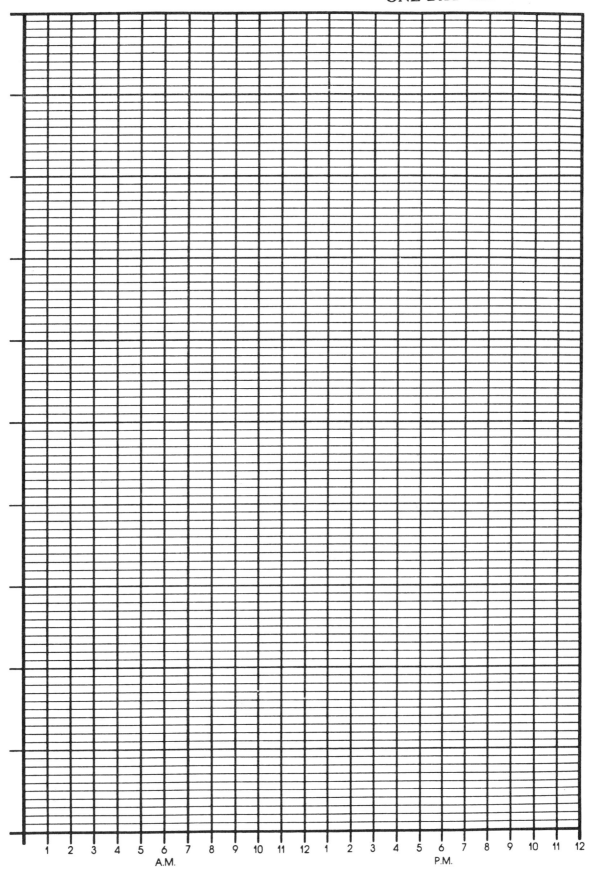

1 2 3 4 5 6 7 8 9 10 11 12 1 2 3 4 5 6 7 8 9 10 11 12

A.M.   P.M.

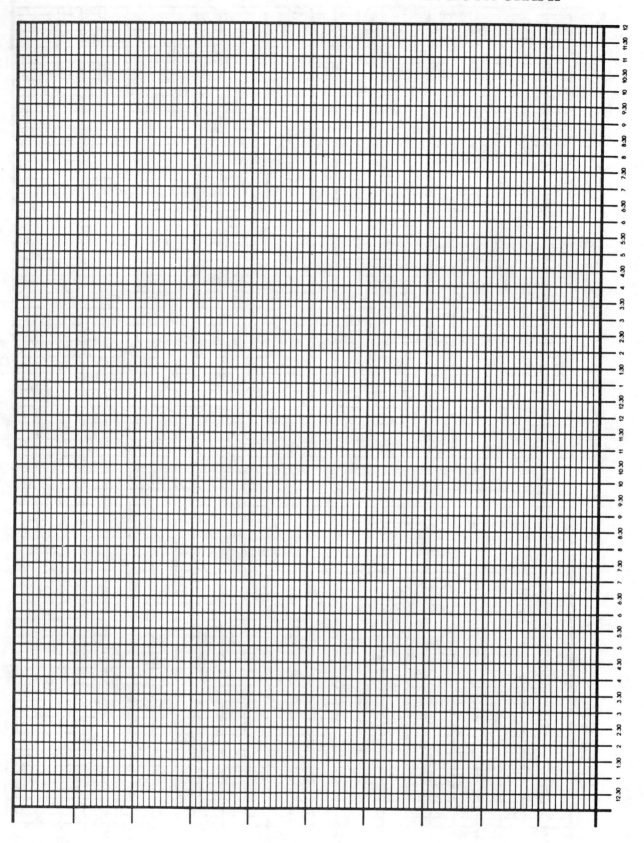

SEVEN DAY GRAPH

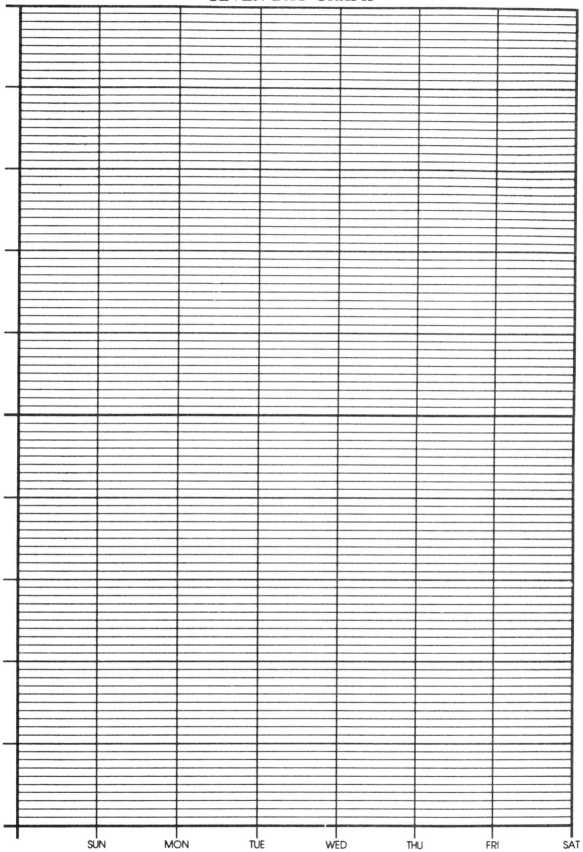

SUN   MON   TUE   WED   THU   FRI   SAT

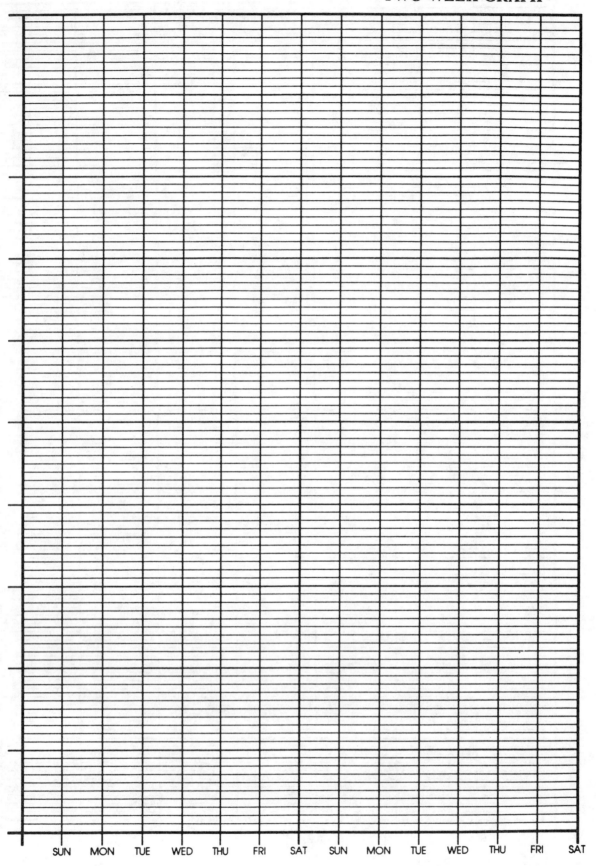

SUN MON TUE WED THU FRI SAT SUN MON TUE WED THU FRI SAT

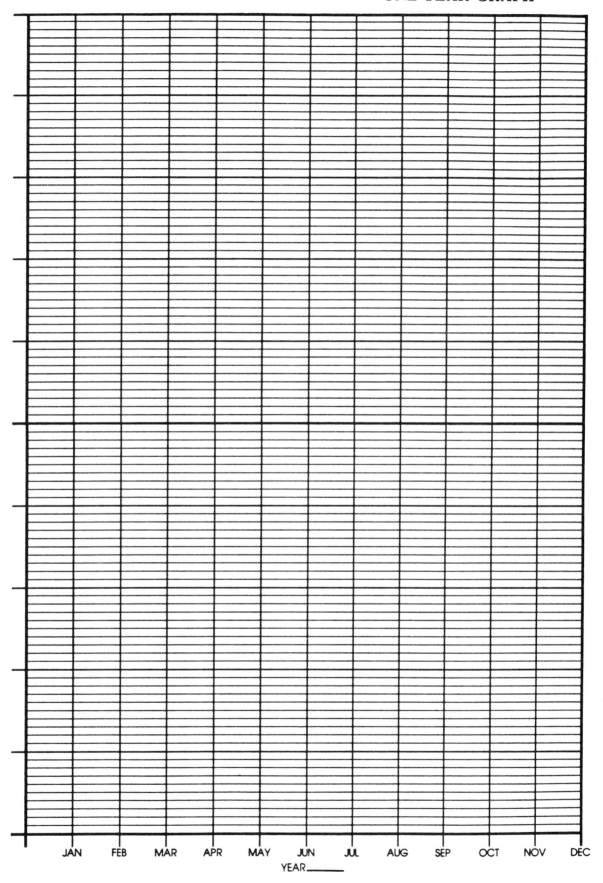

JAN   FEB   MAR   APR   MAY   JUN   JUL   AUG   SEP   OCT   NOV   DEC

YEAR_____

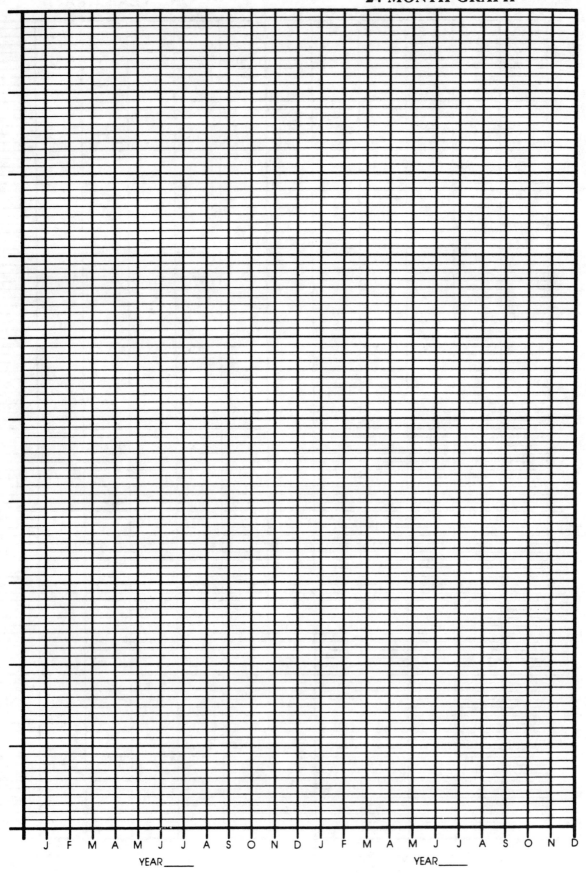

TWO YEAR GRAPH

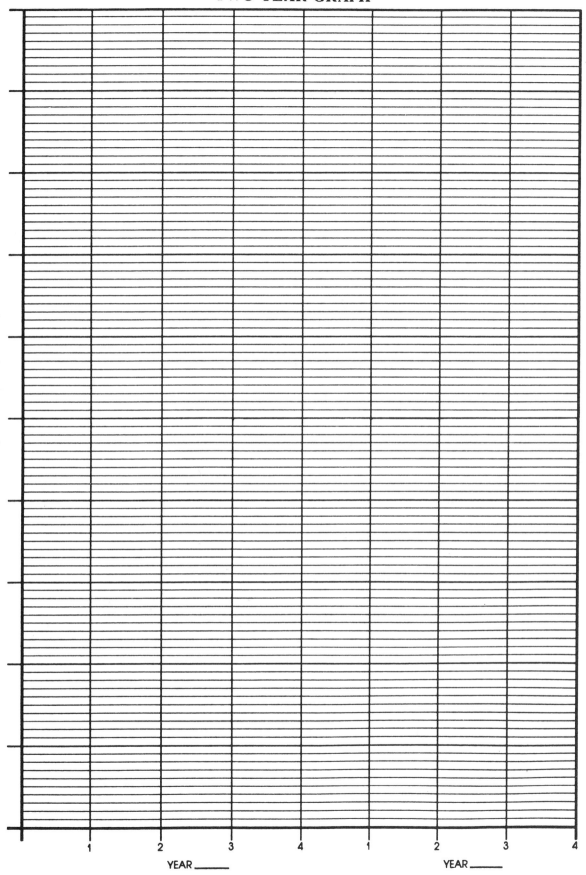

THREE YEAR GRAPH

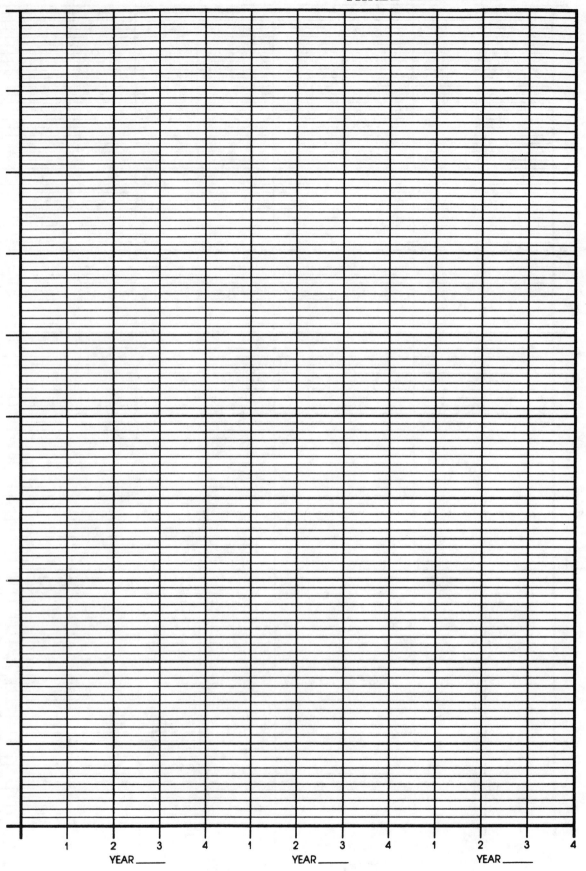

1 2 3 4 1 2 3 4 1 2 3 4

YEAR_____ YEAR_____ YEAR_____

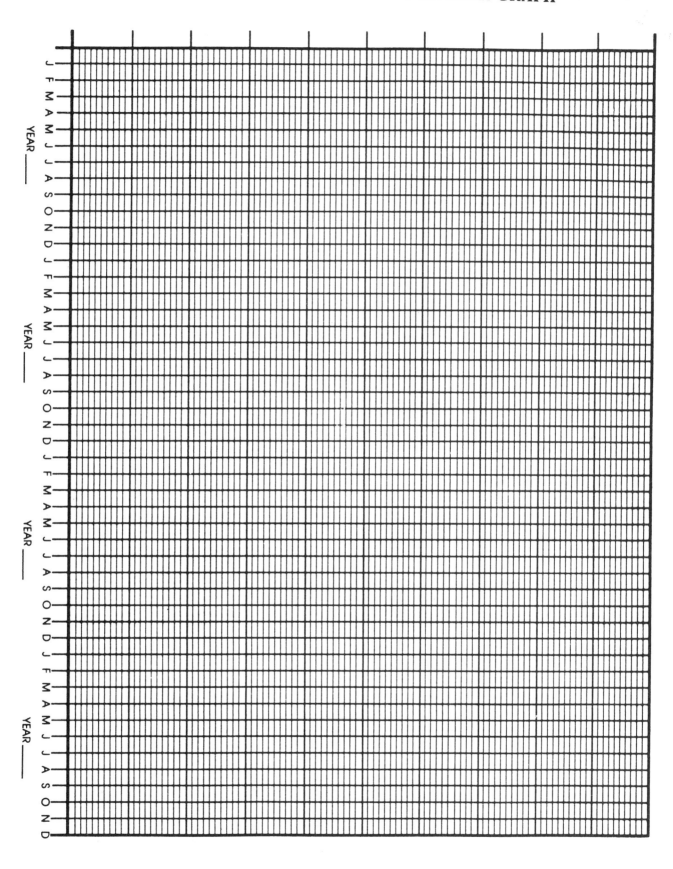

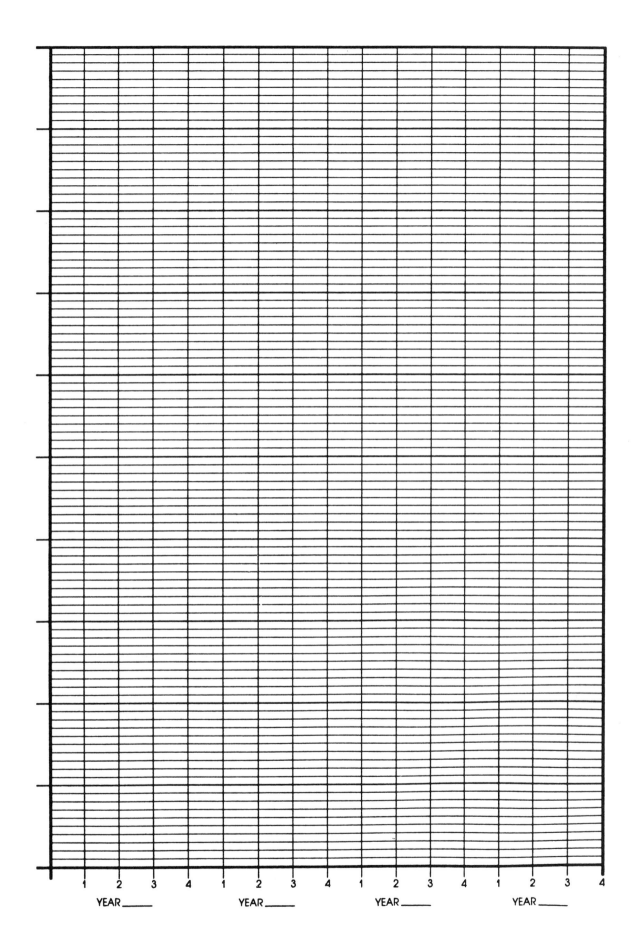

YEAR_____   YEAR_____   YEAR_____   YEAR_____

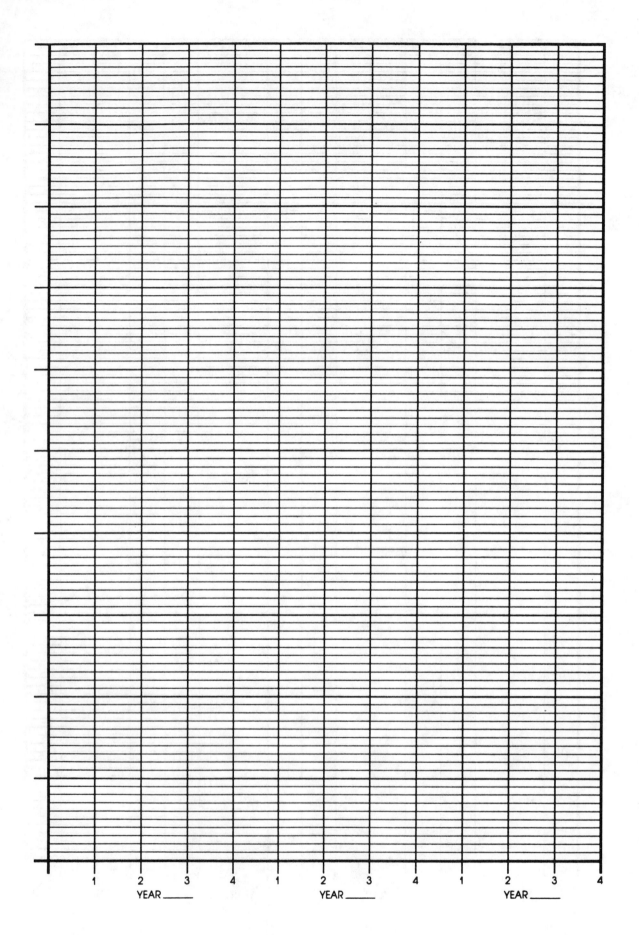

1   2   3   4   1   2   3   4   1   2   3   4

YEAR _____   YEAR _____   YEAR _____

B 404

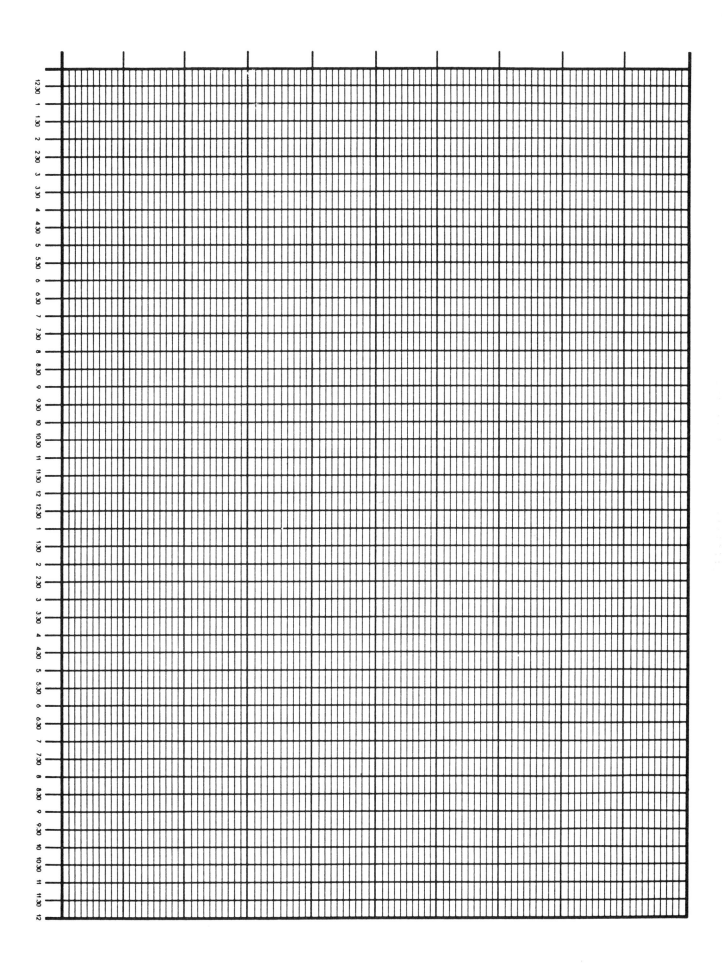

B 405

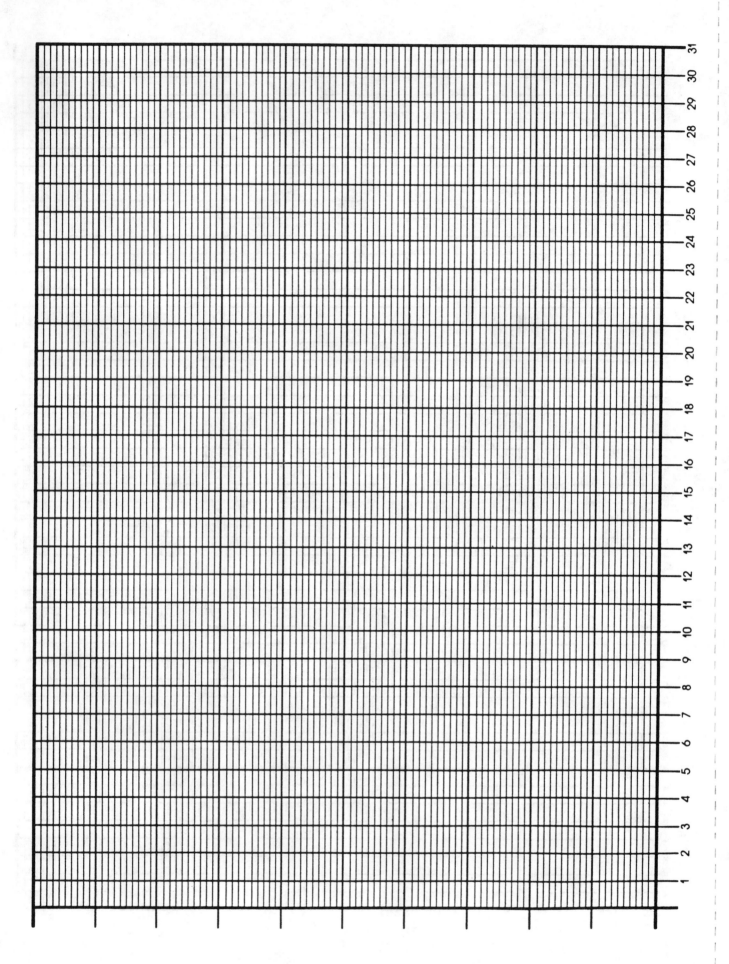

B 406

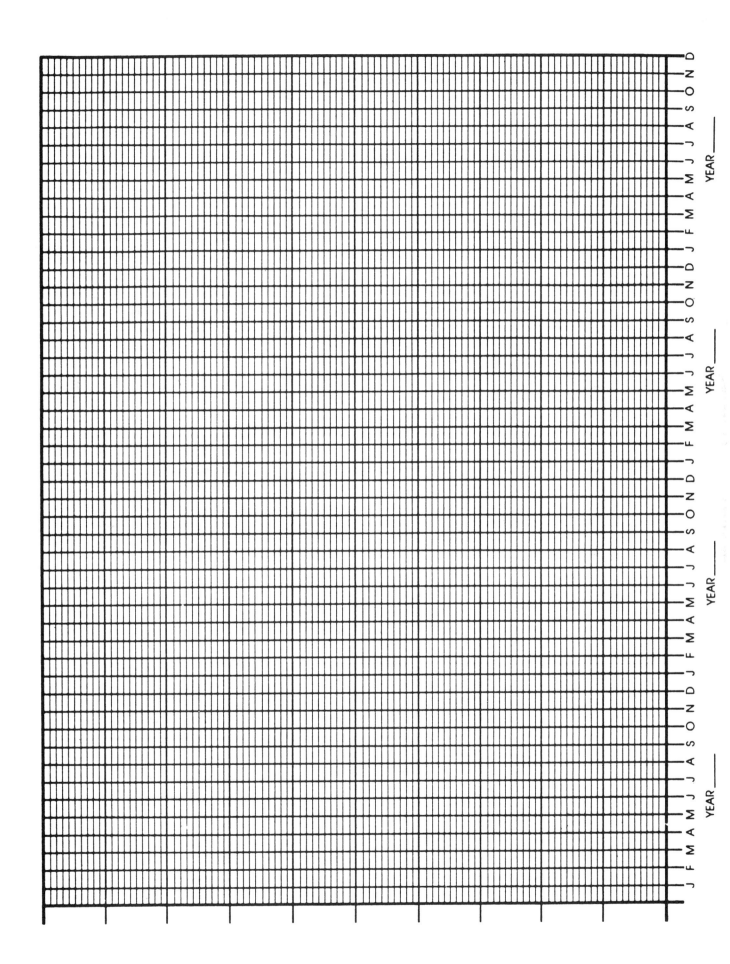

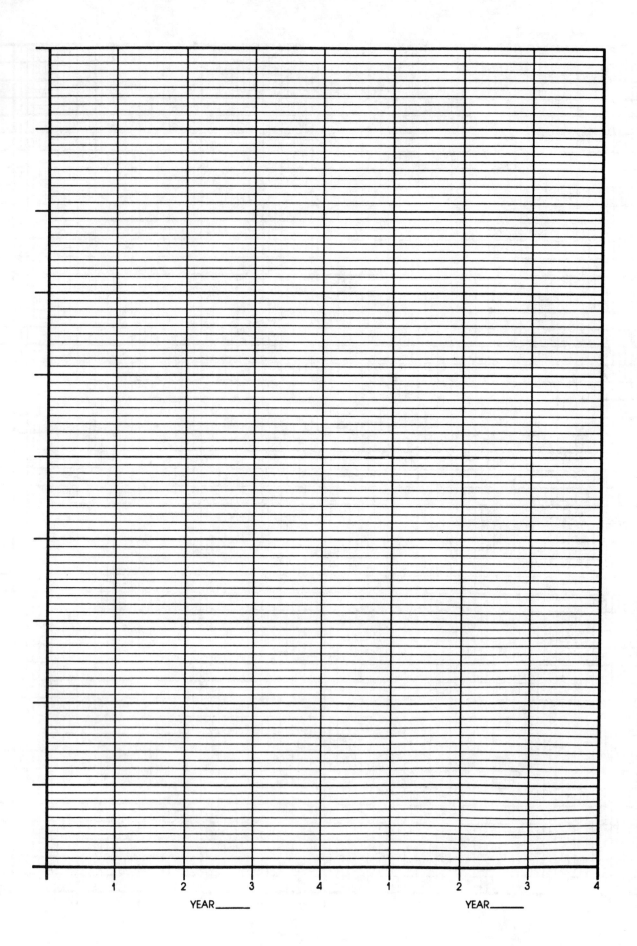

1 2 3 4 1 2 3 4

YEAR_____   YEAR_____

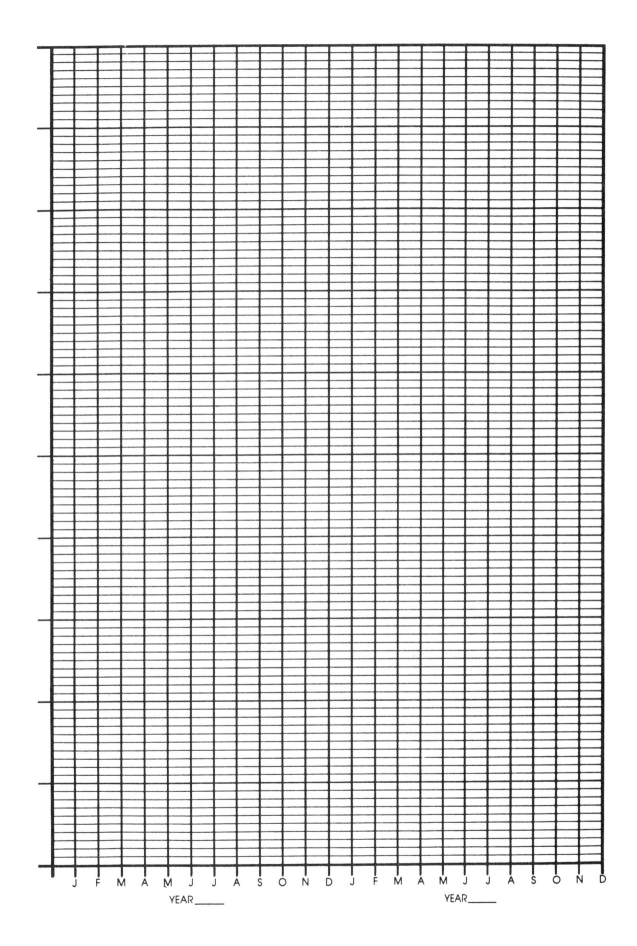

J F M A M J J A S O N D J F M A M J J A S O N D

YEAR_____ YEAR_____

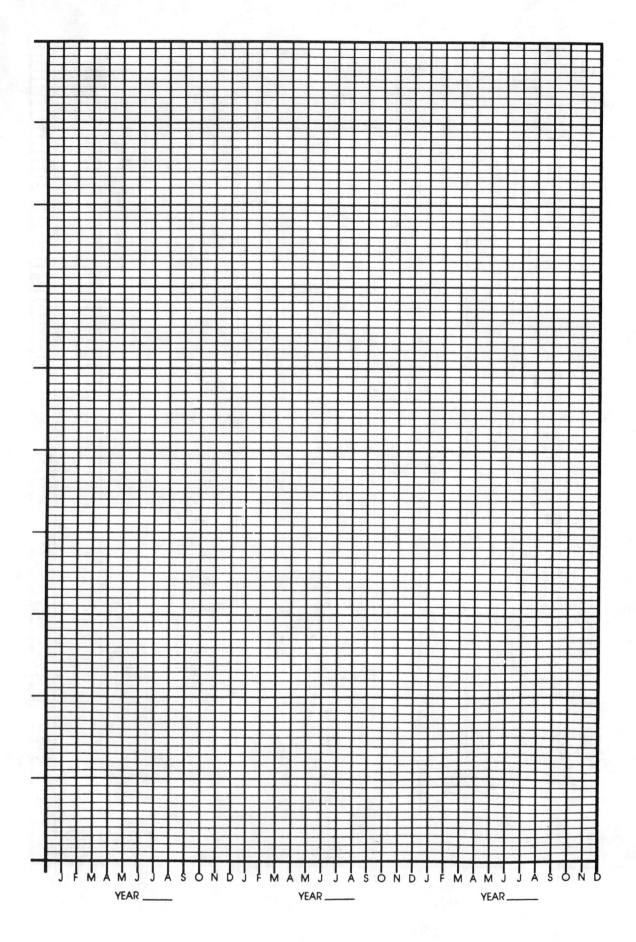

J F M A M J J A S O N D J F M A M J J A S O N D J F M A M J J A S O N D

YEAR _____   YEAR _____   YEAR _____

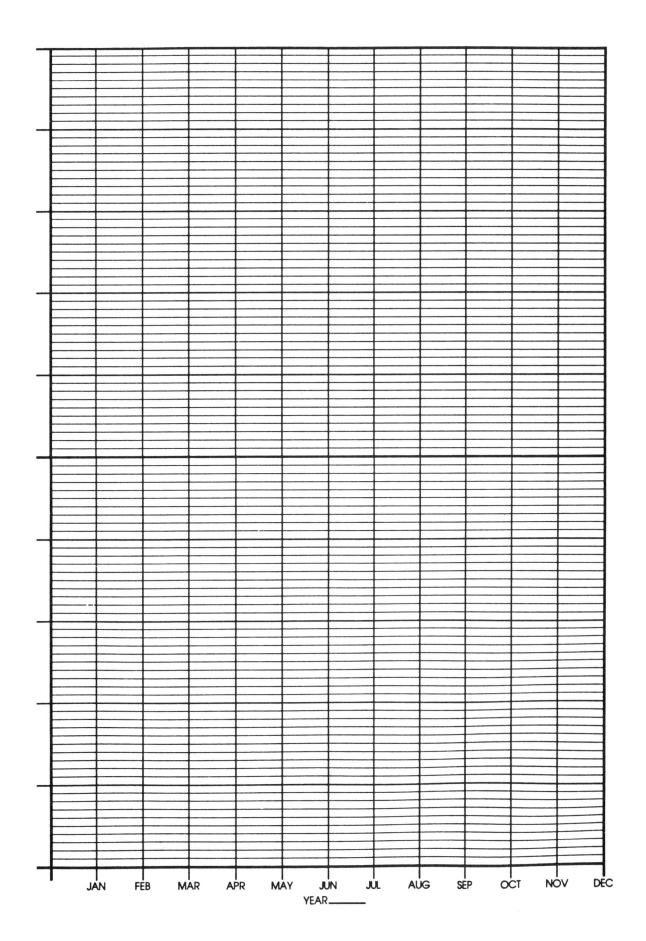

JAN FEB MAR APR MAY JUN JUL AUG SEP OCT NOV DEC

YEAR_____

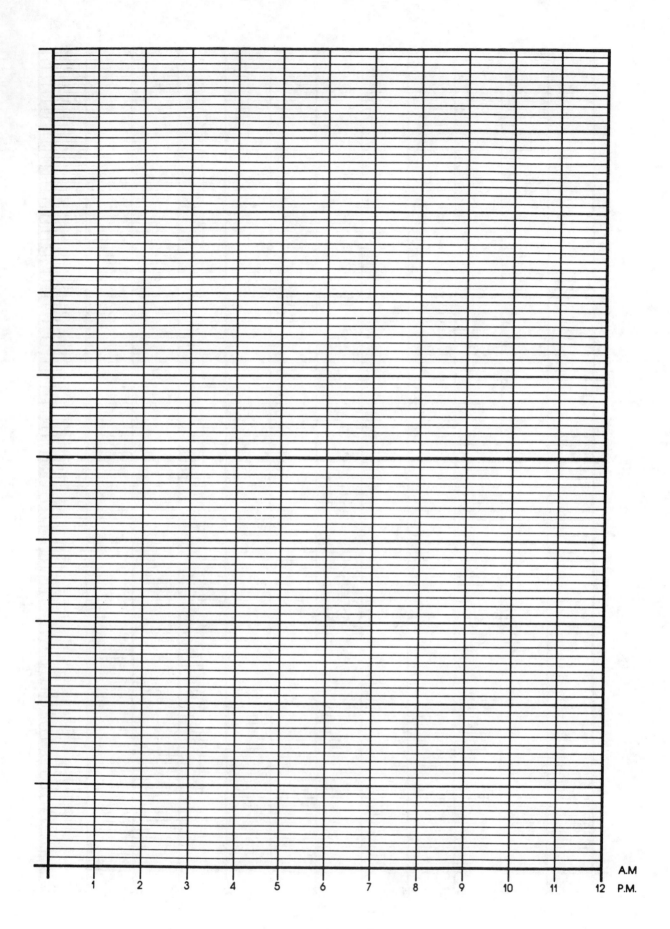

A.M

1   2   3   4   5   6   7   8   9   10   11   12

P.M.

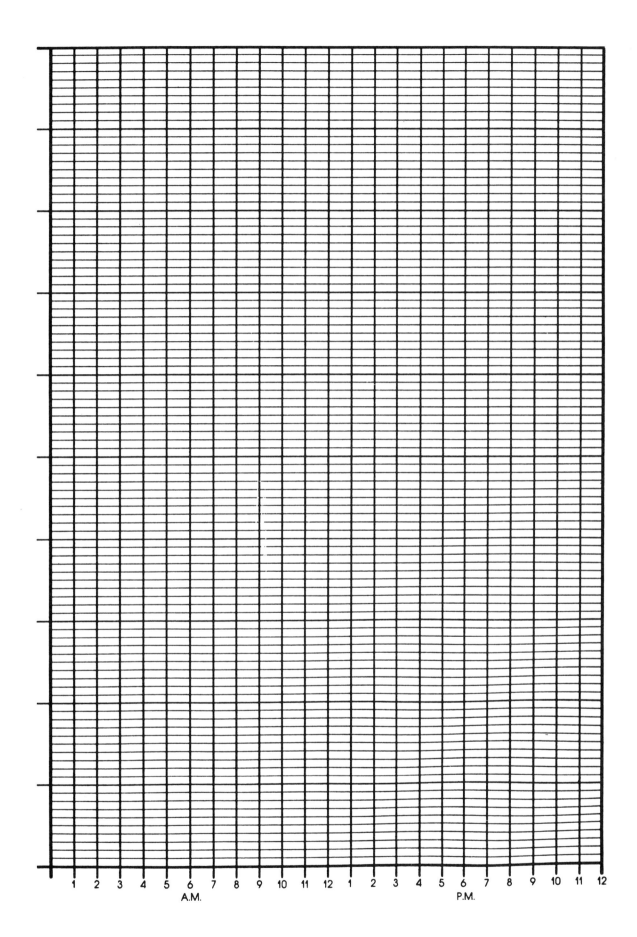

1 2 3 4 5 6 7 8 9 10 11 12 1 2 3 4 5 6 7 8 9 10 11 12
A.M.   P.M.

B 413

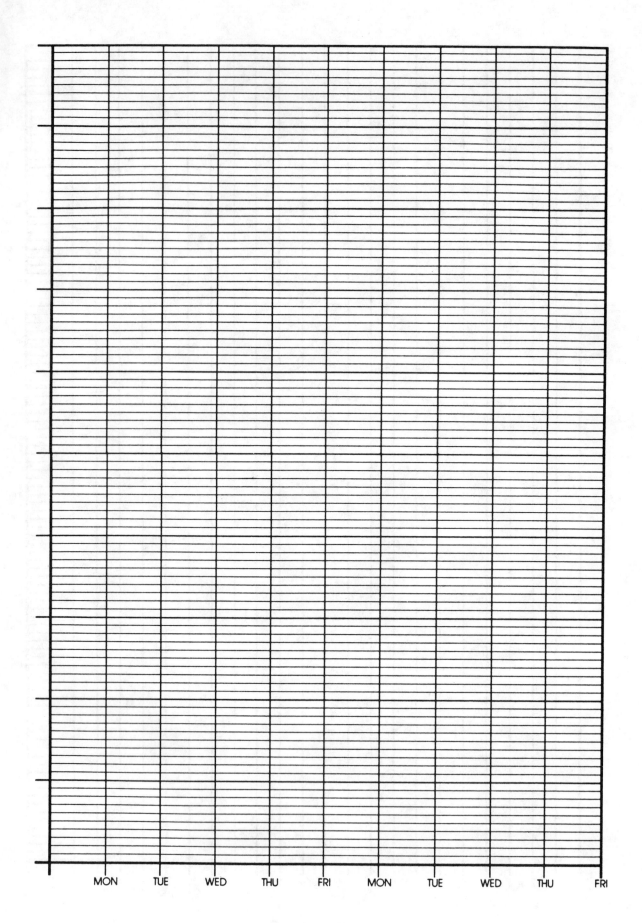

MON   TUE   WED   THU   FRI   MON   TUE   WED   THU   FRI

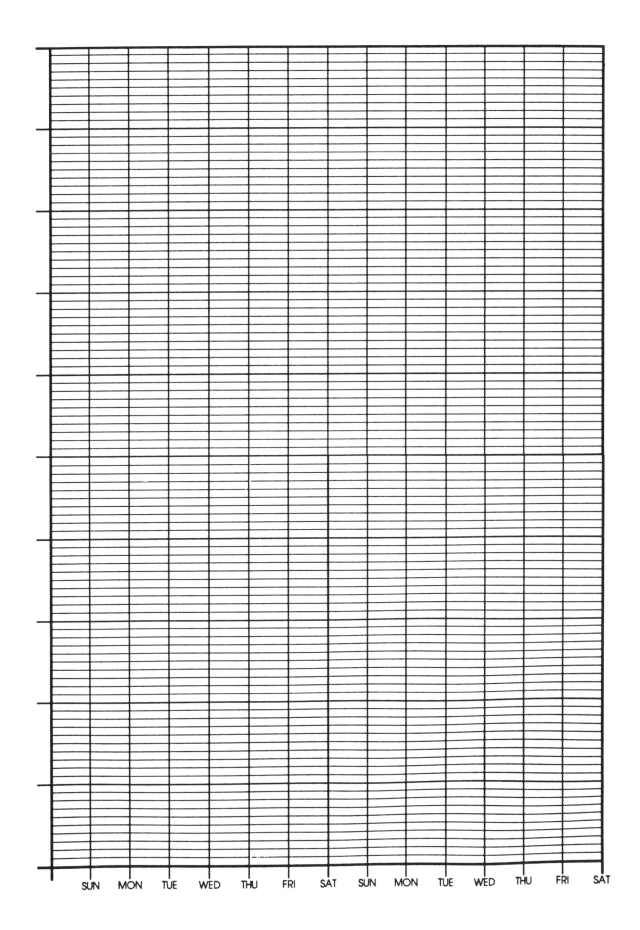

SUN   MON   TUE   WED   THU   FRI   SAT   SUN   MON   TUE   WED   THU   FRI   SAT

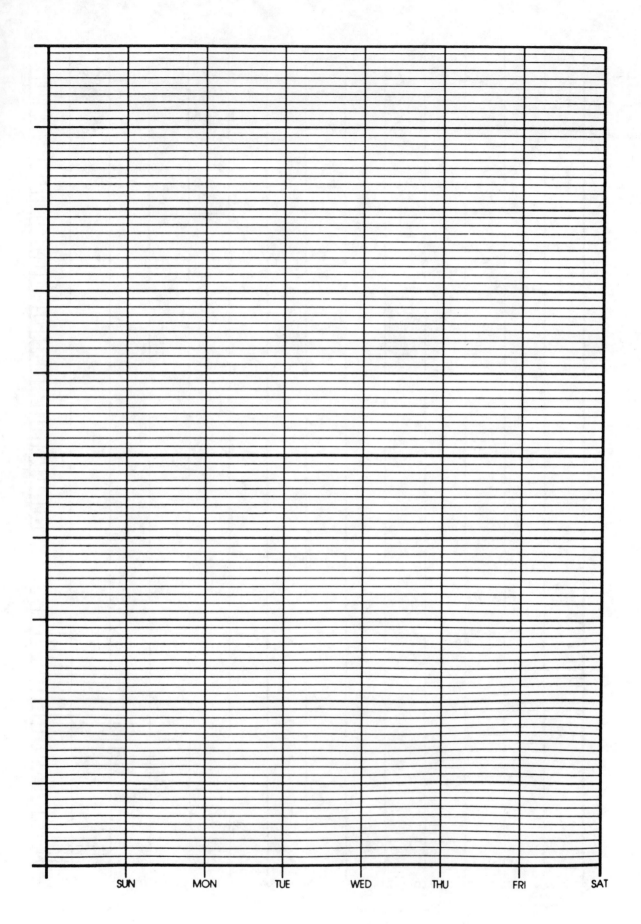

SUN   MON   TUE   WED   THU   FRI   SAT

1 2 3 4 5 6 7 8 9 10 11 12 1 2 3 4 5 6 7 8 9 10 11 12

A.M.   P.M.

JAN FEB MAR APR MAY JUN JUL AUG SEP OCT NOV DEC

VEAR

B 418

SUN MON TUE WED THU FRI SAT SUN MON TUE WED THU FRI SAT

A.M

P.M.

1   2   3   4   5   6   7   8   9   10   11   12

B 420

B 421

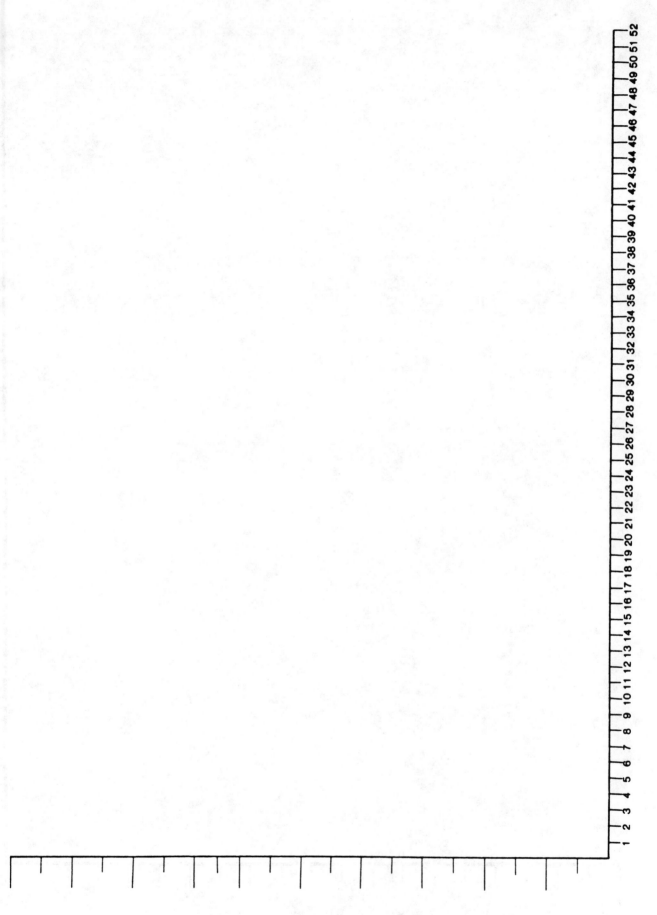

B 422

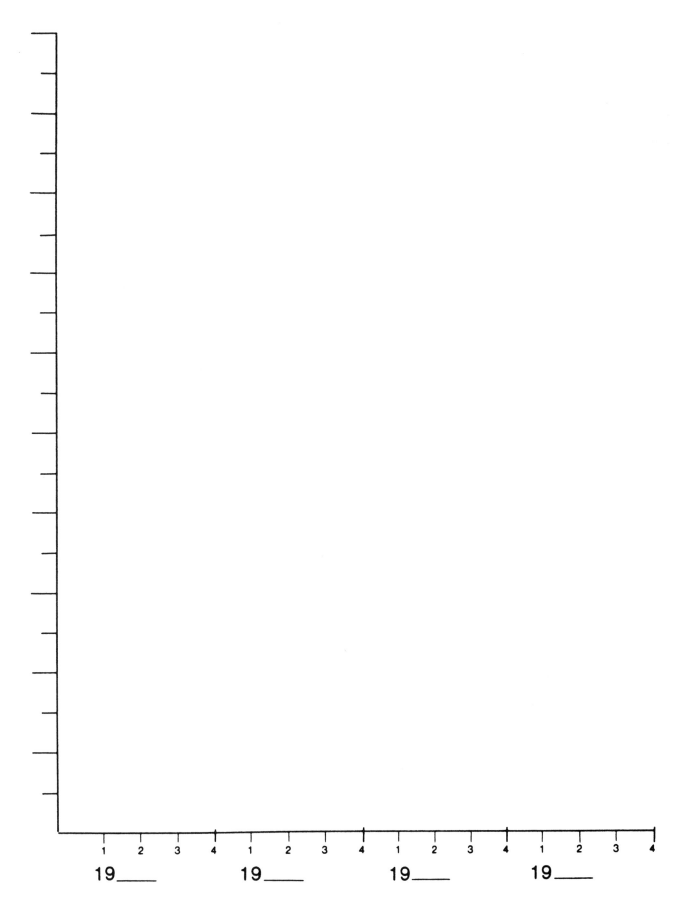

19____ 19____ 19____ 19____

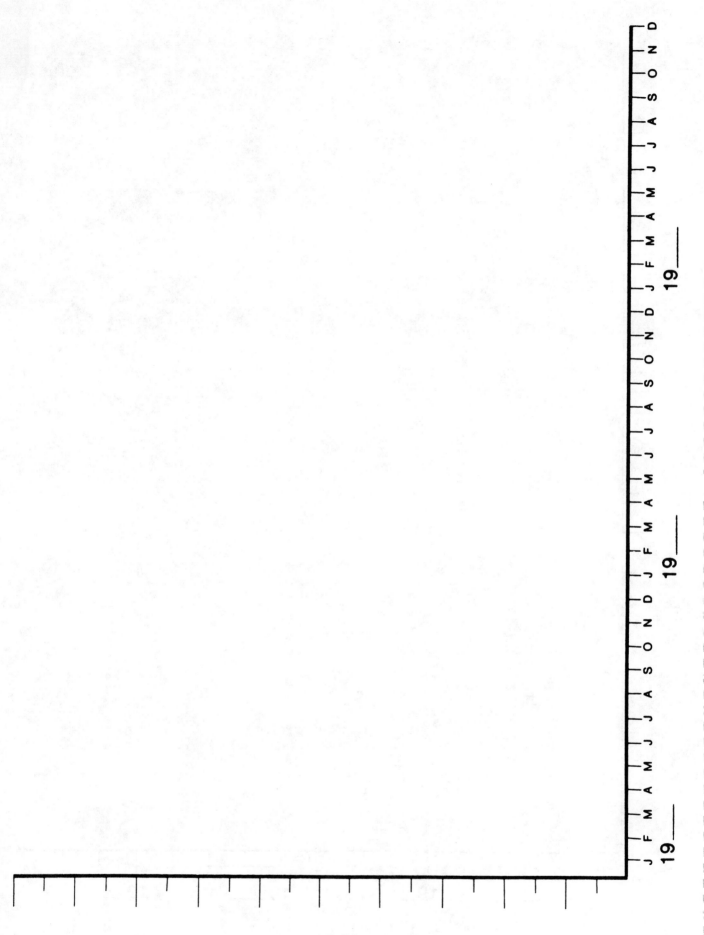

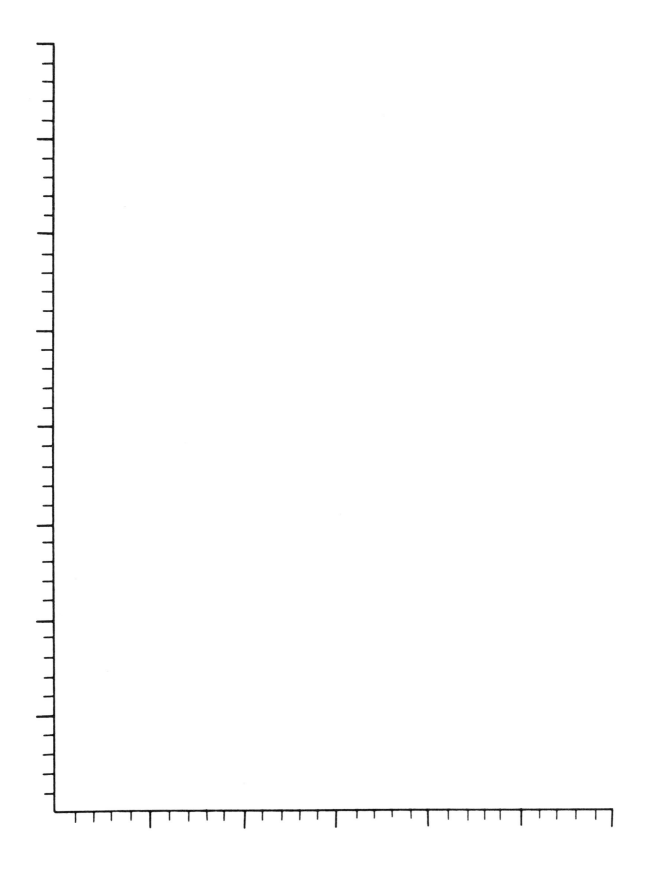

JAN | FEB | MAR | APR | MAY | JUN | JUL | AUG | SEP | OCT | NOV | DEC

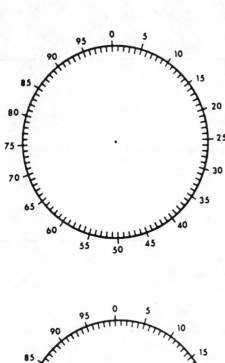
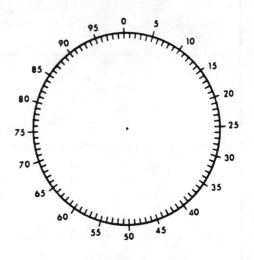
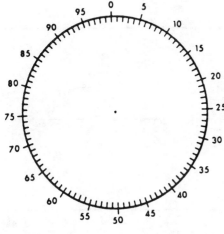
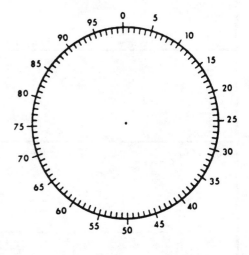
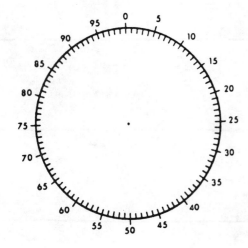
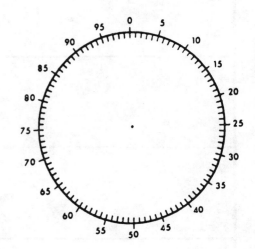

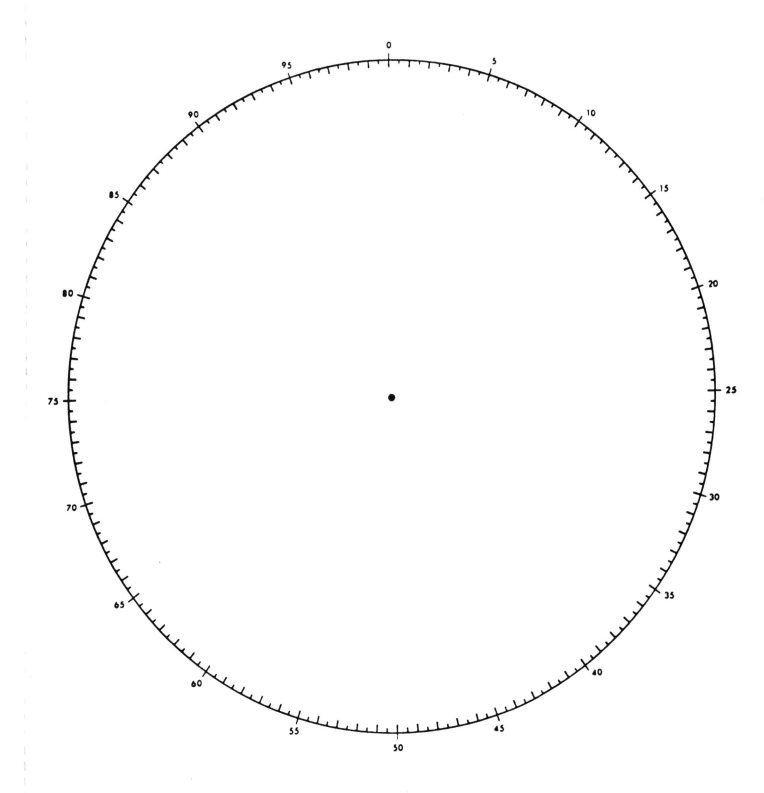

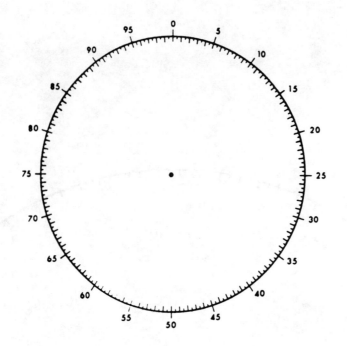

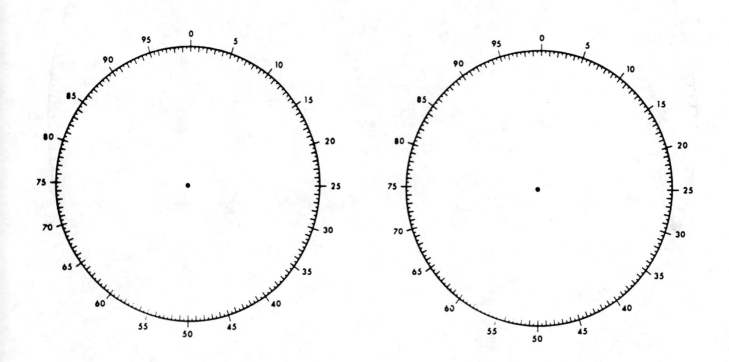

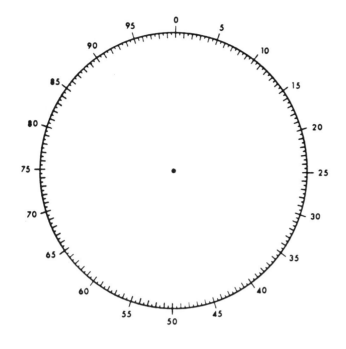
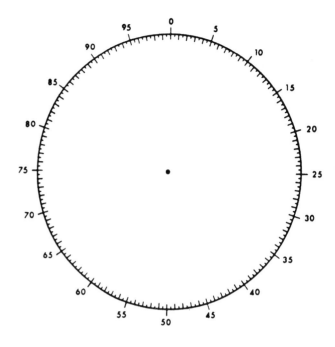
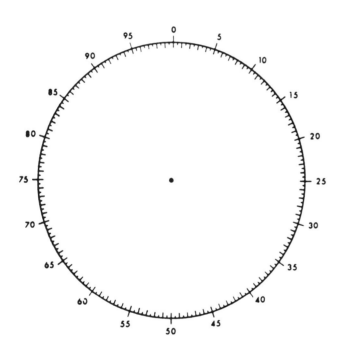
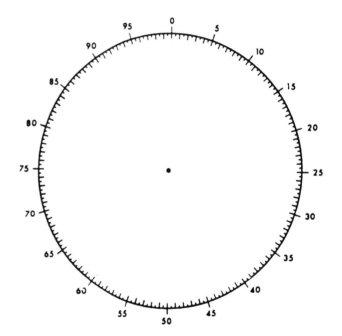

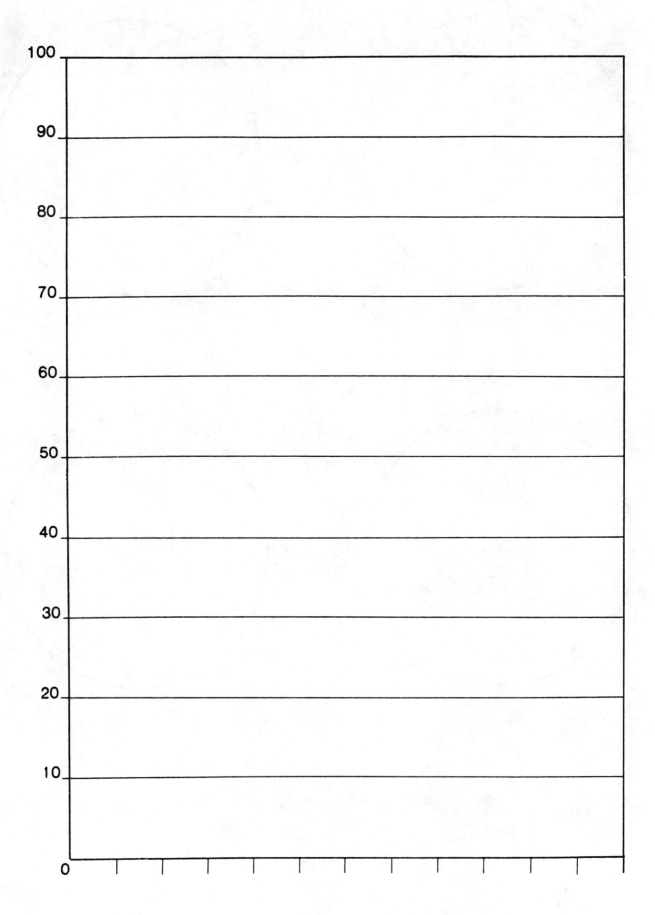

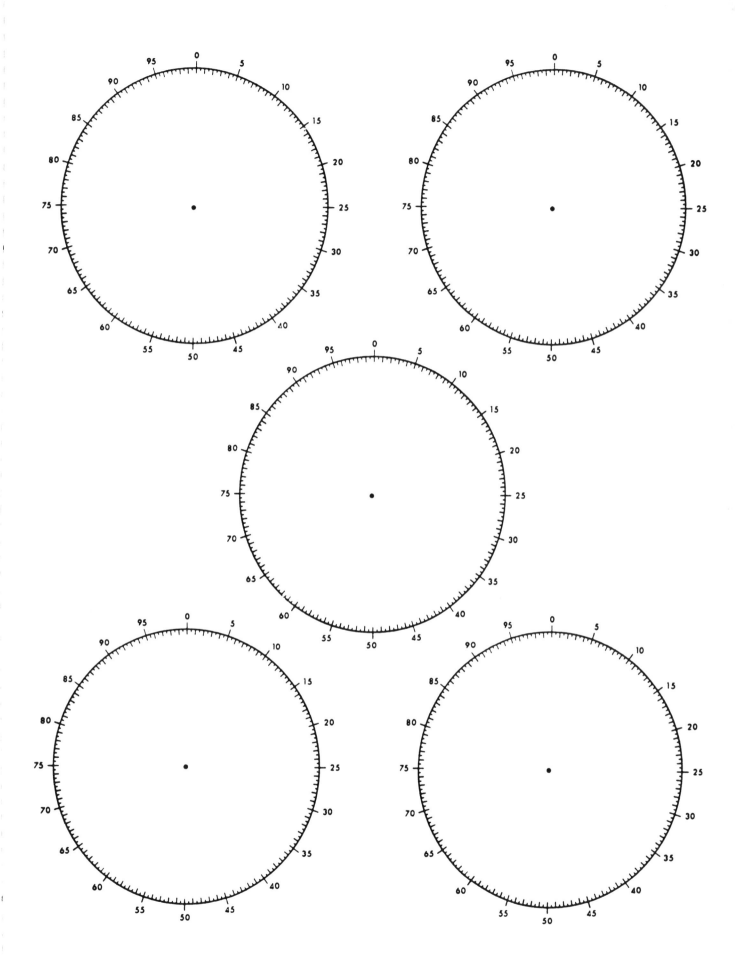

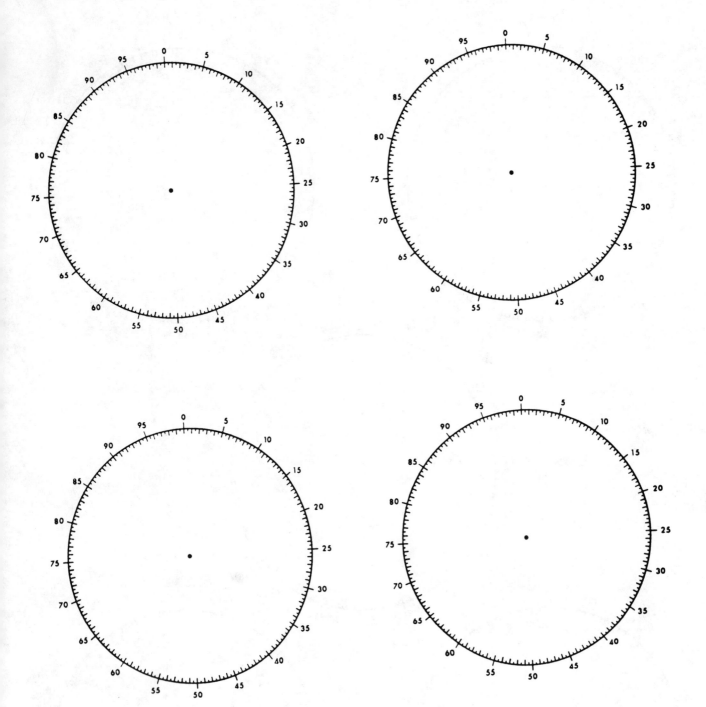

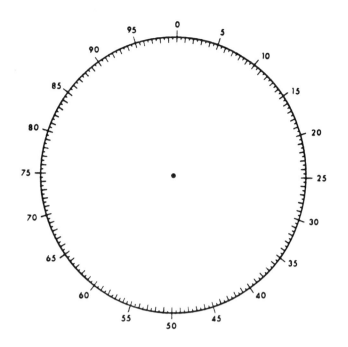

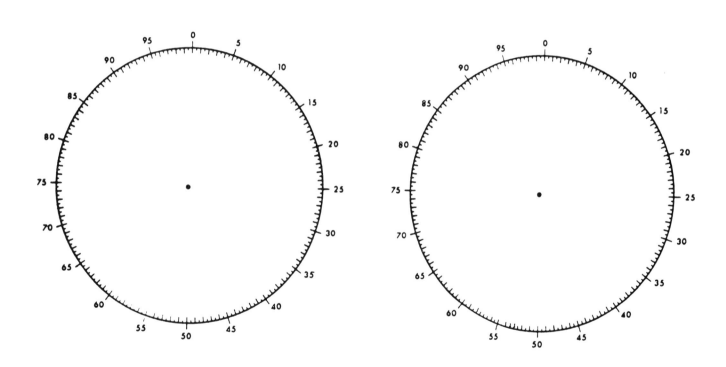

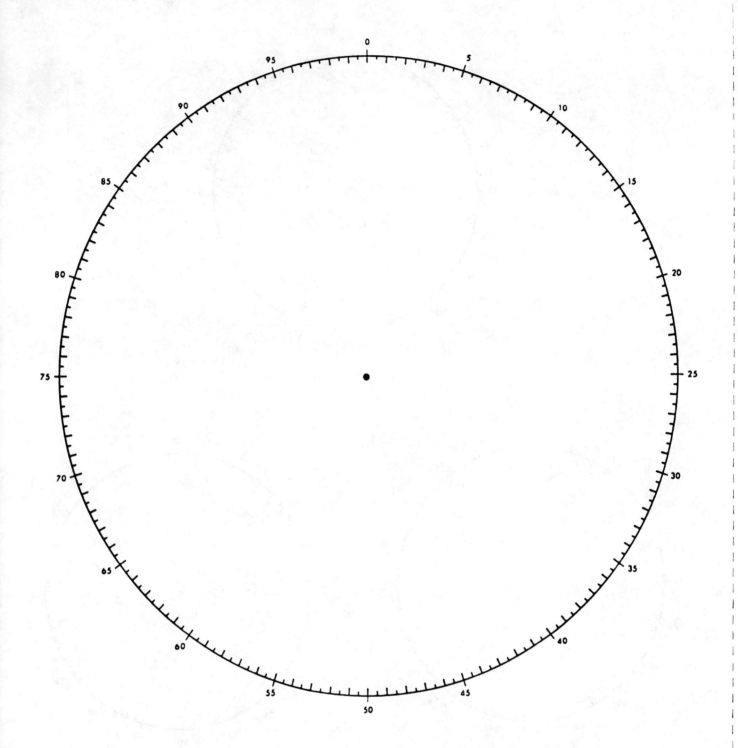

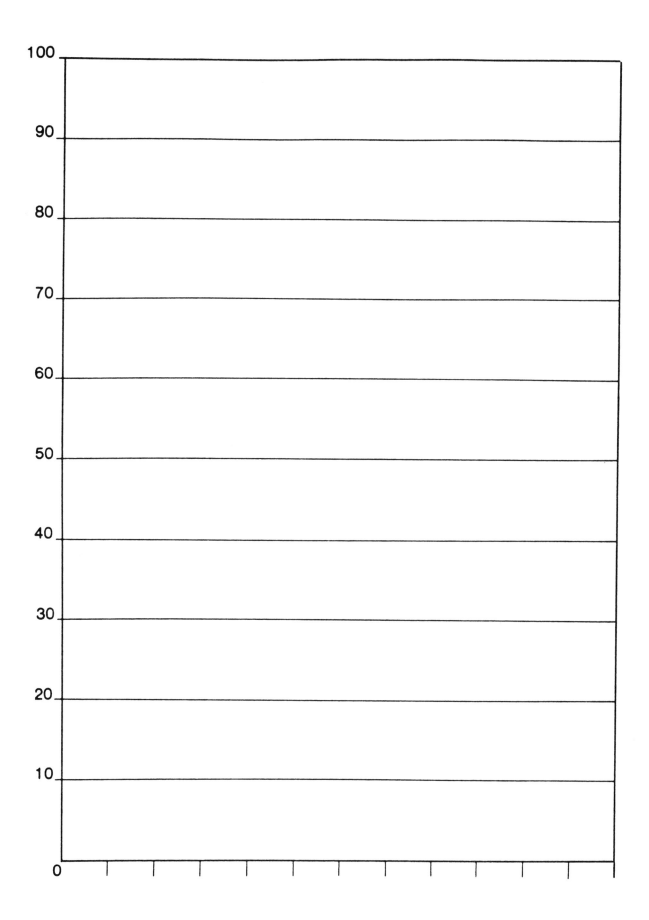

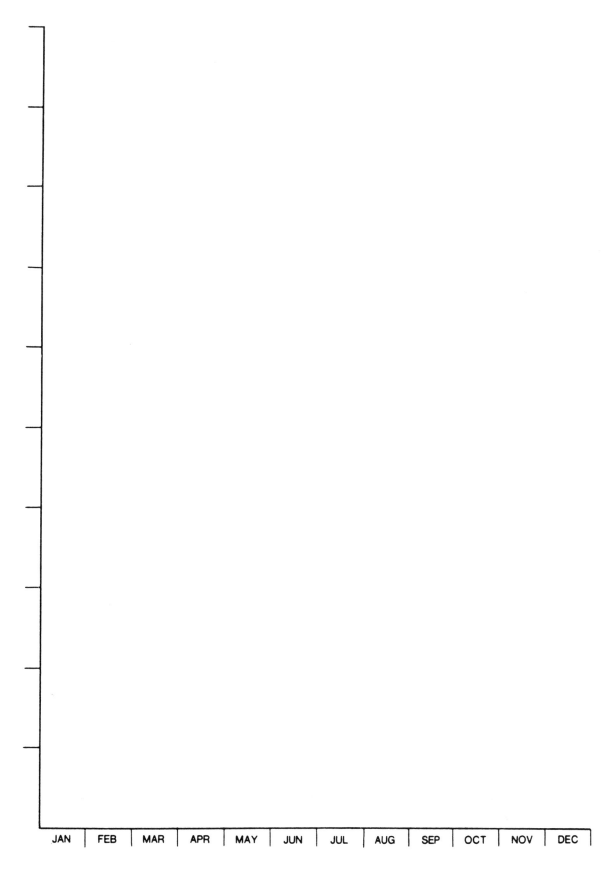

JAN | FEB | MAR | APR | MAY | JUN | JUL | AUG | SEP | OCT | NOV | DEC

B 439

1 2 3 4 1 2 3 4 1 2 3 4 1 2 3 4

19____ 19____ 19____ 19____

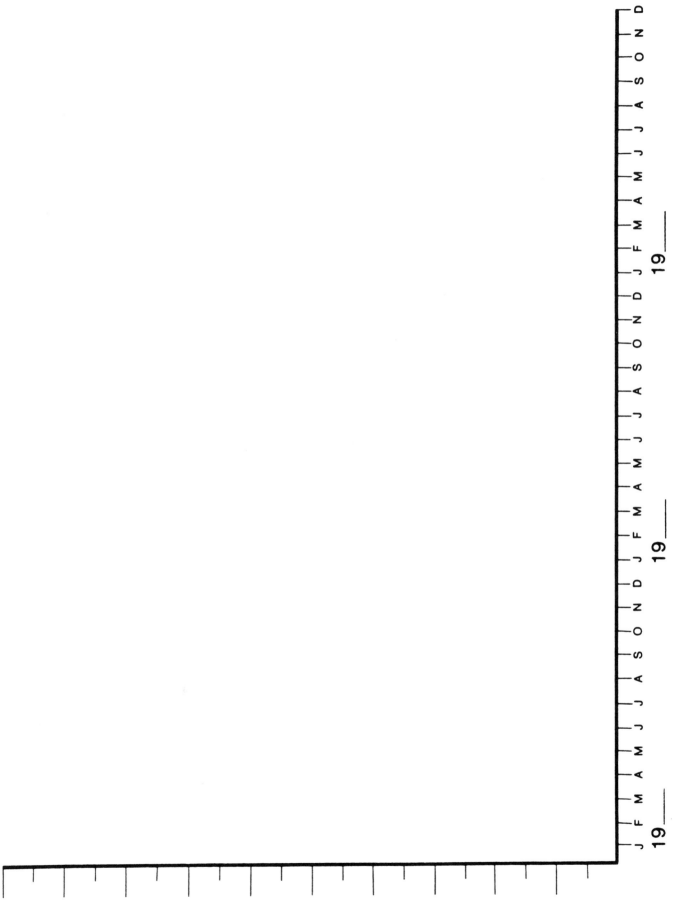

B 442

Maps

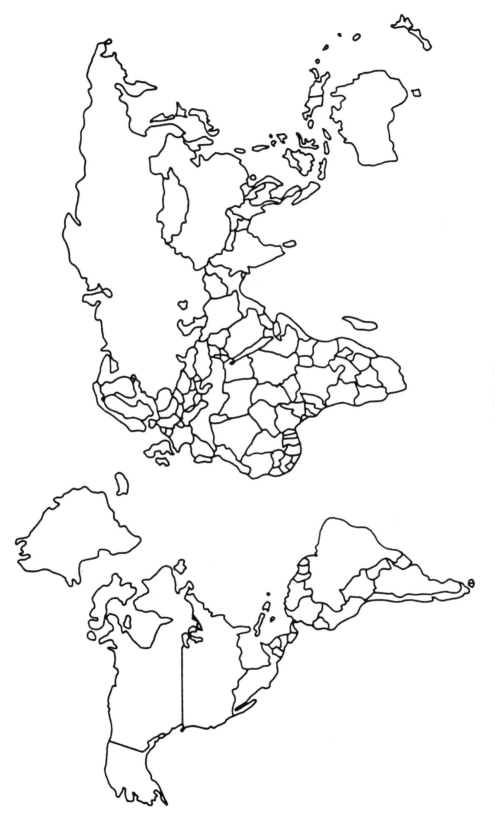

WORLD

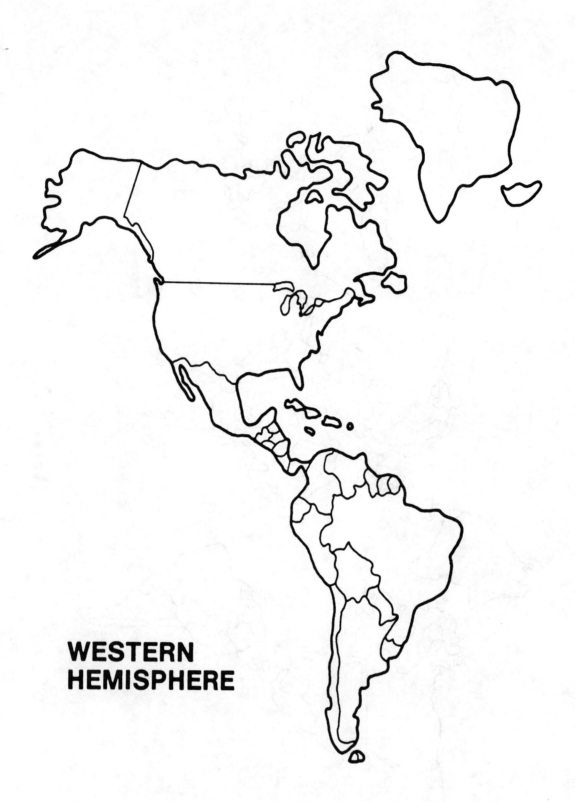

**WESTERN
HEMISPHERE**

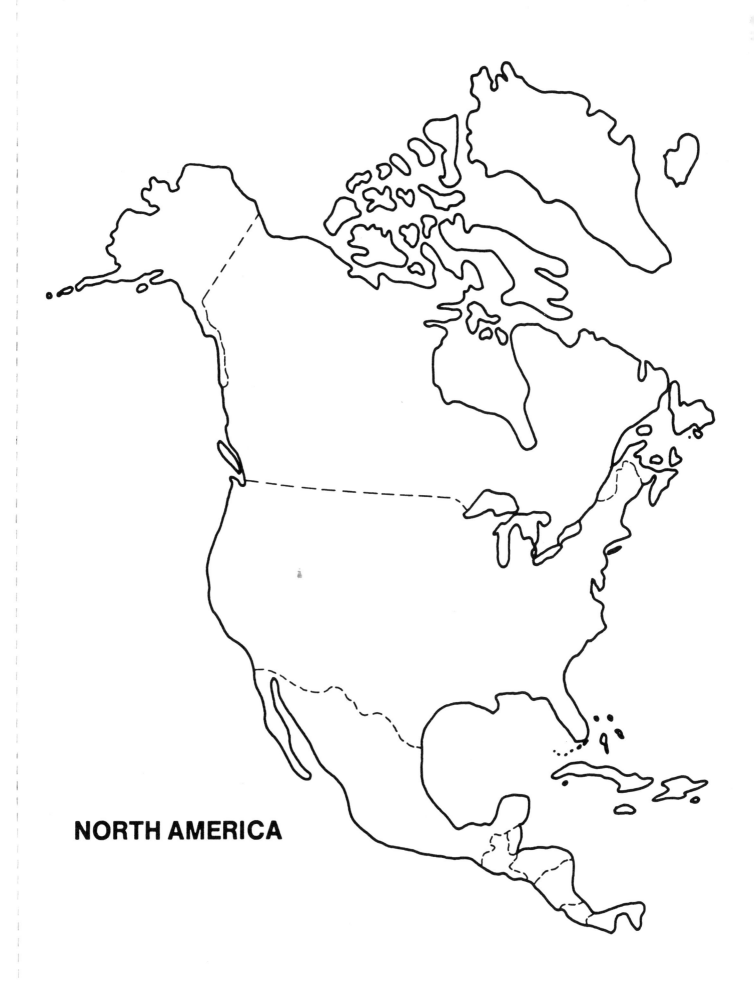

NORTH AMERICA

CENTRAL
AMERICA

VENEZUELA

ATLANTIC OCEAN

COLOMBIA

GUYANA

SURINAM

FRENCH
GUYANA

ECUADOR

PERU

BRAZIL

BOLIVIA

PACIFIC OCEAN

CHILE

PARAGUAY

ARGENTINA

URUGUAY

SOUTH AMERICA

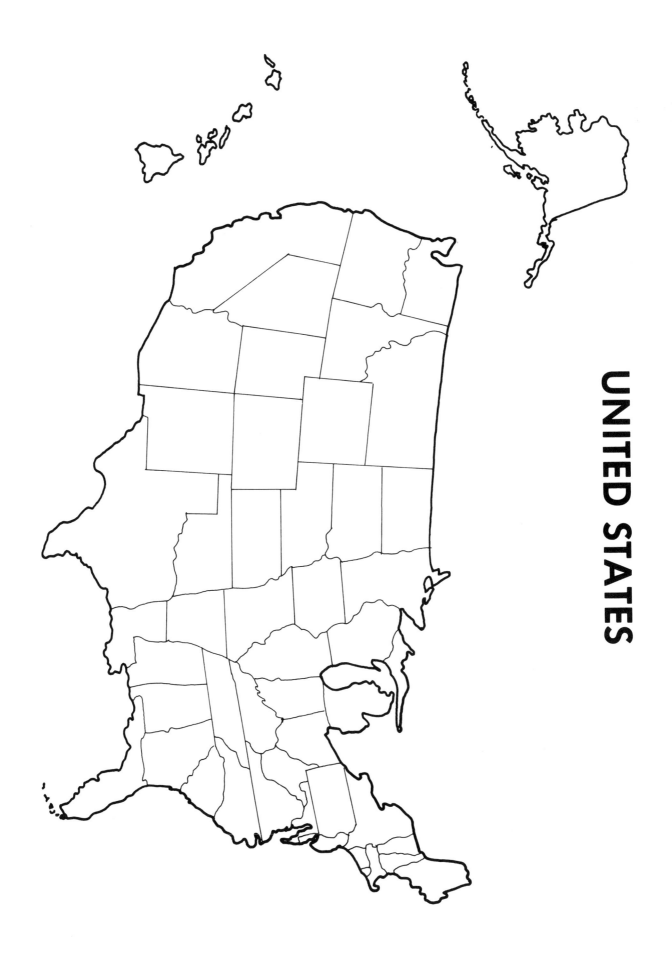

UNITED STATES

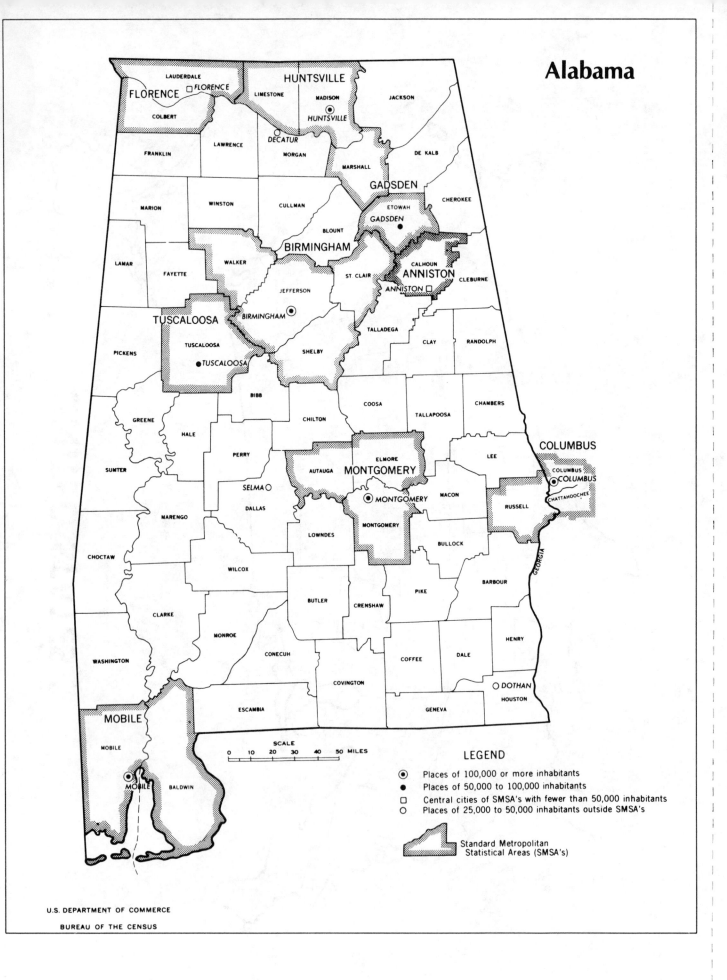

Alabama

LAUDERDALE
FLORENCE   □ FLORENCE
HUNTSVILLE
COLBERT
LIMESTONE
MADISON
⊙ HUNTSVILLE
JACKSON
FRANKLIN
LAWRENCE
DECATUR
MORGAN
MARSHALL
DE KALB
MARION
WINSTON
CULLMAN
GADSDEN
ETOWAH
● GADSDEN
CHEROKEE
BLOUNT
BIRMINGHAM
LAMAR
WALKER
ST. CLAIR
CALHOUN
ANNISTON
ANNISTON □
CLEBURNE
FAYETTE
JEFFERSON
TUSCALOOSA
⊙ BIRMINGHAM
PICKENS
TUSCALOOSA
● TUSCALOOSA
SHELBY
TALLADEGA
CLAY
RANDOLPH
BIBB
GREENE
HALE
CHILTON
COOSA
TALLAPOOSA
CHAMBERS
COLUMBUS
PERRY
ELMORE
LEE
COLUMBUS
⊙ COLUMBUS
SUMTER
SELMA ○
AUTAUGA
MONTGOMERY
MACON
RUSSELL
CHATTAHOOCHEE
MARENGO
DALLAS
⊙ MONTGOMERY
MONTGOMERY
CHOCTAW
WILCOX
LOWNDES
BULLOCK
GEORGIA
CLARKE
BUTLER
CRENSHAW
PIKE
BARBOUR
MONROE
HENRY
WASHINGTON
CONECUH
COFFEE
DALE
COVINGTON
○ DOTHAN
HOUSTON
MOBILE
ESCAMBIA
GENEVA
MOBILE
⊙ MOBILE
BALDWIN

SCALE
0 10 20 30 40 50 MILES

LEGEND

⊙ Places of 100,000 or more inhabitants
● Places of 50,000 to 100,000 inhabitants
□ Central cities of SMSA's with fewer than 50,000 inhabitants
○ Places of 25,000 to 50,000 inhabitants outside SMSA's

Standard Metropolitan
Statistical Areas (SMSA's)

U.S. DEPARTMENT OF COMMERCE

BUREAU OF THE CENSUS

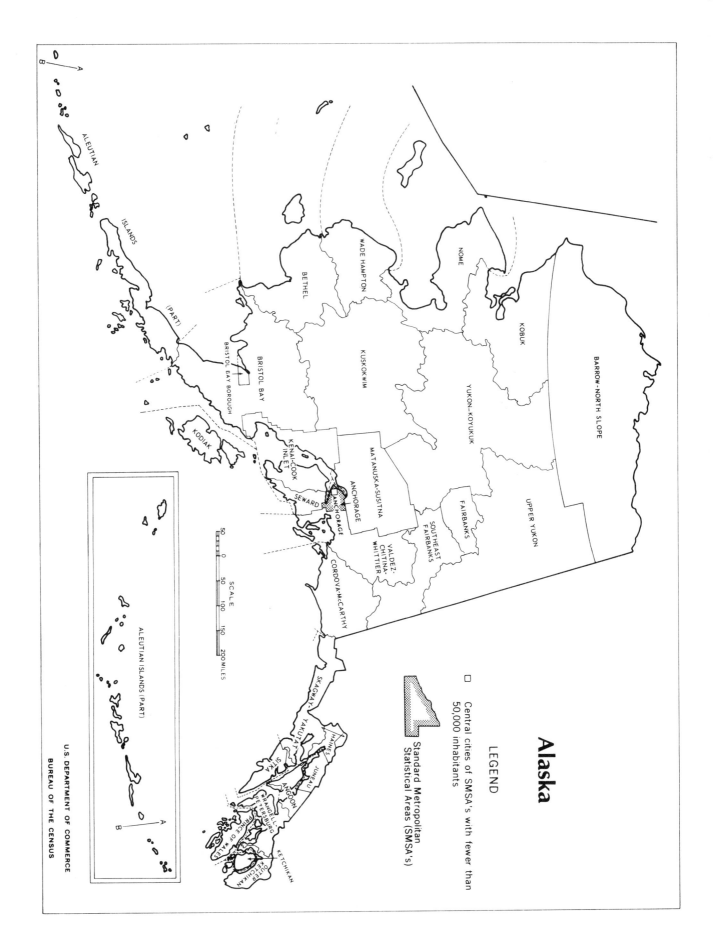

Alaska

LEGEND

□ Central cities of SMSA's with fewer than 50,000 inhabitants

▨ Standard Metropolitan Statistical Areas (SMSA's)

ALEUTIAN ISLANDS

BRISTOL BAY BOROUGH

BRISTOL BAY

(PART)

KODIAK

BETHEL

WADE HAMPTON

NOME

KOBUK

BARROW-NORTH SLOPE

KUSKOKWIM

YUKON-KOYUKUK

UPPER YUKON

KENAI-COOK INLET

MATANUSKA-SUSITNA

ANCHORAGE

SEWARD

SOUTHEAST FAIRBANKS

FAIRBANKS

VALDEZ-CHITINA-WHITTIER

CORDOVA-McCARTHY

SKAGWAY-YAKUTAT

HAINES

SITKA

JUNEAU

ANGOON

WRANGELL-PETERSBURG

PRINCE OF WALES

OUTER KETCHIKAN

KETCHIKAN

SCALE

50   0   50   100   150   200 MILES

ALEUTIAN ISLANDS (PART)

B

A

B

A

U.S. DEPARTMENT OF COMMERCE

BUREAU OF THE CENSUS

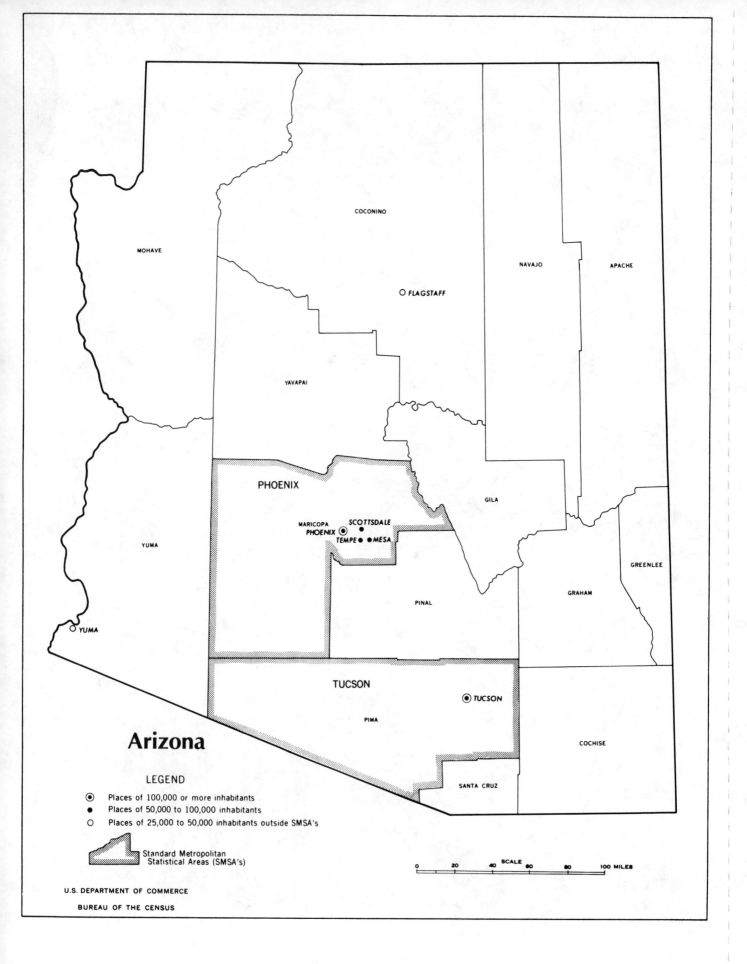

Arizona

LEGEND

⊙ Places of 100,000 or more inhabitants

● Places of 50,000 to 100,000 inhabitants

○ Places of 25,000 to 50,000 inhabitants outside SMSA's

Standard Metropolitan
Statistical Areas (SMSA's)

SCALE

0   20   40   60   80   100 MILES

U.S. DEPARTMENT OF COMMERCE

BUREAU OF THE CENSUS

Map labels: MOHAVE, COCONINO, NAVAJO, APACHE, ○ FLAGSTAFF, YAVAPAI, PHOENIX, GILA, MARICOPA, SCOTTSDALE, ⊙ PHOENIX, TEMPE, ● MESA, YUMA, ○ YUMA, PINAL, GRAHAM, GREENLEE, TUCSON, ⊙ TUCSON, PIMA, COCHISE, SANTA CRUZ

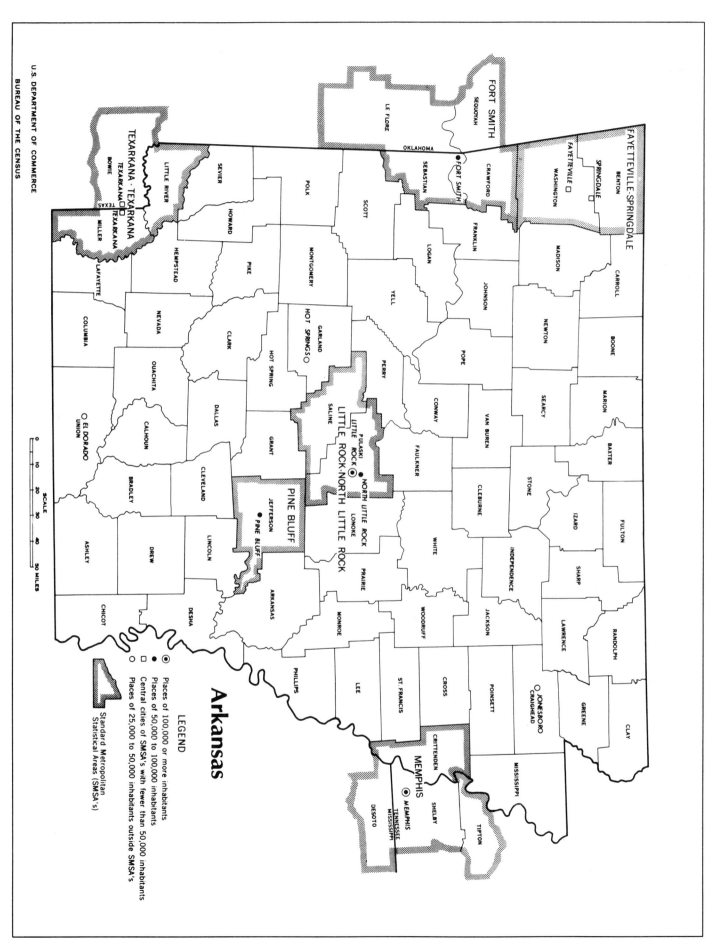

U.S. DEPARTMENT OF COMMERCE
BUREAU OF THE CENSUS

Arkansas

LEGEND

⊚ Places of 100,000 or more inhabitants
● Places of 50,000 to 100,000 inhabitants
□ Central cities of SMSA's with fewer than 50,000 inhabitants
○ Places of 25,000 to 50,000 inhabitants outside SMSA's

Standard Metropolitan
Statistical Areas (SMSA's)

SCALE
0
10
20
30
40
50 MILES

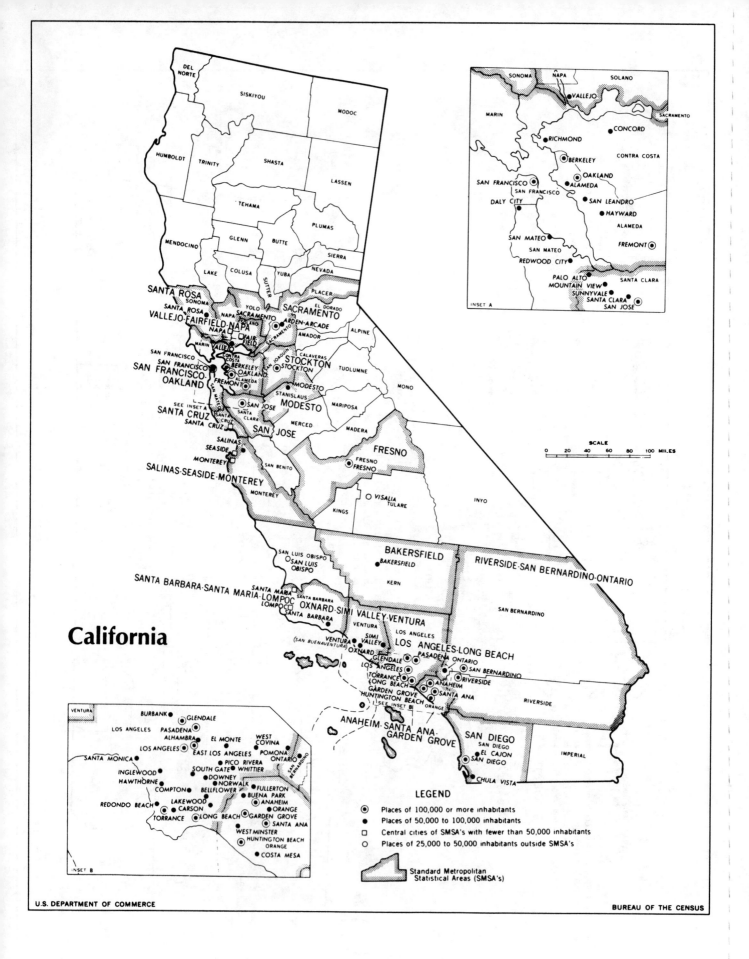

California

LEGEND

⊙ Places of 100,000 or more inhabitants
● Places of 50,000 to 100,000 inhabitants
□ Central cities of SMSA's with fewer than 50,000 inhabitants
○ Places of 25,000 to 50,000 inhabitants outside SMSA's

Standard Metropolitan
Statistical Areas (SMSA's)

SCALE
0   20   40   60   80   100 MILES

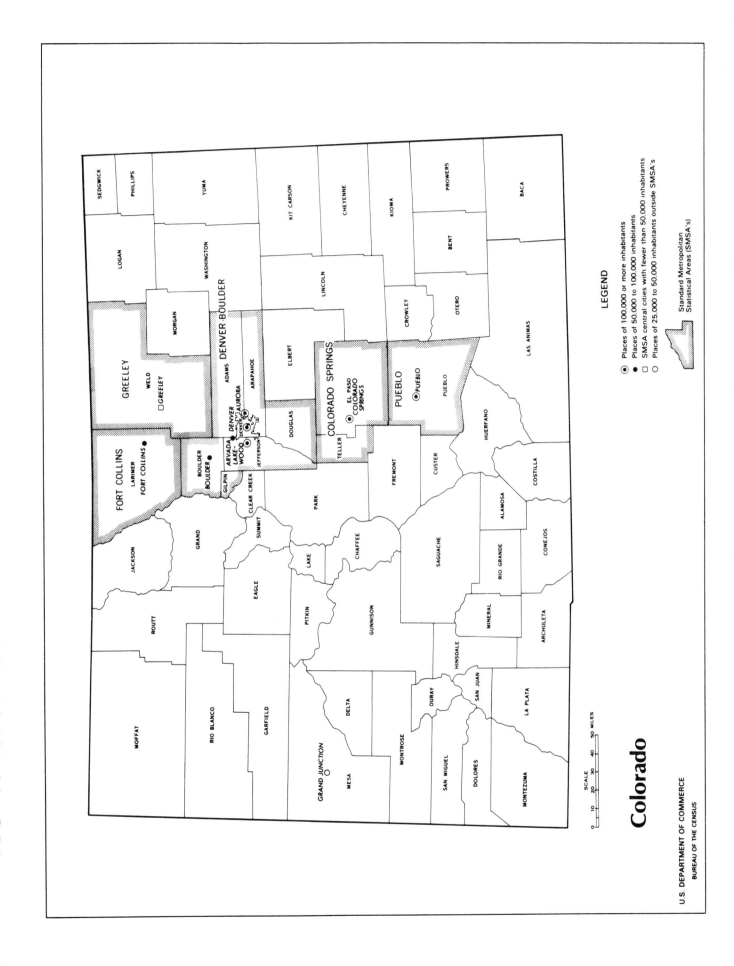

Colorado

U.S. DEPARTMENT OF COMMERCE
BUREAU OF THE CENSUS

LEGEND

⊙ Places of 100,000 or more inhabitants
● Places of 50,000 to 100,000 inhabitants
□ SMSA central cities with fewer than 50,000 inhabitants
○ Places of 25,000 to 50,000 inhabitants outside SMSA's

Standard Metropolitan
Statistical Areas (SMSA's)

SCALE
0 10 20 30 40 50 MILES

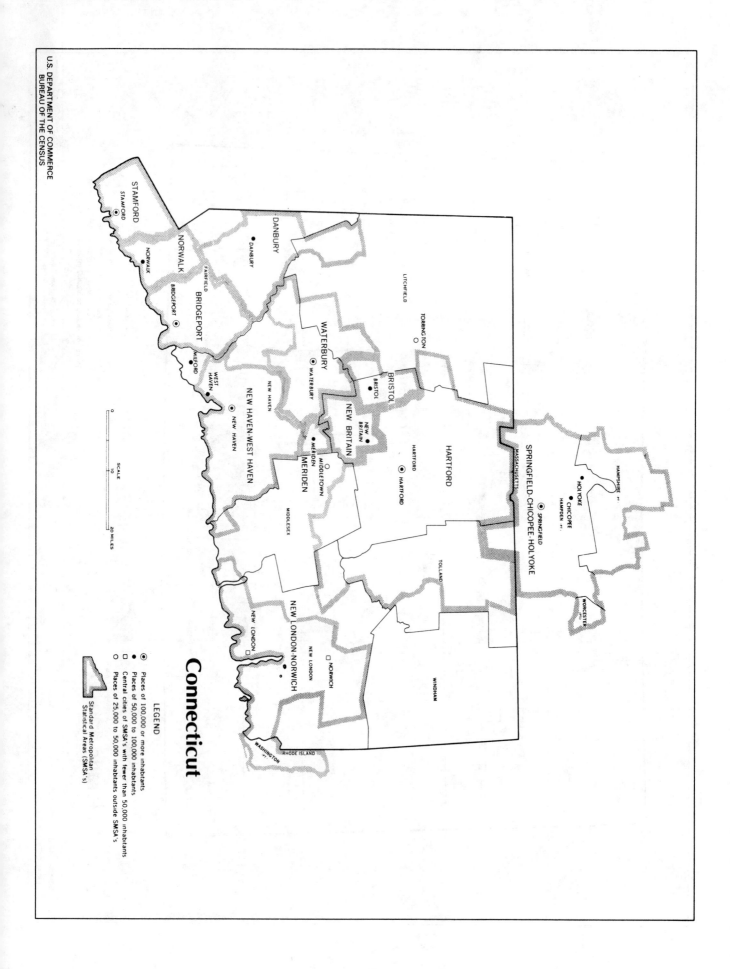

Connecticut

U.S. DEPARTMENT OF COMMERCE
BUREAU OF THE CENSUS

LEGEND

⊙ Places of 100,000 or more inhabitants
● Places of 50,000 to 100,000 inhabitants
▢ Central cities of SMSA's with fewer than 50,000 inhabitants
○ Places of 25,000 to 50,000 inhabitants outside SMSA's

Standard Metropolitan
Statistical Areas (SMSA's)

SCALE

0   10   20 MILES

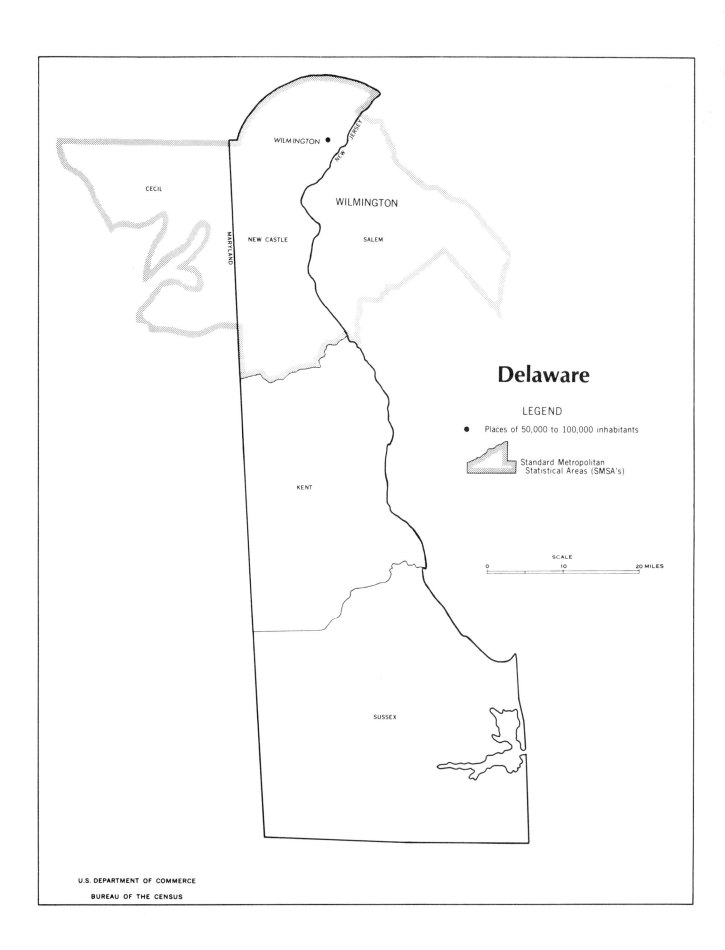

Delaware

LEGEND

● Places of 50,000 to 100,000 inhabitants

Standard Metropolitan
Statistical Areas (SMSA's)

SCALE

0   10   20 MILES

WILMINGTON ●

CECIL

WILMINGTON

NEW CASTLE

SALEM

MARYLAND

NEW JERSEY

KENT

SUSSEX

U.S. DEPARTMENT OF COMMERCE

BUREAU OF THE CENSUS

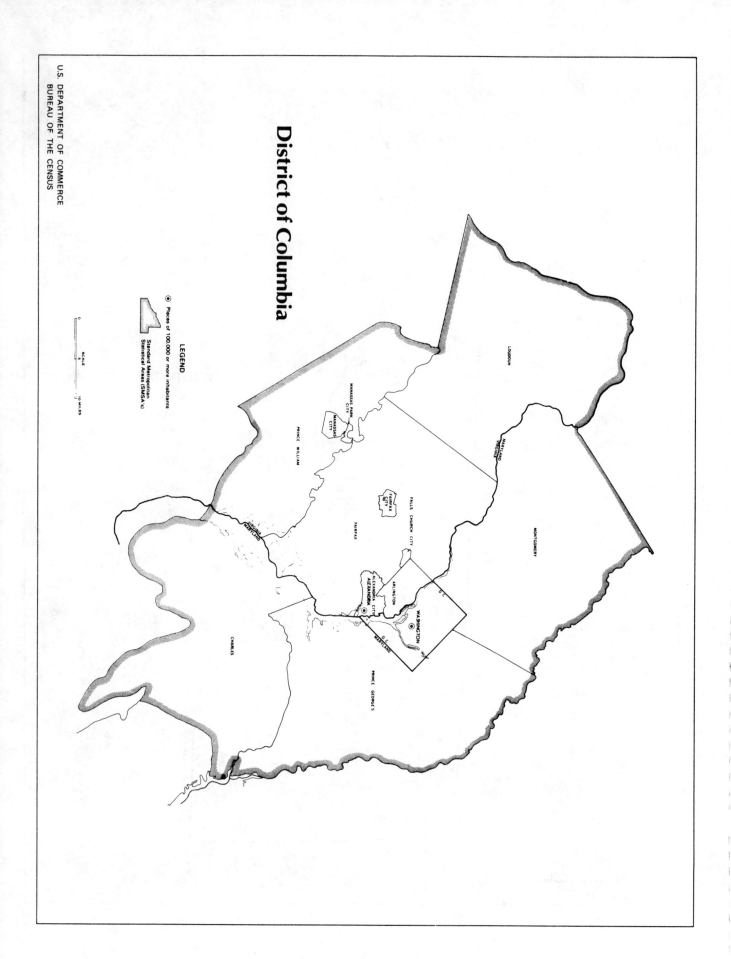

District of Columbia

U.S. DEPARTMENT OF COMMERCE
BUREAU OF THE CENSUS

LEGEND

◉ Places of 100,000 or more inhabitants

Standard Metropolitan
Statistical Areas (SMSA's)

SCALE

0   5   10 MILES

LOUDOUN

MARYLAND
VIRGINIA

MONTGOMERY

PRINCE WILLIAM

MANASSAS PARK
CITY

MANASSAS
CITY

FAIRFAX
CITY

FALLS CHURCH CITY

FAIRFAX

VIRGINIA
MARYLAND

ALEXANDRIA CITY
ALEXANDRIA

ARLINGTON

D. C.

WASHINGTON

D. C.
MARYLAND

CHARLES

PRINCE GEORGES

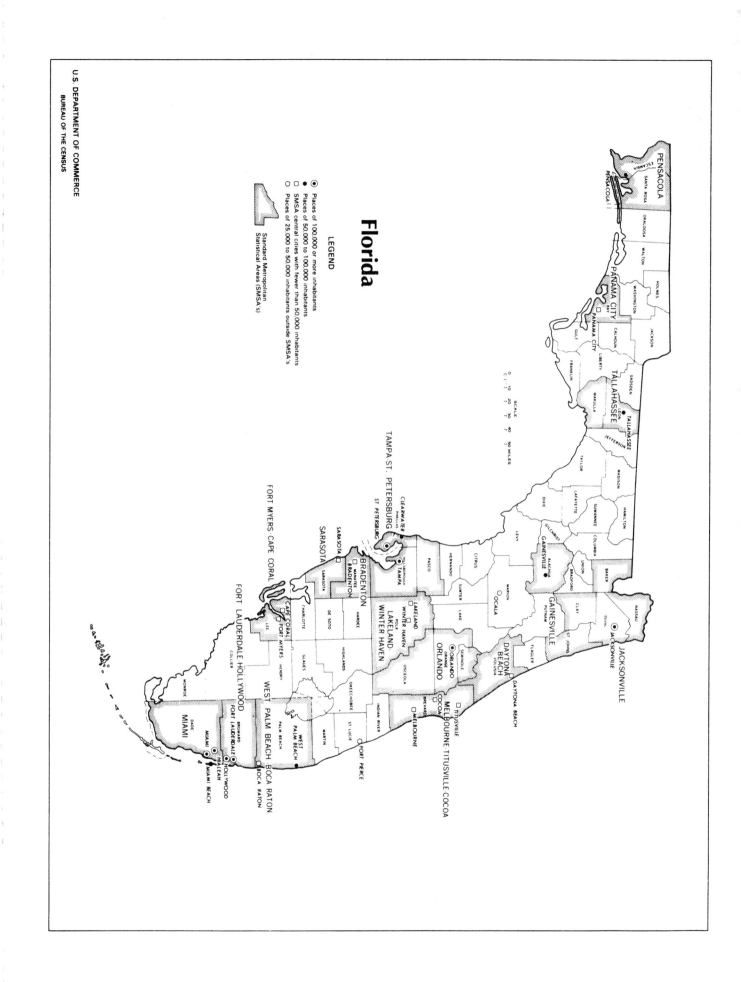

Florida

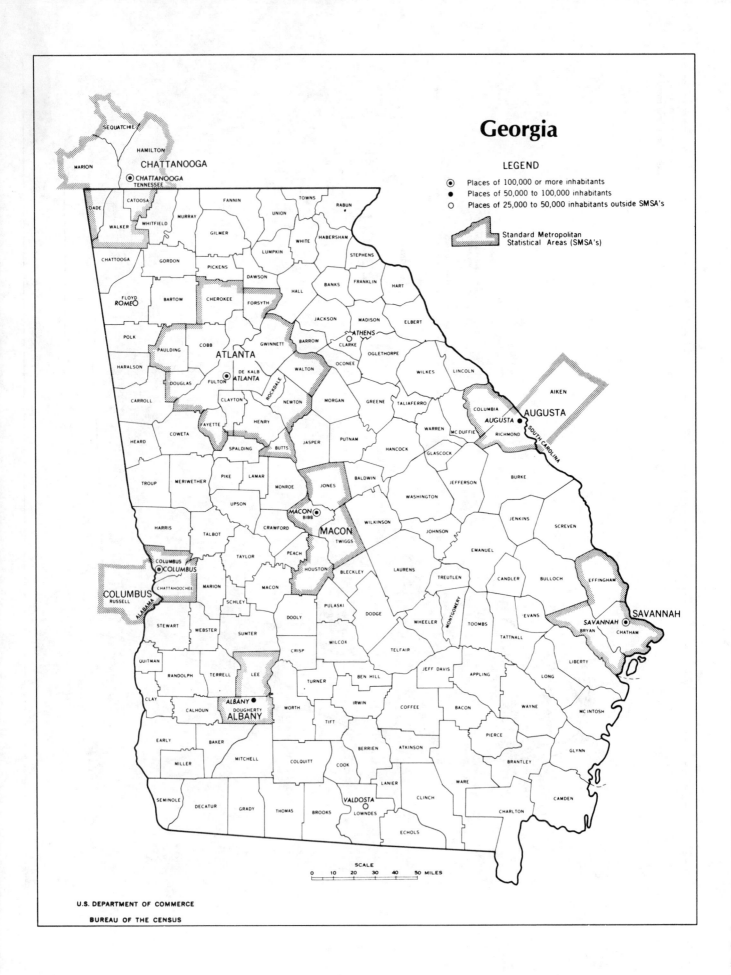

Georgia

LEGEND

⊙ Places of 100,000 or more inhabitants

● Places of 50,000 to 100,000 inhabitants

○ Places of 25,000 to 50,000 inhabitants outside SMSA's

Standard Metropolitan Statistical Areas (SMSA's)

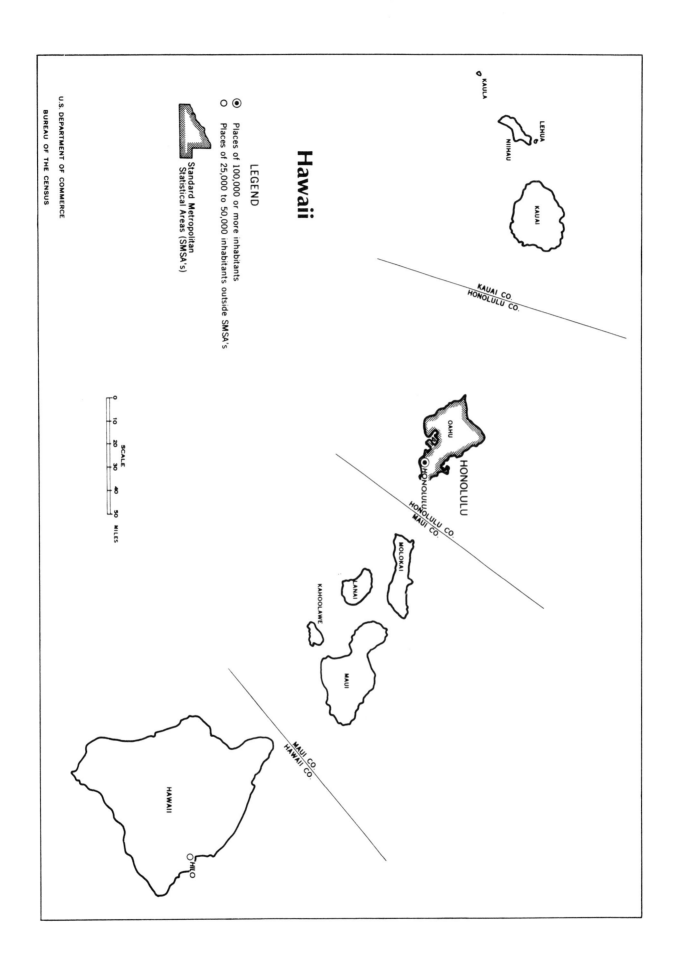

Hawaii

LEGEND

⊙ Places of 100,000 or more inhabitants
○ Places of 25,000 to 50,000 inhabitants outside SMSA's

Standard Metropolitan
Statistical Areas (SMSA's)

SCALE

0
10
20
30
40
50 MILES

U.S. DEPARTMENT OF COMMERCE
BUREAU OF THE CENSUS

KAULA

LEHUA

NIIHAU

KAUAI

KAUAI CO.
HONOLULU CO.

OAHU

HONOLULU

HONOLULU

HONOLULU CO.
MAUI CO.

MOLOKAI

LANAI

KAHOOLAWE

MAUI

MAUI CO.
HAWAII CO.

HAWAII

HILO

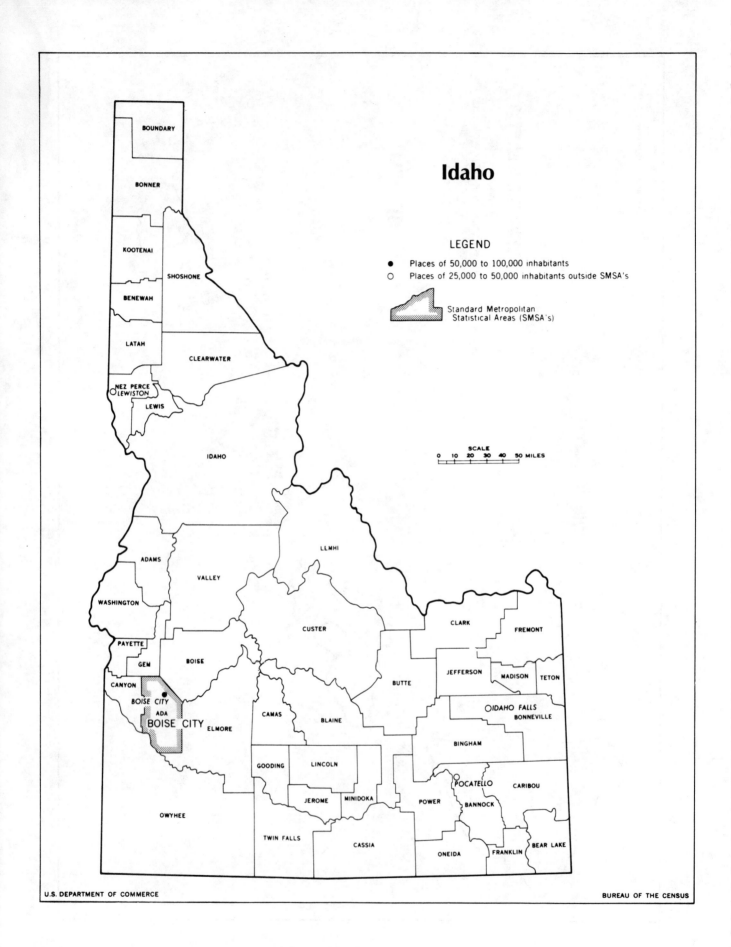

Idaho

LEGEND

● Places of 50,000 to 100,000 inhabitants

○ Places of 25,000 to 50,000 inhabitants outside SMSA's

Standard Metropolitan Statistical Areas (SMSA's)

SCALE

0 10 20 30 40 50 MILES

BOUNDARY

BONNER

KOOTENAI

SHOSHONE

BENEWAH

LATAH

CLEARWATER

NEZ PERCE
○LEWISTON

LEWIS

IDAHO

ADAMS

VALLEY

LEMHI

WASHINGTON

CUSTER

CLARK

FREMONT

PAYETTE

BOISE

JEFFERSON

MADISON

TETON

GEM

BUTTE

CANYON

●
BOISE CITY

ADA

BOISE CITY ELMORE

CAMAS

BLAINE

○IDAHO FALLS
BONNEVILLE

BINGHAM

GOODING

LINCOLN

○POCATELLO

CARIBOU

JEROME

MINIDOKA

POWER

BANNOCK

OWYHEE

TWIN FALLS

CASSIA

ONEIDA

FRANKLIN

BEAR LAKE

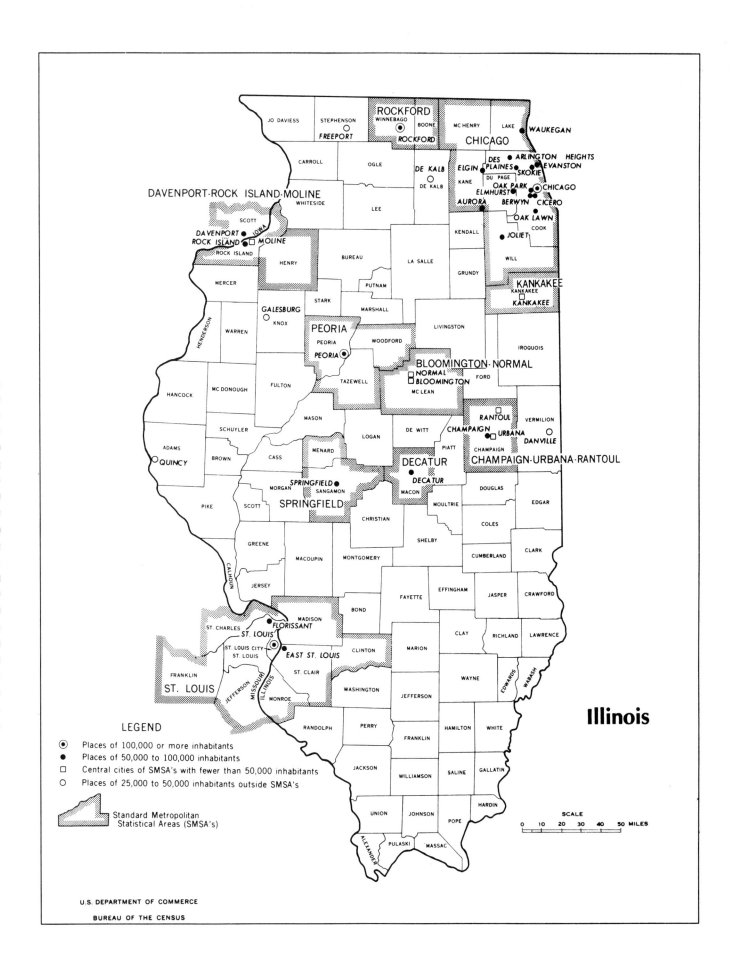

Illinois

LEGEND

⊙   Places of 100,000 or more inhabitants
●   Places of 50,000 to 100,000 inhabitants
□   Central cities of SMSA's with fewer than 50,000 inhabitants
○   Places of 25,000 to 50,000 inhabitants outside SMSA's

Standard Metropolitan
Statistical Areas (SMSA's)

SCALE

0   10   20   30   40   50 MILES

U.S. DEPARTMENT OF COMMERCE

BUREAU OF THE CENSUS

Indiana

LEGEND

- ◉ Places of 100,000 or more inhabitants
- ● Places of 50,000 to 100,000 inhabitants
- ☐ SMSA central cities with fewer than 50,000 inhabitants
- ○ Places of 25,000 to 50,000 inhabitants outside SMSA's

Standard Metropolitan
Statistical Areas (SMSA's)

SCALE

0   10   20   30   40   50 MILES

U.S. DEPARTMENT OF COMMERCE
BUREAU OF THE CENSUS

B 464

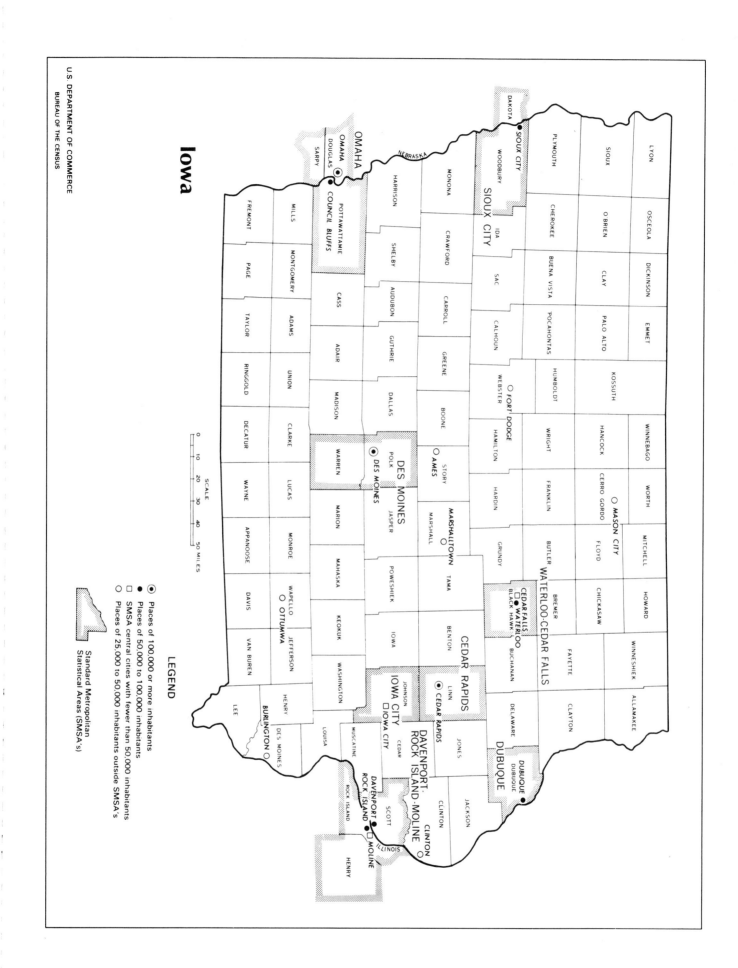

Iowa

U.S. DEPARTMENT OF COMMERCE
BUREAU OF THE CENSUS

LEGEND

- ⊙ Places of 100,000 or more inhabitants
- ● Places of 50,000 to 100,000 inhabitants
- ☐ SMSA central cities with fewer than 50,000 inhabitants
- ○ Places of 25,000 to 50,000 inhabitants outside SMSA's

Standard Metropolitan
Statistical Areas (SMSA's)

SCALE
0 10 20 30 40 50 MILES

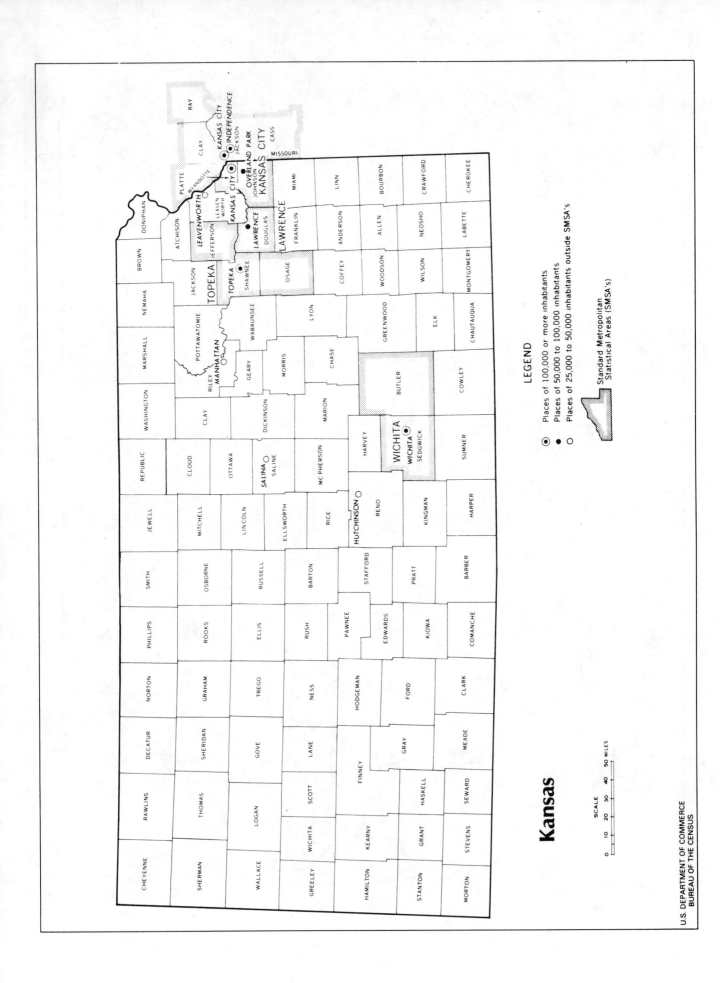

Kansas

U.S. DEPARTMENT OF COMMERCE
BUREAU OF THE CENSUS

SCALE

0   10   20   30   40   50 MILES

LEGEND

⊙ Places of 100,000 or more inhabitants

● Places of 50,000 to 100,000 inhabitants

○ Places of 25,000 to 50,000 inhabitants outside SMSA's

Standard Metropolitan
Statistical Areas (SMSA's)

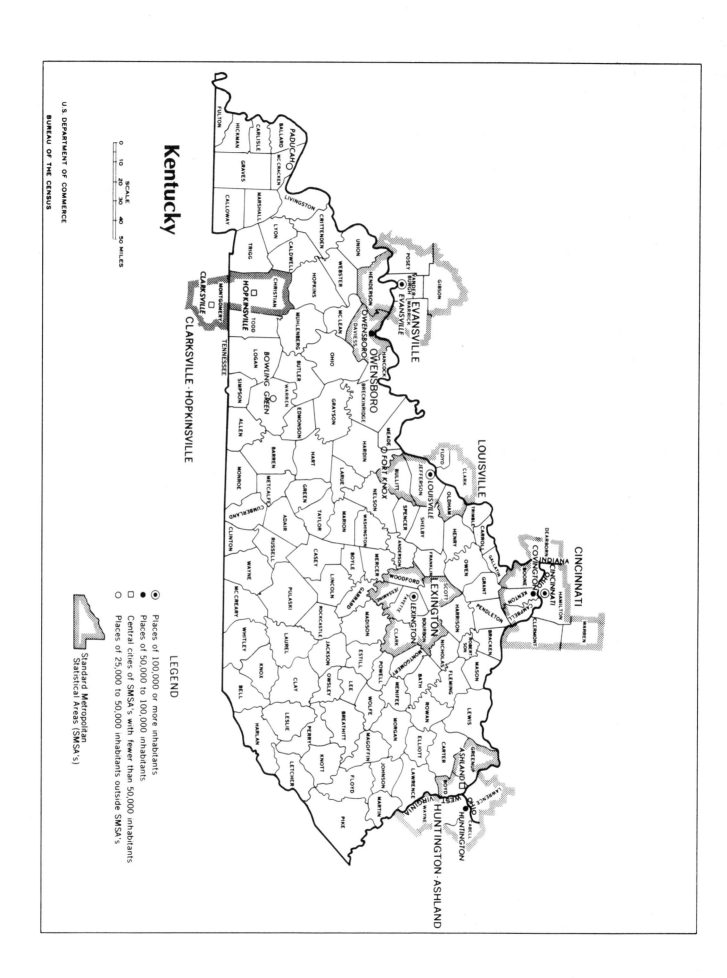

Kentucky

SCALE
0 10 20 30 40 50 MILES

U.S. DEPARTMENT OF COMMERCE
BUREAU OF THE CENSUS

LEGEND

⊙ Places of 100,000 or more inhabitants
● Places of 50,000 to 100,000 inhabitants
□ Central cities of SMSA's with fewer than 50,000 inhabitants
○ Places of 25,000 to 50,000 inhabitants outside SMSA's

Standard Metropolitan
Statistical Areas (SMSA's)

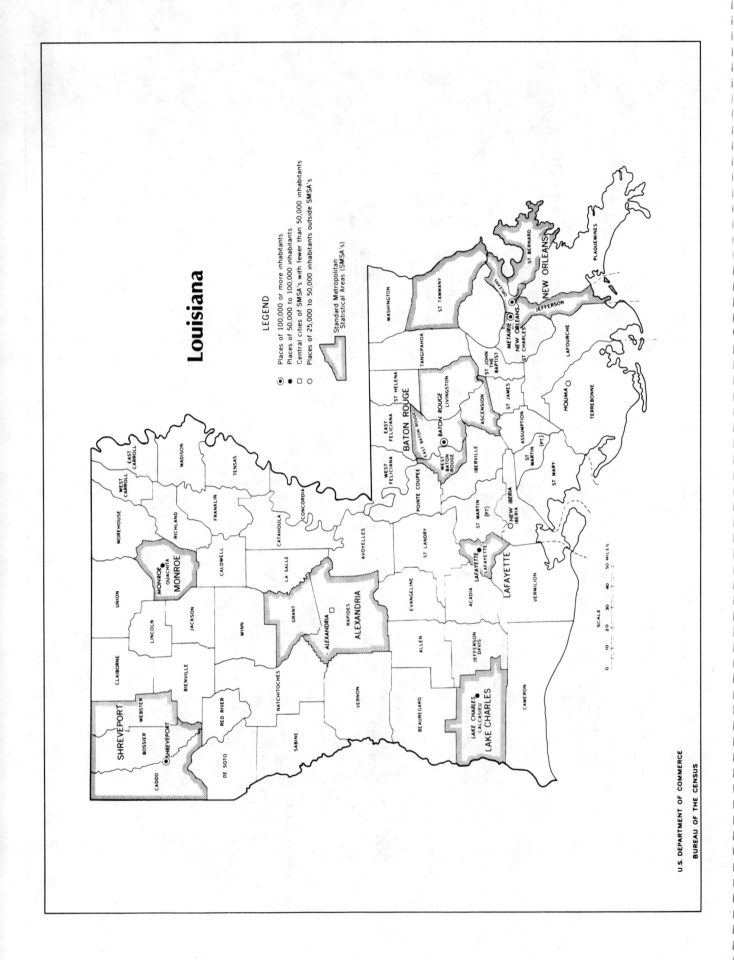

Louisiana

U.S. DEPARTMENT OF COMMERCE
BUREAU OF THE CENSUS

B 468

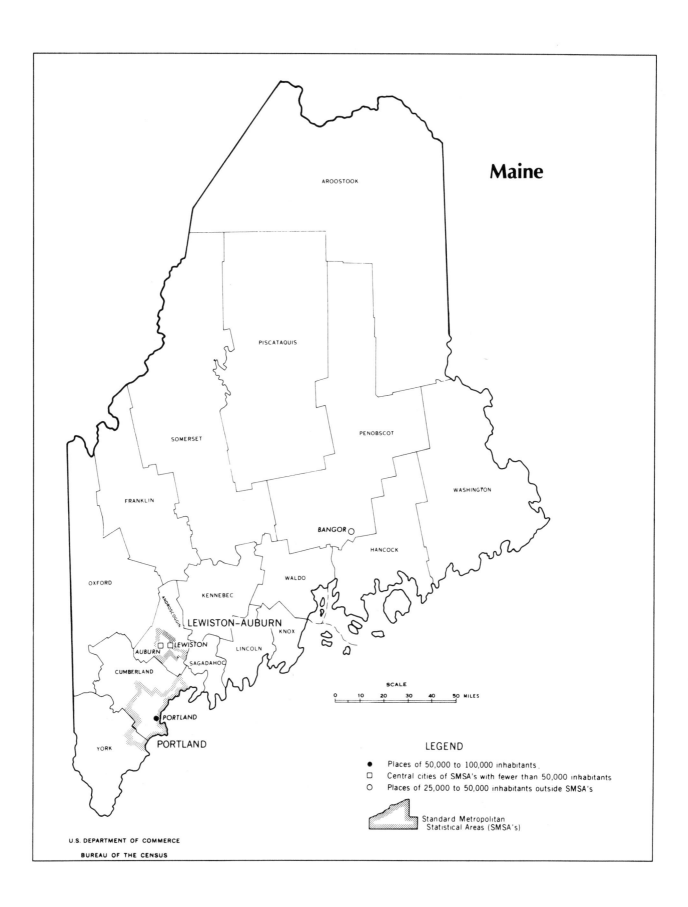

Maine

BANGOR ○

LEWISTON-AUBURN

□ AUBURN □ LEWISTON

● PORTLAND

PORTLAND

AROOSTOOK

PISCATAQUIS

SOMERSET

PENOBSCOT

WASHINGTON

FRANKLIN

OXFORD

KENNEBEC

WALDO

HANCOCK

ANDROSCOGGIN

KNOX

LINCOLN

SAGADAHOC

CUMBERLAND

YORK

SCALE

0   10   20   30   40   50 MILES

LEGEND

● Places of 50,000 to 100,000 inhabitants.
□ Central cities of SMSA's with fewer than 50,000 inhabitants
○ Places of 25,000 to 50,000 inhabitants outside SMSA's

Standard Metropolitan
Statistical Areas (SMSA's)

U.S. DEPARTMENT OF COMMERCE

BUREAU OF THE CENSUS

Maryland

SCALE
0 10 20 30 MILES

SCALE
0 10 20 30 MILES

LEGEND

- ◉ Places of 100,000 or more inhabitants
- ● Places of 50,000 to 100,000 inhabitants
- ○ Places of 25,000 to 50,000 inhabitants outside SMSA's

Standard Metropolitan
Statistical Areas (SMSA's)

U.S. DEPARTMENT OF COMMERCE
BUREAU OF THE CENSUS

GARRETT

ALLEGANY
○ CUMBERLAND

WASHINGTON
○ HAGERSTOWN

FREDERICK

CARROLL

BALTIMORE

BALTIMORE
◉ BALTIMORE CITY

HARFORD

CECIL

WILMINGTON
NEW CASTLE
DELAWARE
NEW JERSEY
SALEM
● WILMINGTON

MONTGOMERY

HOWARD

ANNE ARUNDEL

KENT

QUEEN ANNES

CAROLINE

LOUDOUN

VIRGINIA

FAIRFAX CITY
FALLS CHURCH CITY
FAIRFAX
ARLINGTON
ALEXANDRIA CITY
◉ ALEXANDRIA

MANASSAS CITY
MANASSAS PARK CITY
PRINCE WILLIAM

PRINCE GEORGES

WASHINGTON
◉ WASHINGTON
D C

CHARLES

CALVERT

ST MARYS

DORCHESTER

TALBOT

WICOMICO

SOMERSET

WORCESTER

B 470

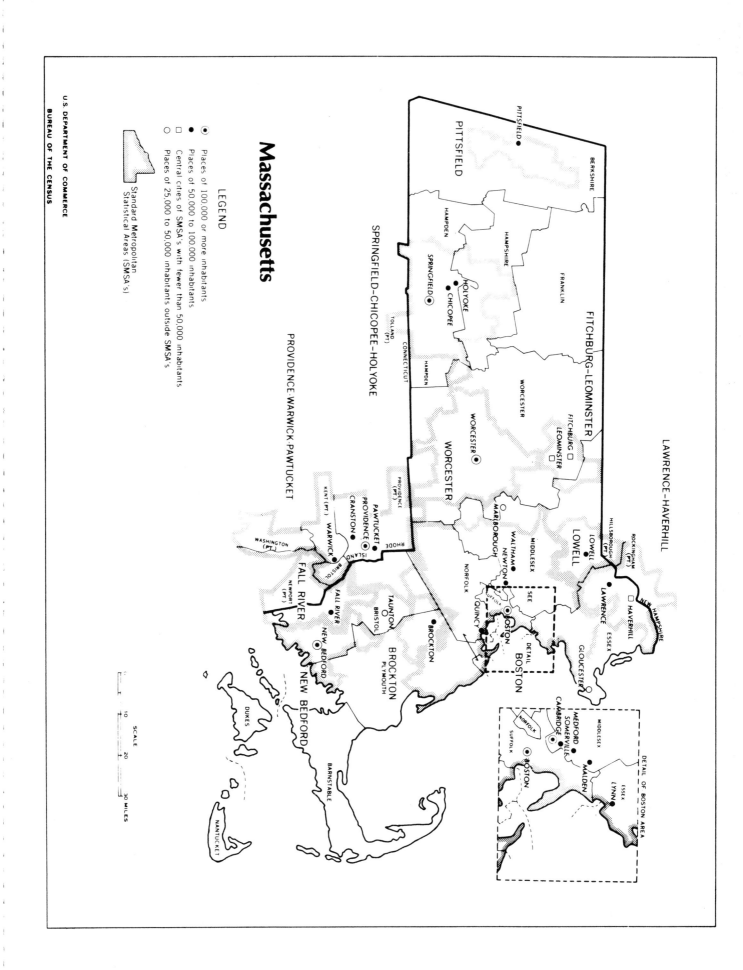

Massachusetts

U.S. DEPARTMENT OF COMMERCE
BUREAU OF THE CENSUS

LEGEND

⊙ Places of 100,000 or more inhabitants
● Places of 50,000 to 100,000 inhabitants
□ Central cities of SMSA's with fewer than 50,000 inhabitants
○ Places of 25,000 to 50,000 inhabitants outside SMSA's

Standard Metropolitan
Statistical Areas (SMSA's)

SCALE

0   10   20   30 MILES

PITTSFIELD

BERKSHIRE

HAMPDEN

HAMPSHIRE

FRANKLIN

SPRINGFIELD-CHICOPEE-HOLYOKE

SPRINGFIELD ⊙
HOLYOKE ●
CHICOPEE ●

TOLLAND (PT)

CONNECTICUT

HAMPDEN

WORCESTER

FITCHBURG-LEOMINSTER

FITCHBURG □
LEOMINSTER □

LAWRENCE-HAVERHILL

WORCESTER ⊙

MARLBOROUGH ○

WALTHAM ●

MIDDLESEX

NEWTON ●

NORFOLK

SUFFOLK

QUINCY ●

LOWELL ●

HILLSBOROUGH (PT)

ROCKINGHAM (PT)

NEW HAMPSHIRE

LAWRENCE ●

HAVERHILL □

ESSEX

GLOUCESTER ○

SEE DETAIL

BOSTON ⊙

BOSTON

PROVIDENCE-WARWICK-PAWTUCKET

KENT (PT)

WASHINGTON (PT)

PROVIDENCE (PT)

PAWTUCKET ●

PROVIDENCE ●

CRANSTON ●

WARWICK ●

RHODE ISLAND

BRISTOL

NEWPORT (PT)

FALL RIVER

FALL RIVER ●

TAUNTON ○

BRISTOL

BROCKTON

NEW BEDFORD ⊙

BROCKTON ●

PLYMOUTH

NEW BEDFORD

BARNSTABLE

DUKES

NANTUCKET

DETAIL OF BOSTON AREA

NORFOLK

SUFFOLK

CAMBRIDGE ⊙

MEDFORD ●

SOMERVILLE ●

MIDDLESEX

MALDEN ●

BOSTON ⊙

LYNN ●

ESSEX

LEGEND

- ⊙ Places of 100,000 or more inhabitants
- ● Places of 50,000 to 100,000 inhabitants
- □ SMSA central cities with fewer than 50,000 inhabitants
- ○ Places of 25,000 to 50,000 inhabitants outside SMSA's

Standard Metropolitan Statistical Areas (SMSA's)

1. DEARBORN HEIGHTS
2. PONTIAC
3. ROSEVILLE
4. ROYAL OAK
5. ST. CLAIR SHORES
6. SOUTHFIELD
7. STERLING HEIGHTS
8. TAYLOR
9. WESTLAND
10. FARMINGTON HILLS
11. TROY

Michigan

SCALE
0 10 20 30 40 50 MILES

U.S. DEPARTMENT OF COMMERCE
BUREAU OF THE CENSUS

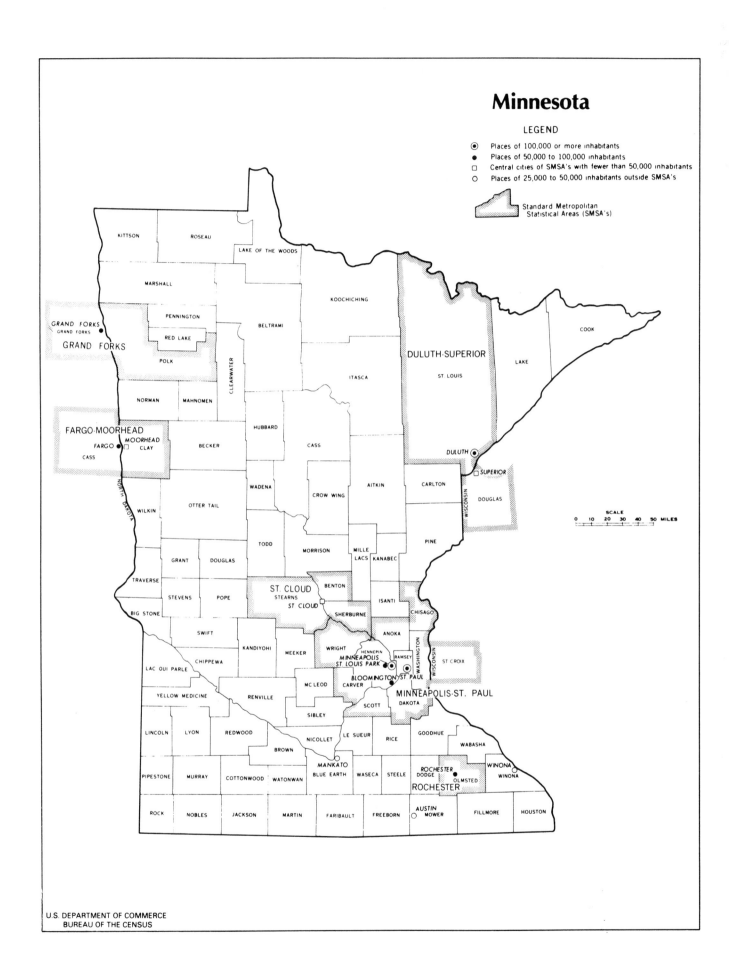

Minnesota

LEGEND

⊙ Places of 100,000 or more inhabitants
● Places of 50,000 to 100,000 inhabitants
□ Central cities of SMSA's with fewer than 50,000 inhabitants
○ Places of 25,000 to 50,000 inhabitants outside SMSA's

Standard Metropolitan Statistical Areas (SMSA's)

KITTSON
ROSEAU
LAKE OF THE WOODS
MARSHALL
KOOCHICHING
PENNINGTON
BELTRAMI
GRAND FORKS
GRAND FORKS
RED LAKE
DULUTH-SUPERIOR
COOK
GRAND FORKS
POLK
CLEARWATER
ITASCA
ST LOUIS
LAKE
NORMAN
MAHNOMEN
FARGO-MOORHEAD
HUBBARD
MOORHEAD
FARGO ● □ CLAY
BECKER
CASS
CASS
WADENA
CROW WING
AITKIN
CARLTON
DULUTH ⊙
NORTH DAKOTA
SUPERIOR □
OTTER TAIL
DOUGLAS
WISCONSIN
WILKIN
TODD
MILLE
LACS
KANABEC
PINE
MORRISON
GRANT
DOUGLAS
TRAVERSE
ST. CLOUD
BENTON
ISANTI
STEARNS
STEVENS
POPE
ST CLOUD
SHERBURNE
CHISAGO
BIG STONE
ANOKA
SWIFT
KANDIYOHI
MEEKER
WRIGHT
HENNEPIN
ST CROIX
CHIPPEWA
MINNEAPOLIS
ST. LOUIS PARK
RAMSEY
WASHINGTON
LAC QUI PARLE
BLOOMINGTON ST. PAUL
WISCONSIN
YELLOW MEDICINE
RENVILLE
MC LEOD
CARVER
MINNEAPOLIS-ST. PAUL
SIBLEY
SCOTT
DAKOTA
LINCOLN
LYON
REDWOOD
NICOLLET
LE SUEUR
RICE
GOODHUE
WABASHA
BROWN
MANKATO
WINONA
PIPESTONE
MURRAY
COTTONWOOD
WATONWAN
BLUE EARTH
WASECA
STEELE
ROCHESTER
DODGE
OLMSTED
WINONA
ROCHESTER
ROCK
NOBLES
JACKSON
MARTIN
FARIBAULT
FREEBORN
AUSTIN
MOWER
FILLMORE
HOUSTON

SCALE
0 10 20 30 40 50 MILES

U.S. DEPARTMENT OF COMMERCE
BUREAU OF THE CENSUS

Mississippi

TIPTON

CRITTENDEN SHELBY

⊙ MEMPHIS
MEMPHIS TENNESSEE

MISSISSIPPI

BENTON ALCORN

DE SOTO

MARSHALL TIPPAH

TUNICA

TATE UNION PRENTISS

TISHOMINGO

PANOLA LAFAYETTE

COAHOMA QUITMAN PONTOTOC LEE ITAWAMBA

YALOBUSHA

TALLAHATCHIE CALHOUN CHICKASAW MONROE

BOLIVAR

GRENADA

CLAY

SUNFLOWER LEFLORE WEBSTER

○ COLUMBUS

CARROLL OKTIBBEHA LOWNDES

○ GREENVILLE CHOCTAW

WASHINGTON MONTGOMERY

HUMPHREYS HOLMES ATTALA WINSTON NOXUBEE

SHARKEY

YAZOO LEAKE NESHOBA KEMPER

ISSAQUENA MADISON

JACKSON

WARREN

○ VICKSBURG JACKSON ⊙ SCOTT NEWTON LAUDERDALE

HINDS RANKIN ○ MERIDIAN

CLAIBORNE SMITH JASPER CLARKE

COPIAH SIMPSON

JEFFERSON

COVINGTON JONES WAYNE

ADAMS FRANKLIN LINCOLN LAWRENCE JEFFERSON DAVIS

○ HATTIESBURG GREENE

WILKINSON AMITE PIKE MARION LAMAR FORREST PERRY

WALTHALL

GEORGE

PEARL RIVER STONE PASCAGOULA-MOSS POINT

JACKSON

BILOXI-GULFPORT MOSS POINT

HARRISON

HANCOCK BILOXI PASCAGOULA

GULFPORT

LEGEND

⊙ Places of 100,000 or more inhabitants
☐ Central cities of SMSA's with fewer than 50,000 inhabitants
○ Places of 25,000 to 50,000 inhabitants outside SMSA's

Standard Metropolitan
Statistical Areas (SMSA's)

SCALE
0 10 20 30 40 50 MILES

U.S. DEPARTMENT OF COMMERCE
BUREAU OF THE CENSUS

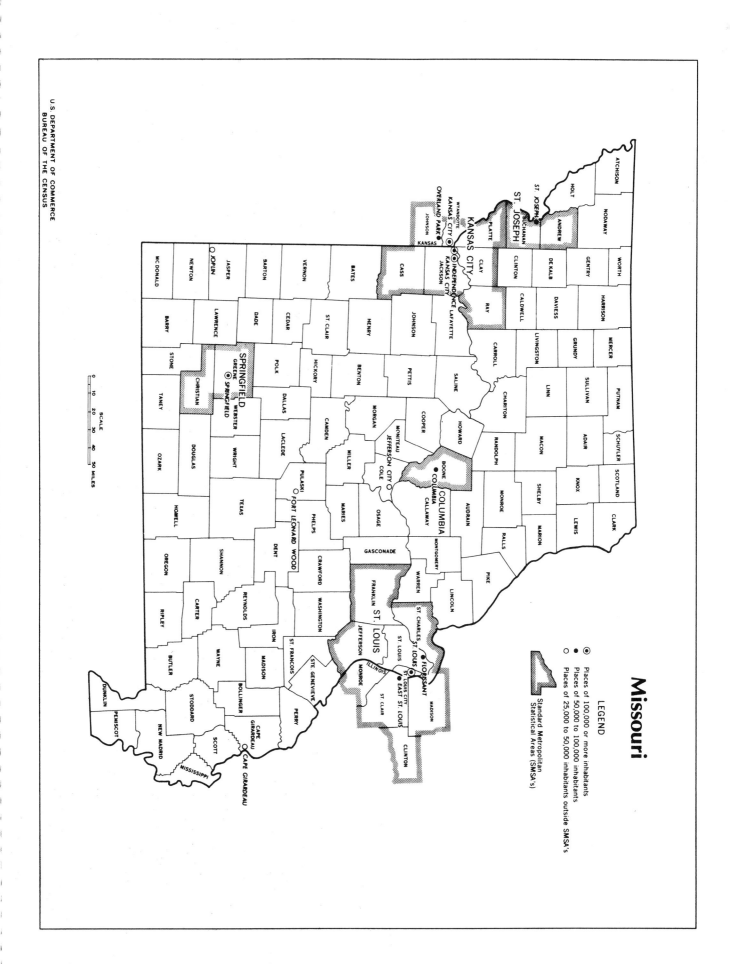

Missouri

LEGEND

◉ Places of 100,000 or more inhabitants

● Places of 50,000 to 100,000 inhabitants

○ Places of 25,000 to 50,000 inhabitants outside SMSA's

Standard Metropolitan
Statistical Areas (SMSA's)

SCALE

0 10 20 30 40 50 MILES

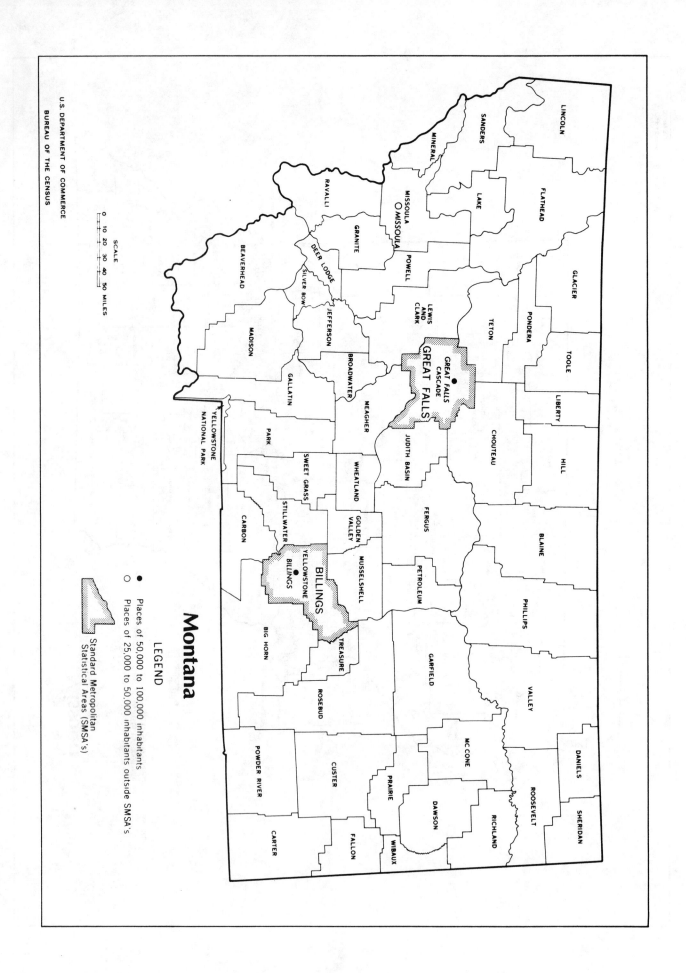

Montana

U.S. DEPARTMENT OF COMMERCE
BUREAU OF THE CENSUS

SCALE

0 10 20 30 40 50 MILES

LEGEND

● Places of 50,000 to 100,000 inhabitants

○ Places of 25,000 to 50,000 inhabitants outside SMSA's

Standard Metropolitan
Statistical Areas (SMSA's)

LINCOLN

SANDERS

MINERAL

RAVALLI

MISSOULA
○ MISSOULA

LAKE

FLATHEAD

GLACIER

GRANITE

POWELL

DEER LODGE

SILVER BOW

BEAVERHEAD

JEFFERSON

LEWIS
AND
CLARK

TETON

PONDERA

TOOLE

LIBERTY

HILL

GREAT FALLS
CASCADE
GREAT FALLS

CHOUTEAU

MADISON

BROADWATER

MEAGHER

JUDITH BASIN

GALLATIN

PARK

SWEET GRASS

WHEATLAND

FERGUS

PETROLEUM

BLAINE

PHILLIPS

YELLOWSTONE
NATIONAL PARK

STILLWATER

GOLDEN
VALLEY

MUSSELSHELL

CARBON

YELLOWSTONE
● BILLINGS
BILLINGS

TREASURE

GARFIELD

VALLEY

DANIELS

BIG HORN

ROSEBUD

CUSTER

MC CONE

PRAIRIE

DAWSON

RICHLAND

ROOSEVELT

SHERIDAN

POWDER RIVER

CARTER

FALLON

WIBAUX

B 476

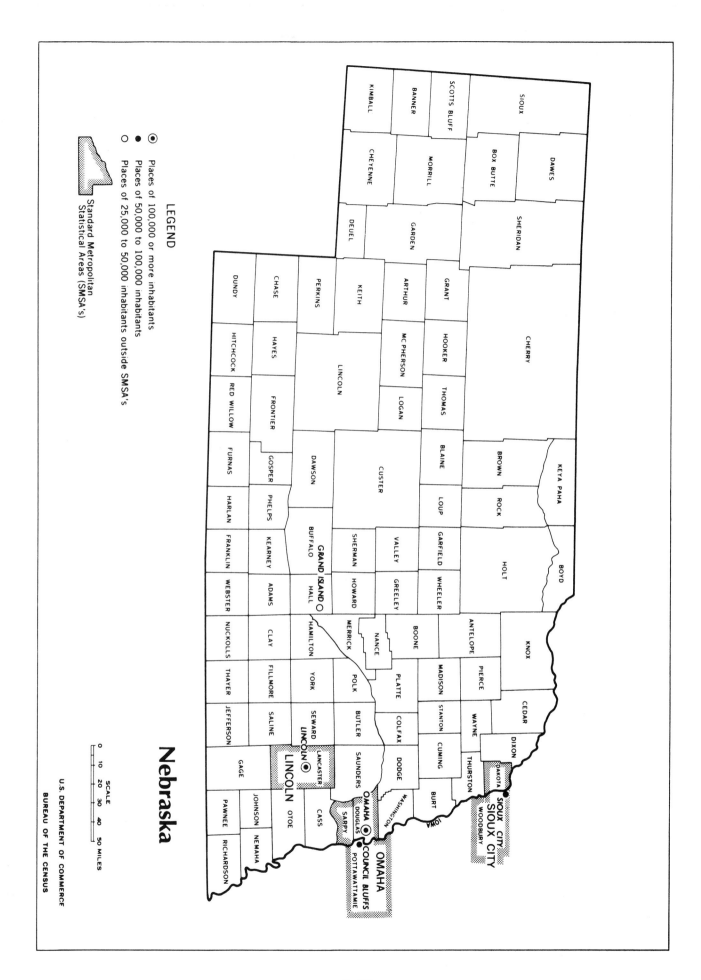

Nebraska

LEGEND

⊙ Places of 100,000 or more inhabitants

● Places of 50,000 to 100,000 inhabitants

○ Places of 25,000 to 50,000 inhabitants outside SMSA's

Standard Metropolitan Statistical Areas (SMSA's)

SCALE

0 10 20 30 40 50 MILES

U.S. DEPARTMENT OF COMMERCE
BUREAU OF THE CENSUS

B 477

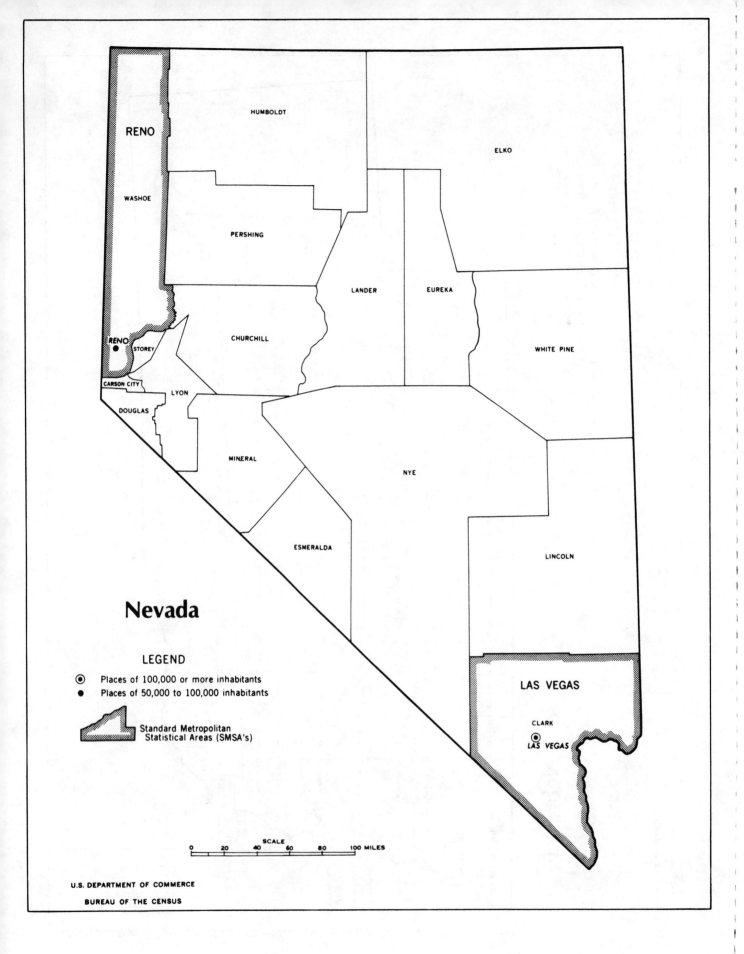

Nevada

LEGEND

⊙ Places of 100,000 or more inhabitants
● Places of 50,000 to 100,000 inhabitants

Standard Metropolitan
Statistical Areas (SMSA's)

RENO

WASHOE

HUMBOLDT

ELKO

PERSHING

LANDER

EUREKA

WHITE PINE

CHURCHILL

RENO
● STOREY

CARSON CITY

LYON

DOUGLAS

MINERAL

NYE

ESMERALDA

LINCOLN

LAS VEGAS

CLARK

⊙ LAS VEGAS

SCALE
0   20   40   60   80   100 MILES

U.S. DEPARTMENT OF COMMERCE

BUREAU OF THE CENSUS

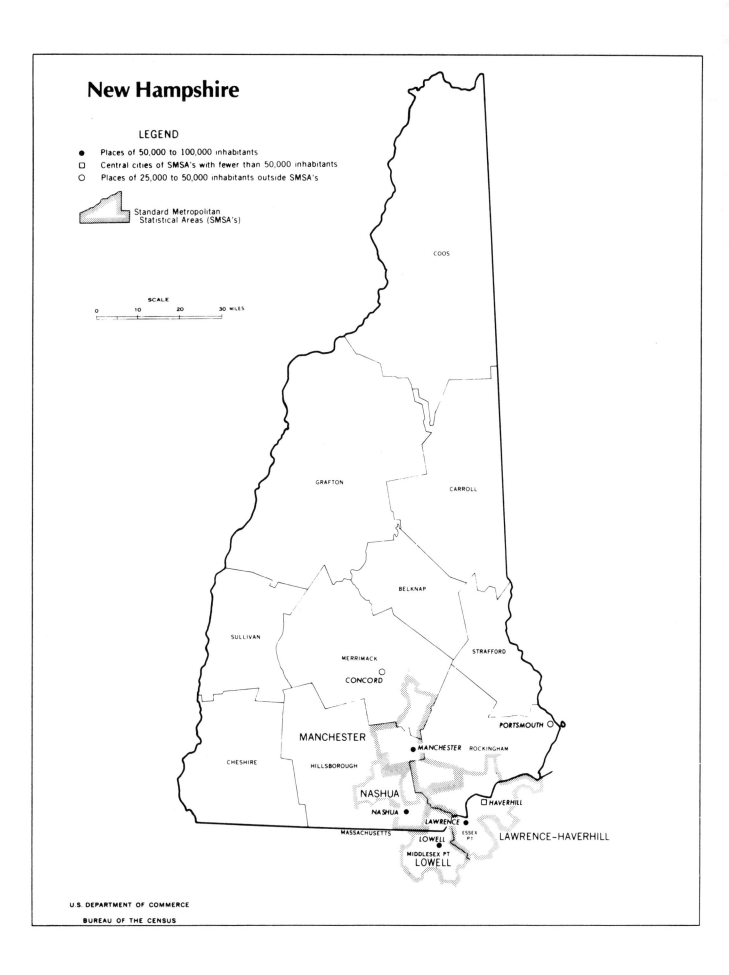

New Hampshire

LEGEND

● Places of 50,000 to 100,000 inhabitants

□ Central cities of SMSA's with fewer than 50,000 inhabitants

○ Places of 25,000 to 50,000 inhabitants outside SMSA's

Standard Metropolitan Statistical Areas (SMSA's)

SCALE

0   10   20   30 MILES

COOS

GRAFTON

CARROLL

BELKNAP

SULLIVAN

STRAFFORD

MERRIMACK

○ CONCORD

CHESHIRE

MANCHESTER

HILLSBOROUGH

PORTSMOUTH ○

● MANCHESTER   ROCKINGHAM

NASHUA

□ HAVERHILL

NASHUA ●

LAWRENCE ●

MASSACHUSETTS   ESSEX PT   LAWRENCE–HAVERHILL

LOWELL ●

MIDDLESEX PT

LOWELL

U.S. DEPARTMENT OF COMMERCE

BUREAU OF THE CENSUS

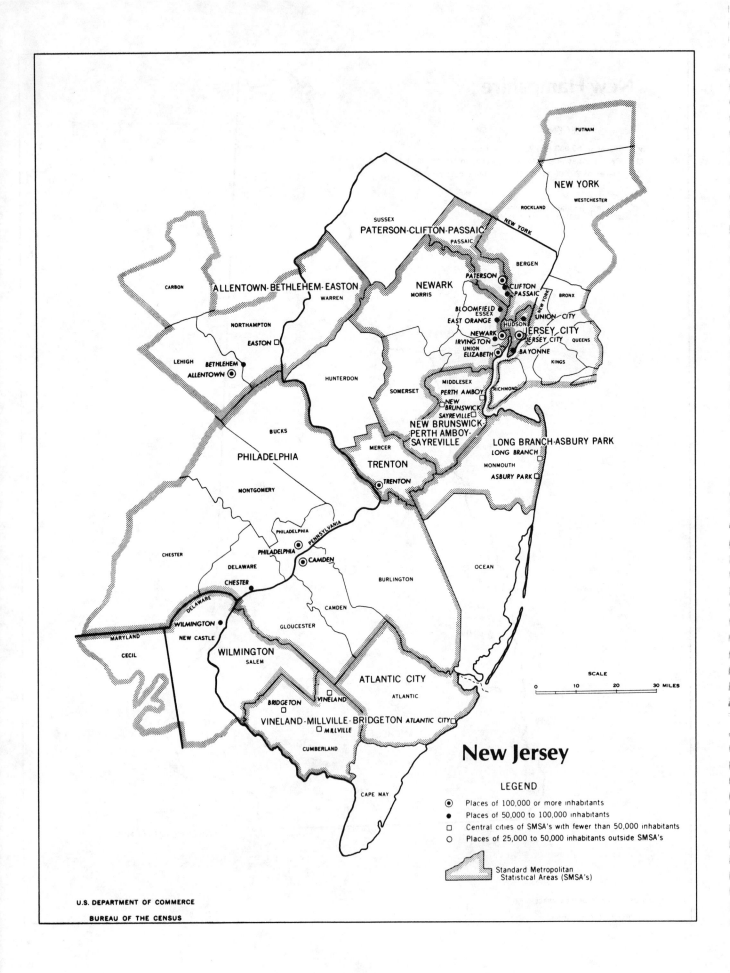

New Jersey

PUTNAM

NEW YORK

ROCKLAND   WESTCHESTER

SUSSEX

PATERSON-CLIFTON-PASSAIC

NEW YORK

PASSAIC

BERGEN

CARBON

ALLENTOWN-BETHLEHEM-EASTON

NEWARK

PATERSON

WARREN   MORRIS   CLIFTON

PASSAIC

BRONX

NORTHAMPTON

BLOOMFIELD

UNION CITY

ESSEX

EAST ORANGE

EASTON

HUDSON   JERSEY CITY

LEHIGH   NEWARK   JERSEY CITY

BETHLEHEM   IRVINGTON

ALLENTOWN   UNION   QUEENS

ELIZABETH   BAYONNE

HUNTERDON   KINGS

MIDDLESEX

SOMERSET   PERTH AMBOY   RICHMOND

NEW
BUCKS   BRUNSWICK

SAYREVILLE

PHILADELPHIA   MERCER   NEW BRUNSWICK-
PERTH AMBOY-   LONG BRANCH-ASBURY PARK
SAYREVILLE
LONG BRANCH

MONMOUTH

TRENTON   ASBURY PARK

MONTGOMERY

TRENTON

PHILADELPHIA
PENNSYLVANIA

CHESTER   OCEAN

PHILADELPHIA

DELAWARE   CAMDEN

CHESTER   BURLINGTON

CAMDEN

DELAWARE

MARYLAND   WILMINGTON

CECIL   NEW CASTLE

GLOUCESTER

WILMINGTON

SALEM   SCALE

ATLANTIC CITY   0   10   20   30 MILES

BRIDGETON   VINELAND   ATLANTIC

VINELAND-MILLVILLE-BRIDGETON ATLANTIC CITY

MILLVILLE

CUMBERLAND

CAPE MAY

LEGEND

- ⊙ Places of 100,000 or more inhabitants
- ● Places of 50,000 to 100,000 inhabitants
- □ Central cities of SMSA's with fewer than 50,000 inhabitants
- ○ Places of 25,000 to 50,000 inhabitants outside SMSA's

Standard Metropolitan
Statistical Areas (SMSA's)

U.S. DEPARTMENT OF COMMERCE

BUREAU OF THE CENSUS

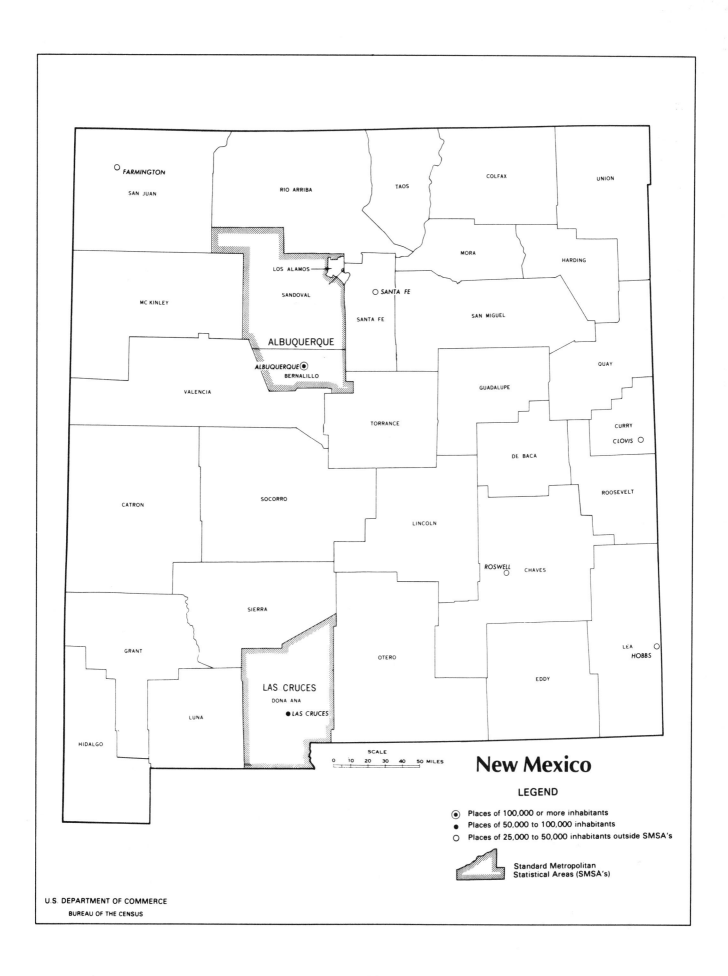

FARMINGTON ◯

SAN JUAN

RIO ARRIBA

TAOS

COLFAX

UNION

MORA

HARDING

MC KINLEY

SANDOVAL

LOS ALAMOS

◯ SANTA FE

SANTA FE

SAN MIGUEL

ALBUQUERQUE

ALBUQUERQUE ◉
BERNALILLO

QUAY

VALENCIA

GUADALUPE

TORRANCE

CURRY

CLOVIS ◯

DE BACA

ROOSEVELT

CATRON

SOCORRO

LINCOLN

ROSWELL ◯   CHAVES

SIERRA

LEA
HOBBS ◯

GRANT

OTERO

EDDY

LAS CRUCES

DONA ANA

● LAS CRUCES

LUNA

HIDALGO

SCALE
0 10 20 30 40 50 MILES

New Mexico

LEGEND

◉ Places of 100,000 or more inhabitants

● Places of 50,000 to 100,000 inhabitants

◯ Places of 25,000 to 50,000 inhabitants outside SMSA's

Standard Metropolitan
Statistical Areas (SMSA's)

U.S. DEPARTMENT OF COMMERCE
BUREAU OF THE CENSUS

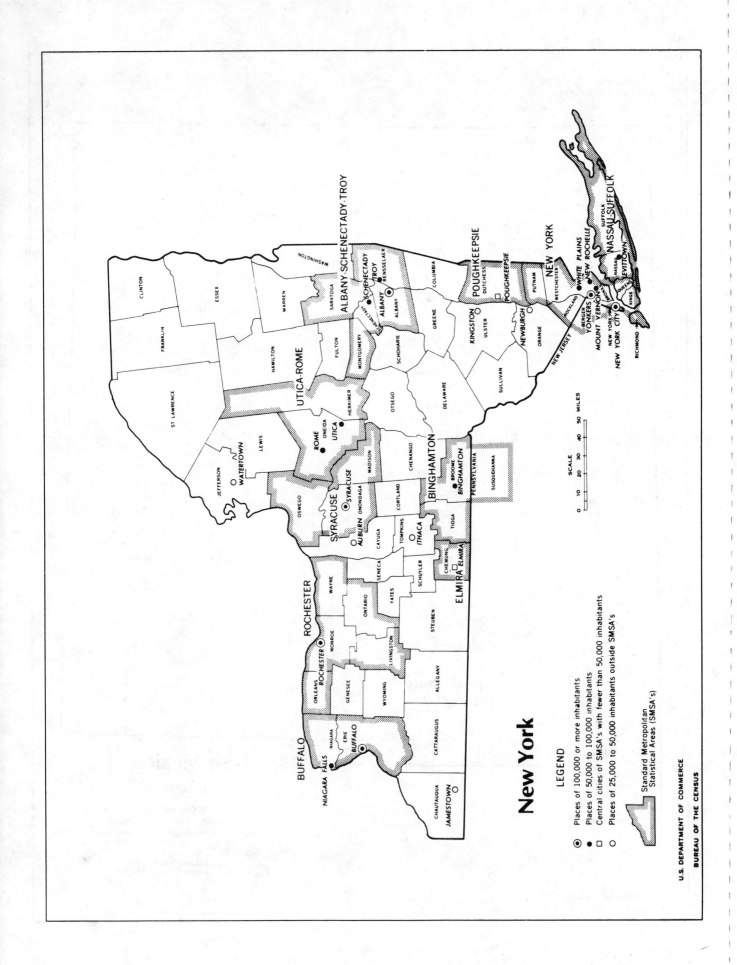

New York

LEGEND

⊙ Places of 100,000 or more inhabitants

● Places of 50,000 to 100,000 inhabitants

□ Central cities of SMSA's with fewer than 50,000 inhabitants

○ Places of 25,000 to 50,000 inhabitants outside SMSA's

Standard Metropolitan
Statistical Areas (SMSA's)

U.S. DEPARTMENT OF COMMERCE

BUREAU OF THE CENSUS

SCALE

0   10   20   30   40   50 MILES

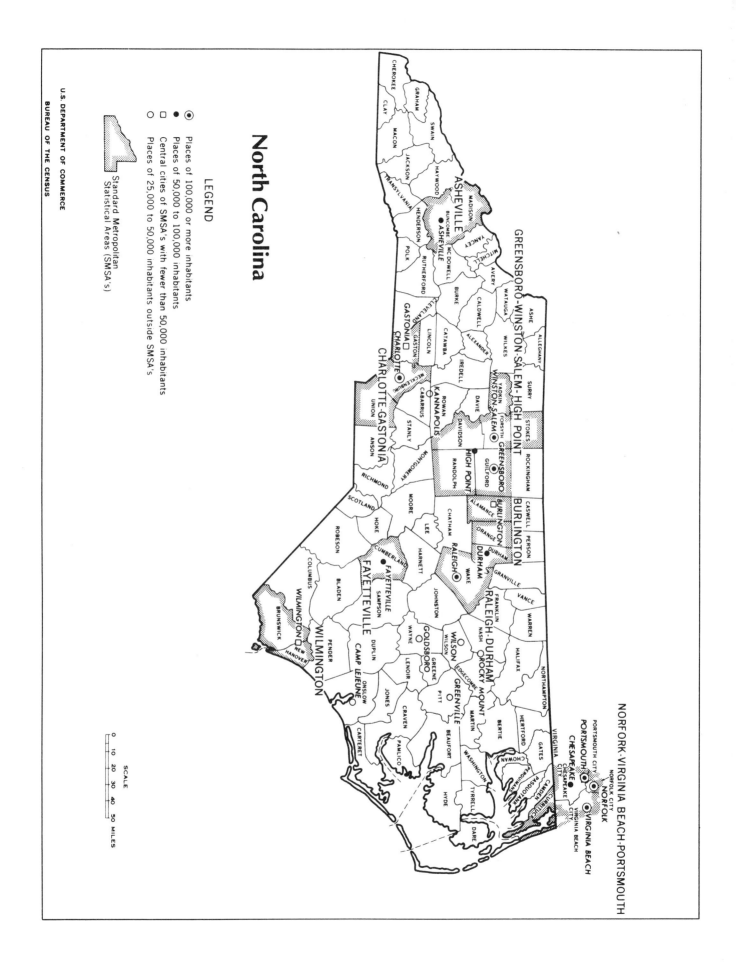

North Carolina

LEGEND

- ⊙ Places of 100,000 or more inhabitants
- ● Places of 50,000 to 100,000 inhabitants
- □ Central cities of SMSA's with fewer than 50,000 inhabitants
- ○ Places of 25,000 to 50,000 inhabitants outside SMSA's

Standard Metropolitan
Statistical Areas (SMSA's)

U.S. DEPARTMENT OF COMMERCE
BUREAU OF THE CENSUS

SCALE

0 10 20 30 40 50 MILES

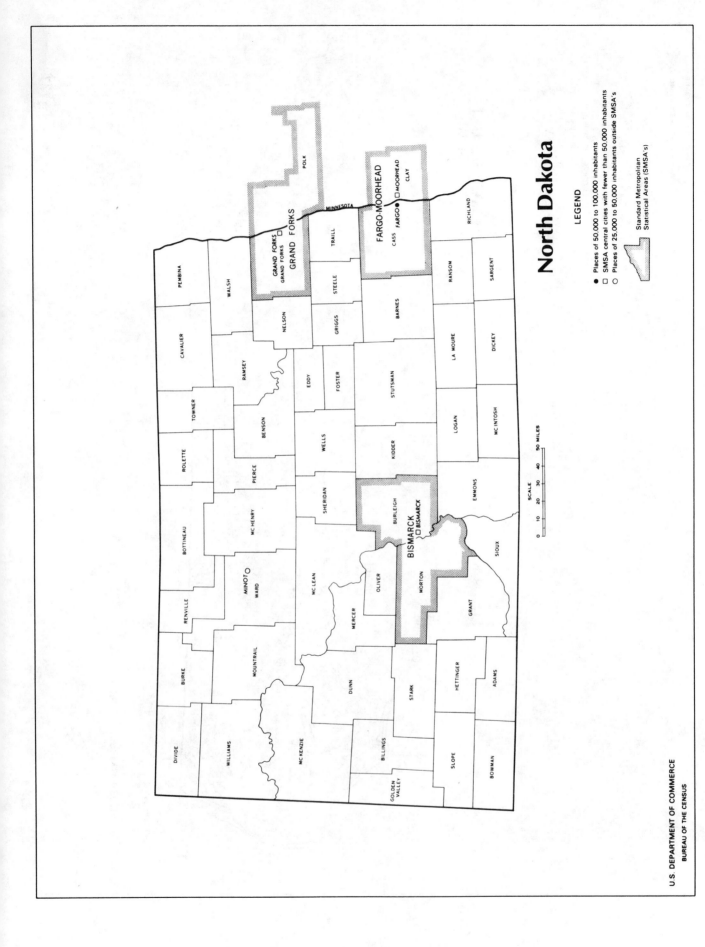

North Dakota

SCALE

0   10   20   30   40   50 MILES

MINNESOTA

GRAND FORKS

FARGO-MOORHEAD

BISMARCK

MINOT

PEMBINA
WALSH
CAVALIER
RAMSEY
TOWNER
BENSON
ROLETTE
PIERCE
BOTTINEAU
McHENRY
WARD
RENVILLE
BURKE
MOUNTRAIL
DIVIDE
WILLIAMS
McKENZIE
DUNN
MERCER
OLIVER
McLEAN
SHERIDAN
WELLS
EDDY
FOSTER
NELSON
STEELE
GRIGGS
TRAILL
BARNES
STUTSMAN
KIDDER
LOGAN
LA MOURE
DICKEY
McINTOSH
EMMONS
BURLEIGH
MORTON
GRANT
SIOUX
STARK
HETTINGER
ADAMS
BILLINGS
GOLDEN VALLEY
SLOPE
BOWMAN
RANSOM
SARGENT
RICHLAND
CLAY
CASS
POLK

GRAND FORKS

MOORHEAD
FARGO

BISMARCK

U.S. DEPARTMENT OF COMMERCE
BUREAU OF THE CENSUS

Ohio

LEGEND

- ⊙ Places of 100,000 or more inhabitants
- ● Places of 50,000 to 100,000 inhabitants
- □ SMSA central cities with fewer than 50,000 inhabitants
- ○ Places of 25,000 to 50,000 inhabitants outside SMSA's

Standard Metropolitan
Statistical Areas (SMSA's)

SCALE
0 10 20 30 40 50 MILES

U.S. DEPARTMENT OF COMMERCE
BUREAU OF THE CENSUS

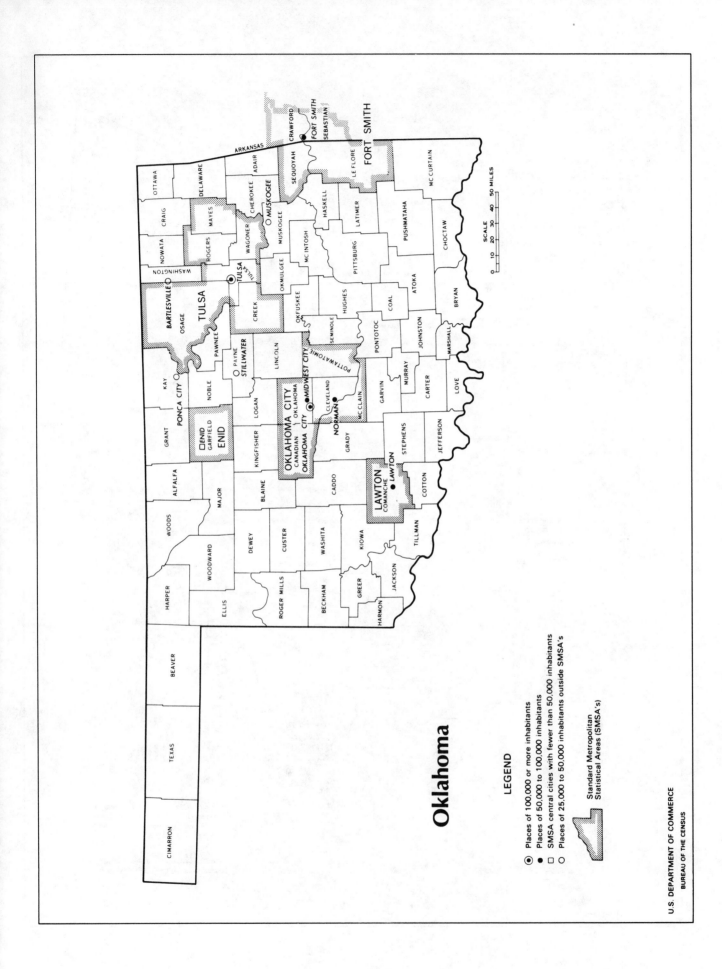

Oklahoma

LEGEND

- ⊙ Places of 100,000 or more inhabitants
- ● Places of 50,000 to 100,000 inhabitants
- □ SMSA central cities with fewer than 50,000 inhabitants
- ○ Places of 25,000 to 50,000 inhabitants outside SMSA's

Standard Metropolitan
Statistical Areas (SMSA's)

SCALE
0 10 20 30 40 50 MILES

U.S. DEPARTMENT OF COMMERCE
BUREAU OF THE CENSUS

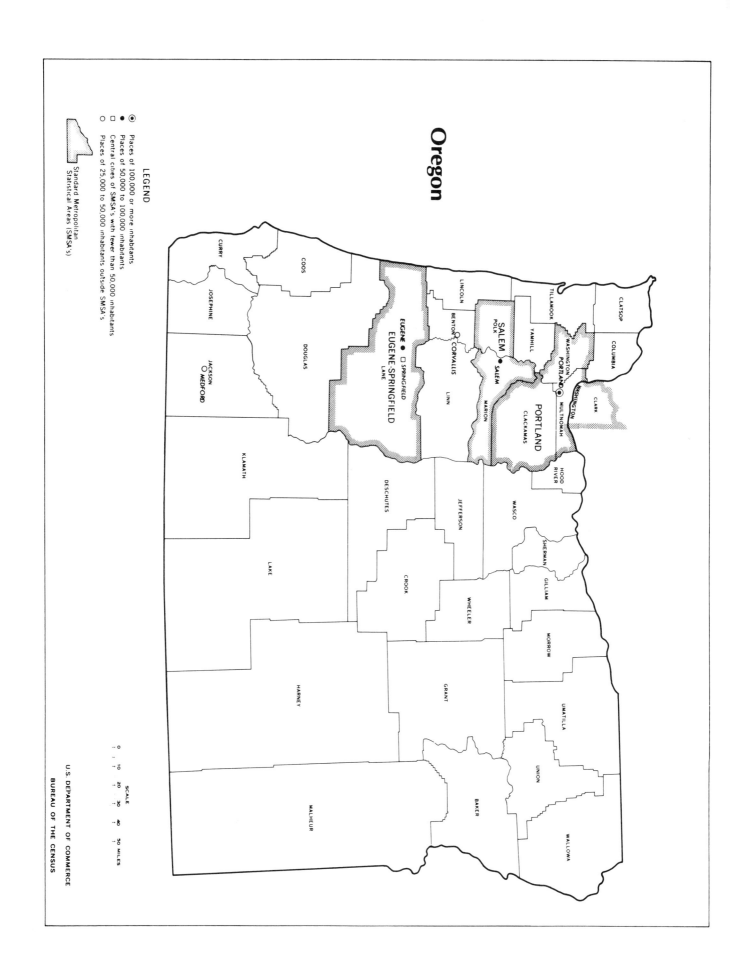

Oregon

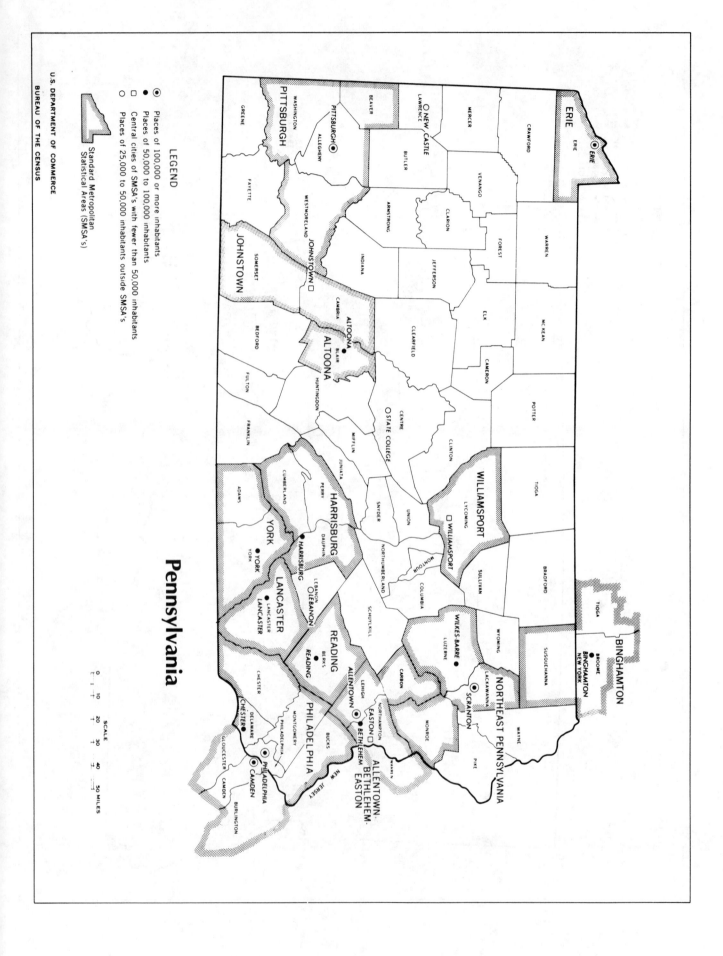

Pennsylvania

U.S. DEPARTMENT OF COMMERCE
BUREAU OF THE CENSUS

LEGEND

⊙ Places of 100,000 or more inhabitants

● Places of 50,000 to 100,000 inhabitants

☐ Central cities of SMSA's with fewer than 50,000 inhabitants

○ Places of 25,000 to 50,000 inhabitants outside SMSA's

◁ Standard Metropolitan Statistical Areas (SMSA's)

SCALE
0 10 20 30 40 50 MILES

Rhode Island

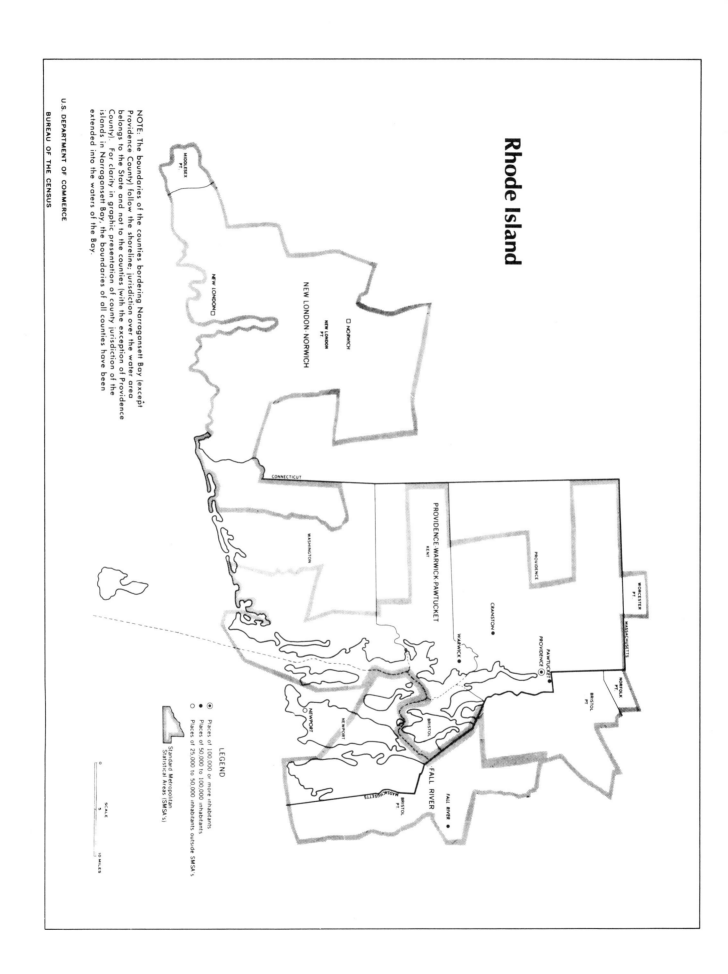

NOTE: The boundaries of the counties bordering Narragansett Bay (except Providence County) follow the shoreline; jurisdiction over the water area belongs to the State and not to the counties (with the exception of Providence County). For clarity in graphic presentation of county jurisdiction of the islands in Narragansett Bay, the boundaries of all counties have been extended into the waters of the Bay.

U.S. DEPARTMENT OF COMMERCE
BUREAU OF THE CENSUS

LEGEND

⊙ Places of 100,000 or more inhabitants

● Places of 50,000 to 100,000 inhabitants

○ Places of 25,000 to 50,000 inhabitants outside SMSA's

Standard Metropolitan Statistical Areas (SMSA's)

SCALE

0   5   10 MILES

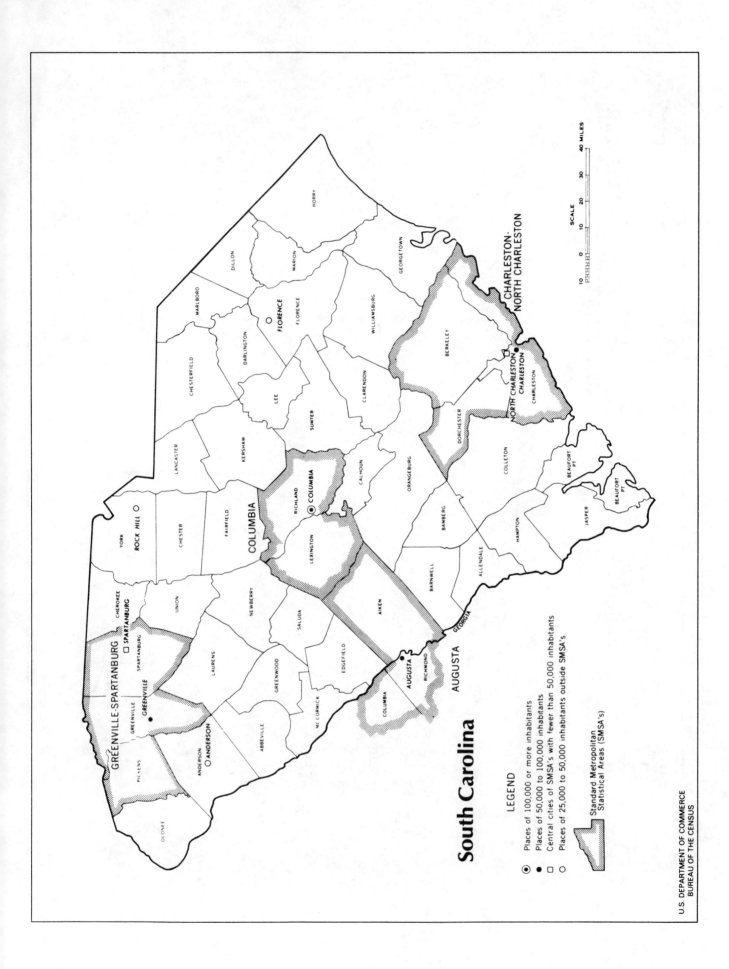

South Carolina

LEGEND

- ⊙ Places of 100,000 or more inhabitants
- ● Places of 50,000 to 100,000 inhabitants
- ☐ Central cities of SMSA's with fewer than 50,000 inhabitants
- ○ Places of 25,000 to 50,000 inhabitants outside SMSA's

Standard Metropolitan
Statistical Areas (SMSA's)

U.S. DEPARTMENT OF COMMERCE
BUREAU OF THE CENSUS

SCALE

10 0 10 20 30 40 MILES

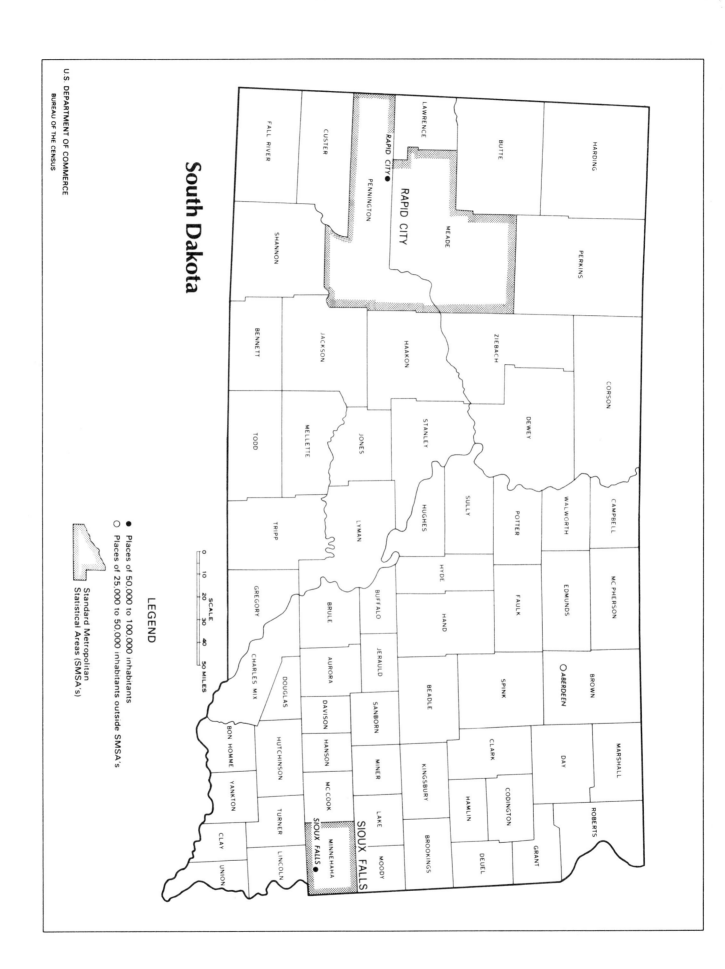

South Dakota

U.S. DEPARTMENT OF COMMERCE
BUREAU OF THE CENSUS

LEGEND

● Places of 50,000 to 100,000 inhabitants
○ Places of 25,000 to 50,000 inhabitants outside SMSA's

Standard Metropolitan
Statistical Areas (SMSA's)

SCALE
0
10
20
30
40
50 MILES

RAPID CITY

RAPID CITY ●

SIOUX FALLS

SIOUX FALLS ●

○ ABERDEEN

HARDING

BUTTE

PERKINS

CORSON

LAWRENCE

MEADE

ZIEBACH

DEWEY

CAMPBELL

MC PHERSON

BROWN

MARSHALL

ROBERTS

PENNINGTON

HAAKON

STANLEY

SULLY

POTTER

WALWORTH

EDMUNDS

DAY

GRANT

FALL RIVER

CUSTER

SHANNON

BENNETT

JACKSON

HUGHES

HYDE

HAND

FAULK

SPINK

CLARK

CODINGTON

DEUEL

TODD

MELLETTE

JONES

LYMAN

BUFFALO

BEADLE

KINGSBURY

HAMLIN

BROOKINGS

TRIPP

GREGORY

BRULE

JERAULD

SANBORN

MINER

LAKE

MOODY

CHARLES MIX

DOUGLAS

AURORA

DAVISON

HANSON

MC COOK

MINNEHAHA

LINCOLN

BON HOMME

HUTCHINSON

TURNER

YANKTON

CLAY

UNION

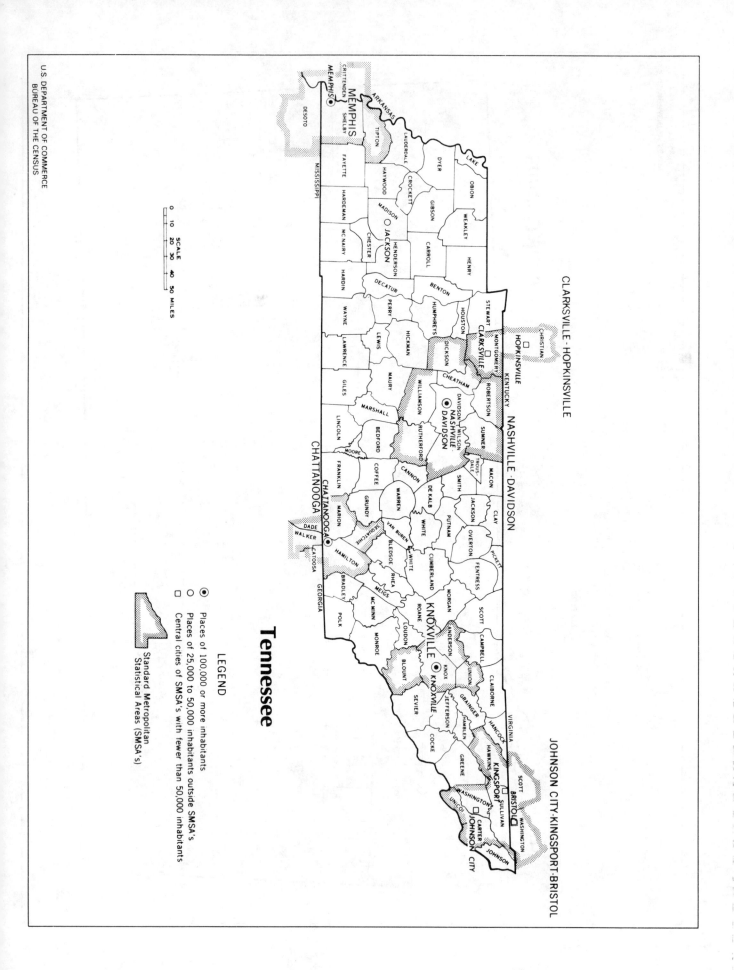

U.S DEPARTMENT OF COMMERCE
BUREAU OF THE CENSUS

Tennessee

LEGEND

- ⊙ Places of 100,000 or more inhabitants
- ○ Places of 25,000 to 50,000 inhabitants outside SMSA's
- ☐ Central cities of SMSA's with fewer than 50,000 inhabitants

Standard Metropolitan
Statistical Areas (SMSA's)

SCALE
0 10 20 30 40 50 MILES

Texas

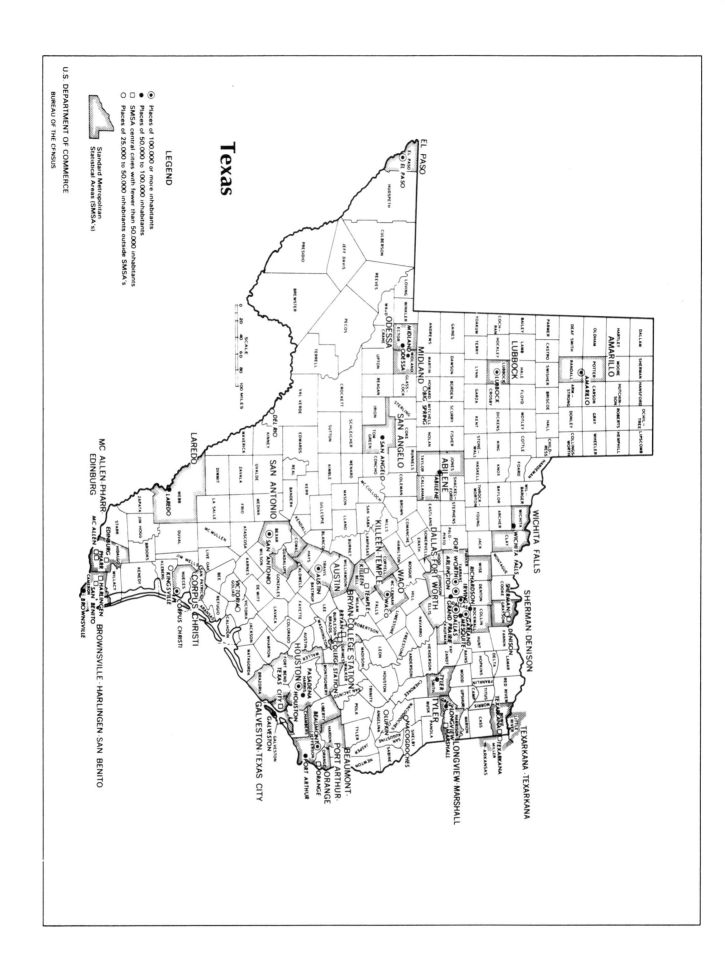

⊙ Places of 100,000 or more inhabitants
● Places of 50,000 to 100,000 inhabitants
□ SMSA central cities with fewer than 50,000 inhabitants
○ Places of 25,000 to 50,000 inhabitants outside SMSA's

Standard Metropolitan
Statistical Areas (SMSA's)

SCALE

U.S. DEPARTMENT OF COMMERCE
BUREAU OF THE CENSUS

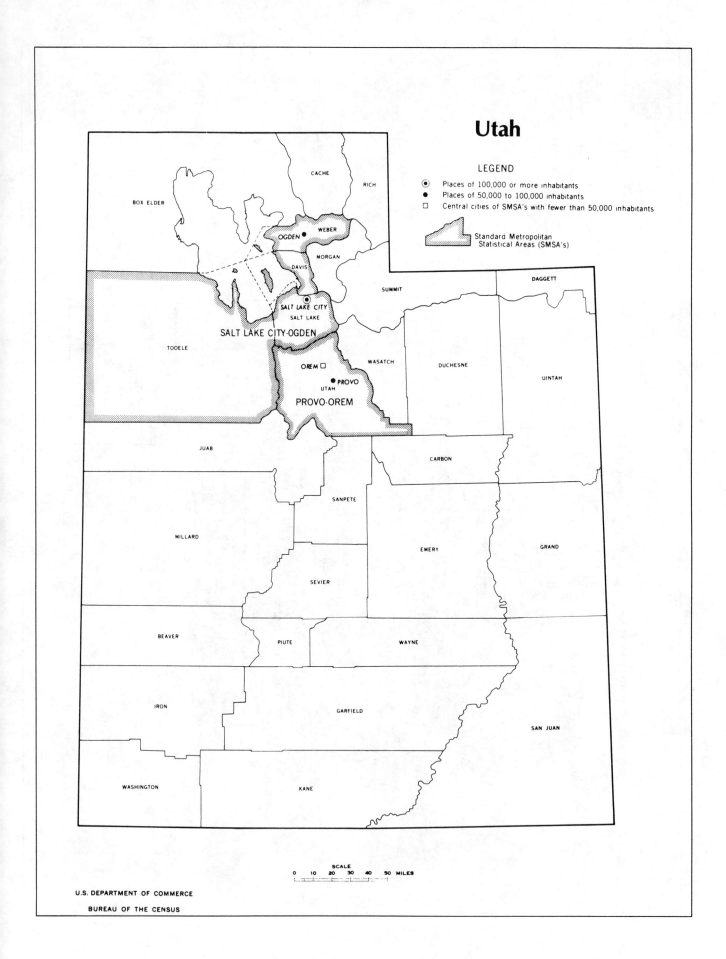

Utah

LEGEND

⊙ Places of 100,000 or more inhabitants

● Places of 50,000 to 100,000 inhabitants

□ Central cities of SMSA's with fewer than 50,000 inhabitants

Standard Metropolitan
Statistical Areas (SMSA's)

BOX ELDER

CACHE

RICH

WEBER

OGDEN ●

MORGAN

DAVIS

SUMMIT

DAGGETT

⊙ SALT LAKE CITY

SALT LAKE

SALT LAKE CITY-OGDEN

TOOELE

WASATCH

DUCHESNE

UINTAH

OREM □

● PROVO

UTAH

PROVO-OREM

JUAB

CARBON

SANPETE

MILLARD

EMERY

GRAND

SEVIER

BEAVER

PIUTE

WAYNE

IRON

GARFIELD

SAN JUAN

WASHINGTON

KANE

SCALE

0 10 20 30 40 50 MILES

U.S. DEPARTMENT OF COMMERCE

BUREAU OF THE CENSUS

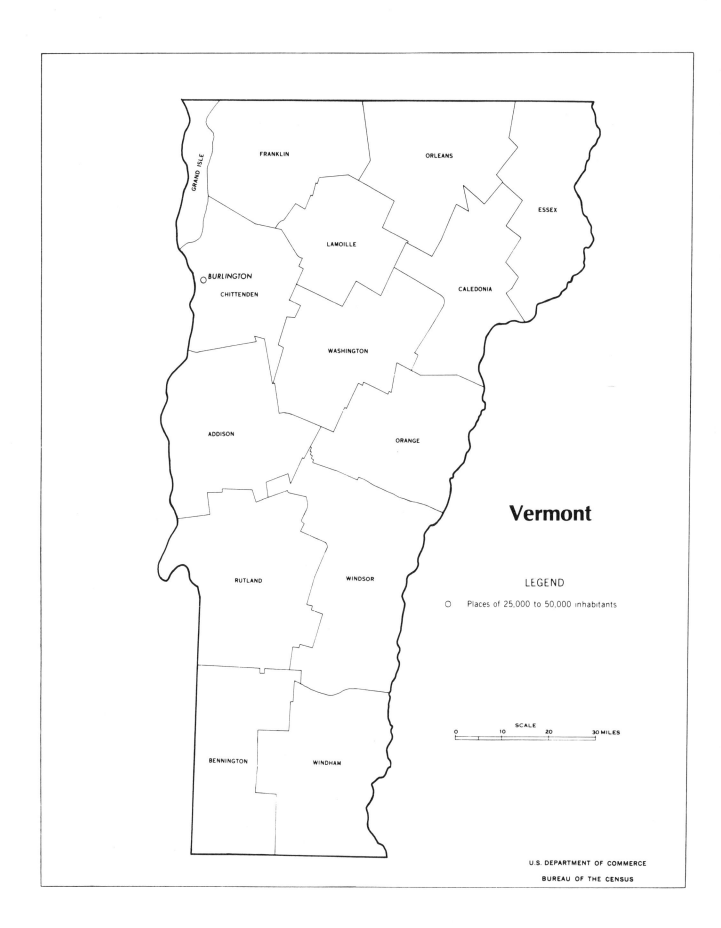

GRAND ISLE

FRANKLIN

ORLEANS

ESSEX

LAMOILLE

○ BURLINGTON

CHITTENDEN

CALEDONIA

WASHINGTON

ADDISON

ORANGE

Vermont

RUTLAND

WINDSOR

LEGEND

○   Places of 25,000 to 50,000 inhabitants

BENNINGTON

WINDHAM

SCALE

0   10   20   30 MILES

U.S. DEPARTMENT OF COMMERCE

BUREAU OF THE CENSUS

Virginia

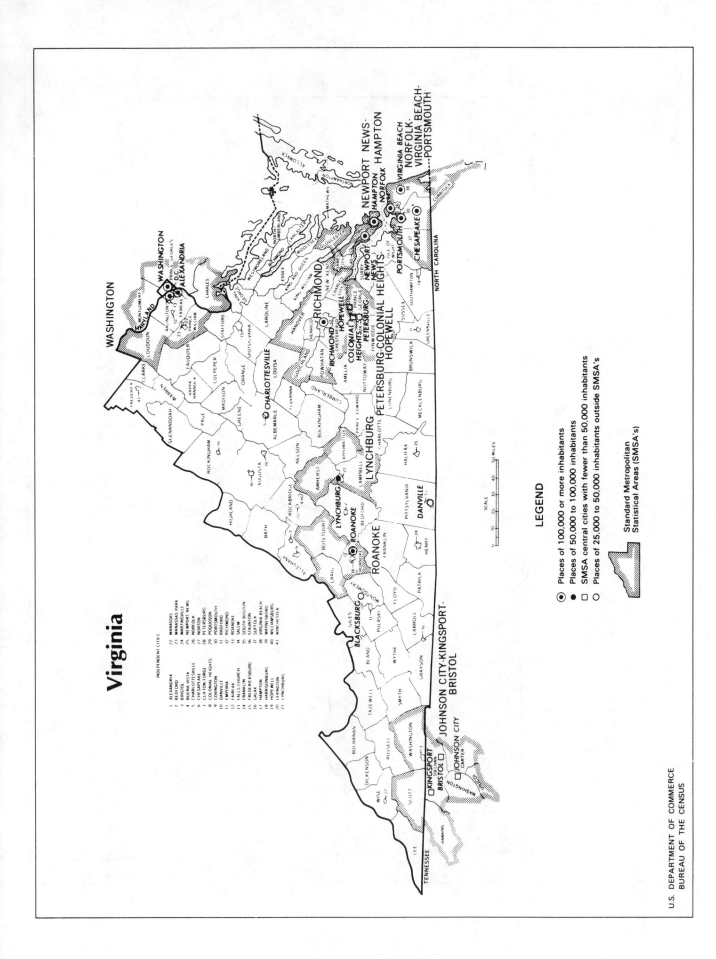

INDEPENDENT CITIES

1	ALEXANDRIA	22	MANASSAS
2	BEDFORD	23	MANASSAS PARK
3	BRISTOL	24	MARTINSVILLE
4	BUENA VISTA	25	NEWPORT NEWS
5	CHARLOTTESVILLE	26	NORFOLK
6	CHESAPEAKE	27	NORTON
7	CLIFTON FORGE	28	PETERSBURG
8	COLONIAL HEIGHTS	29	POQUOSON
9	COVINGTON	30	PORTSMOUTH
10	DANVILLE	31	RADFORD
11	EMPORIA	32	RICHMOND
12	FAIRFAX	33	SALEM
13	FALLS CHURCH	34	SOUTH BOSTON
14	FRANKLIN	35	STAUNTON
15	FRED'KSBURG	36	SUFFOLK
16	GALAX	37	VIRGINIA BEACH
17	HAMPTON	38	WAYNESBORO
18	HARRISONBURG	39	WILLIAMSBURG
19	HOPEWELL	40	WINCHESTER
20	LEXINGTON	41	
21	LYNCHBURG		

SCALE

0 10 20 30 40 50 MILES

LEGEND

- ◉ Places of 100,000 or more inhabitants
- ● Places of 50,000 to 100,000 inhabitants
- ☐ SMSA central cities with fewer than 50,000 inhabitants
- ○ Places of 25,000 to 50,000 inhabitants outside SMSA's

⬡ Standard Metropolitan Statistical Areas (SMSA's)

U.S. DEPARTMENT OF COMMERCE
BUREAU OF THE CENSUS

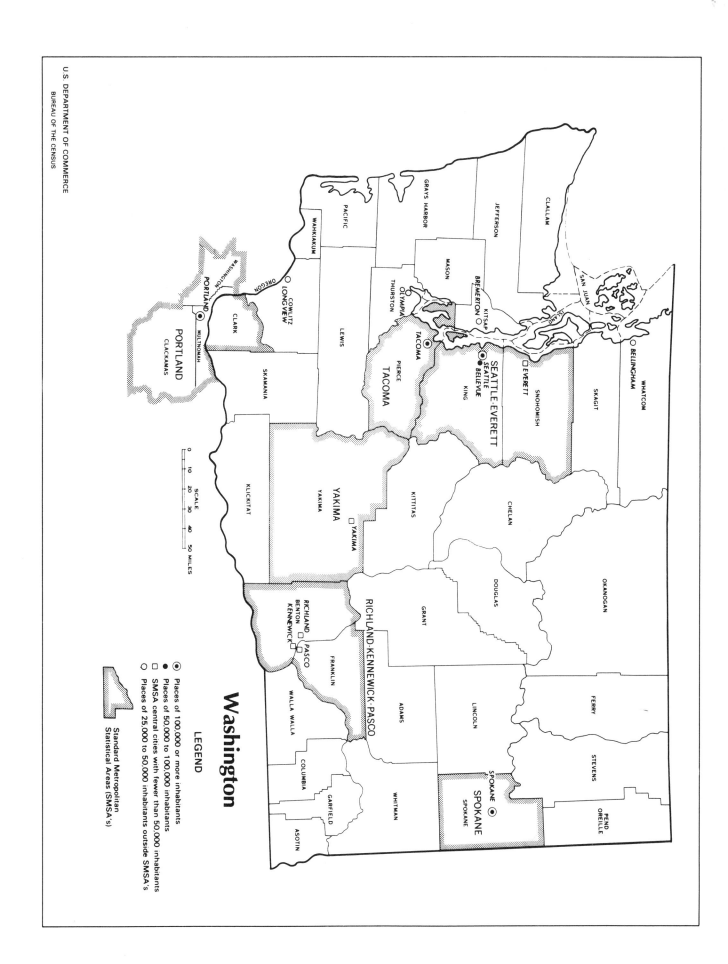

Washington

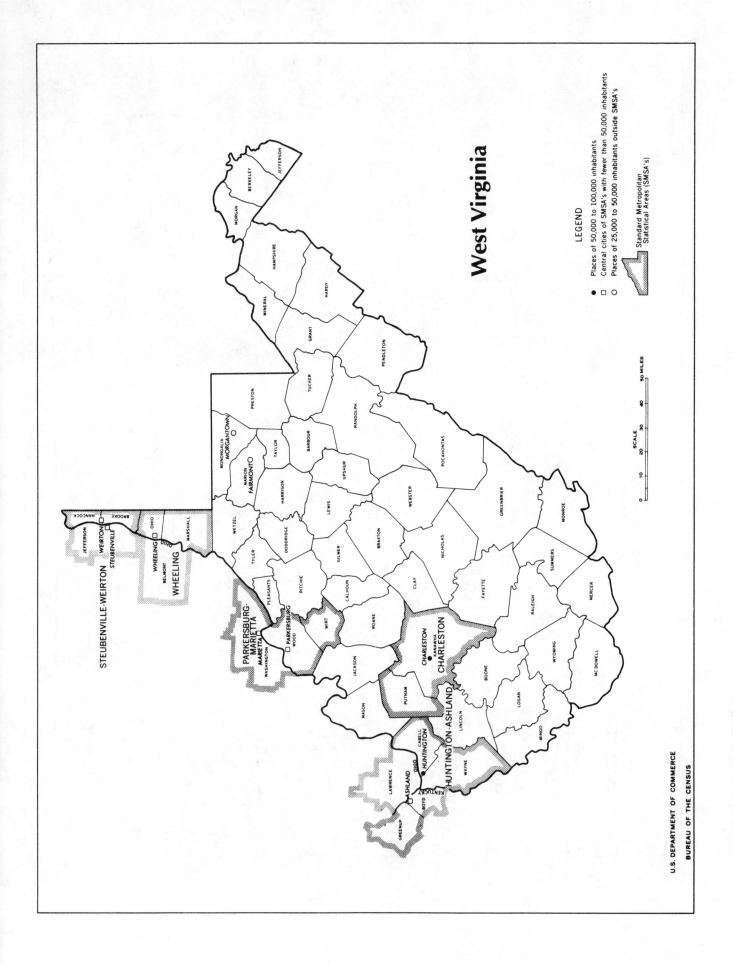

West Virginia

LEGEND

- Places of 50,000 to 100,000 inhabitants
- □ Central cities of SMSA's with fewer than 50,000 inhabitants
- ○ Places of 25,000 to 50,000 inhabitants outside SMSA's

Standard Metropolitan
Statistical Areas (SMSA's)

SCALE

0 10 20 30 40 50 MILES

U.S. DEPARTMENT OF COMMERCE
BUREAU OF THE CENSUS

Wisconsin

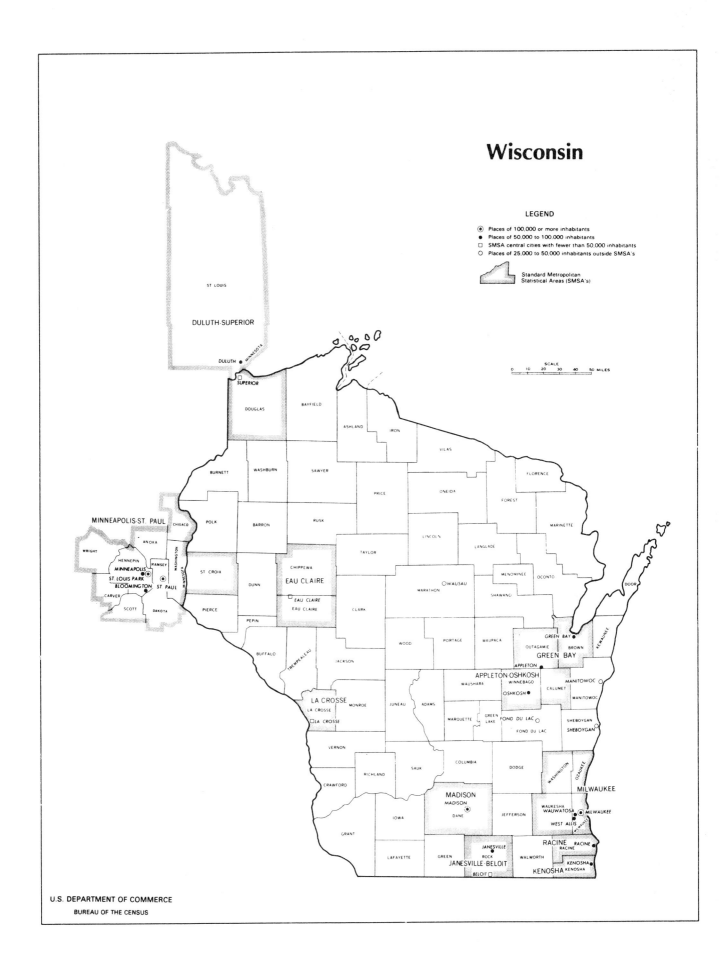

LEGEND

⊙ Places of 100,000 or more inhabitants
● Places of 50,000 to 100,000 inhabitants
□ SMSA central cities with fewer than 50,000 inhabitants
○ Places of 25,000 to 50,000 inhabitants outside SMSA's

Standard Metropolitan
Statistical Areas (SMSA's)

SCALE
0   10   20   30   40   50 MILES

U.S. DEPARTMENT OF COMMERCE
BUREAU OF THE CENSUS

B 499

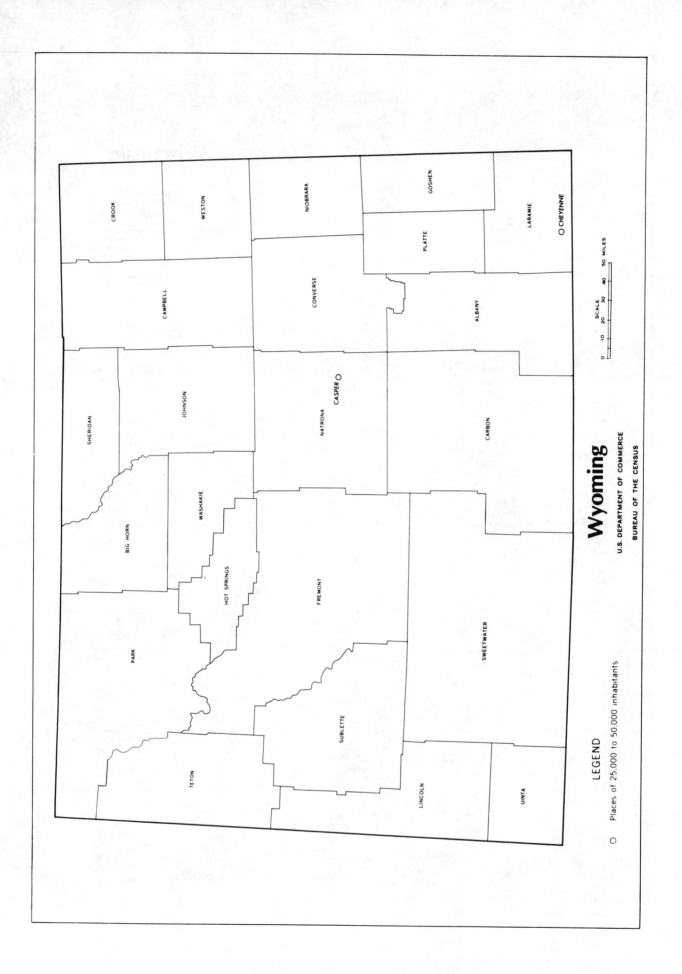

Wyoming

U.S. DEPARTMENT OF COMMERCE

BUREAU OF THE CENSUS

SCALE

0 10 20 30 40 50 MILES

LEGEND

○   Places of 25,000 to 50,000 inhabitants

Cross-Index to the J.K. Lasser Business Forms Series